A PILGRIM MUDDLES THROUGH

Other Books by Robert F. Brodsky

rfoxbro@aol.com

On the Cutting Edge (Gordian Knot Books, 2006)

Songs my Mother Never Sang to Me (FOXBRO Press, 2008)

The World in a Jug (FOXBRO Press, 2010)

A PILGRIM MUDDLES THROUGH

RF BRODSKY

BEING

ANNALS FROM A LIFE

MERCHANDIZING – MORALITY –AUTHORSHIP – LAW – WRITER'S WORKSHOP – OUTRAGED CITIZEN - SAILING - RETIREMENT

FOXBRO PRESS
REDONDO BEACH, CA

A PILGRIM MUDDLES THROUGH: BEING ANNALS FROM A LIFE.
Copyright© 2009 by Robert F. Brodsky.

For information contact Foxbro Press at 110 The Village, #410, Redondo Beach, CA 90277, rfoxbro@aol.com, or 310-937-1811.

ISBN: 978-0-615-27216-0

Library of Congress Control Number: 2009903485

Cover Design: Robert F. Brodsky

Printed in the United States of America

CONTENTS

ACKNOWLEDGEMENT

I became interested in writing at Central High School in Philadelphia, where I did bit articles for our class paper. In my Freshman year at Cornell, I successfully competed to become a reporter for the Cornell Daily Sun, whose Associate Editor – and my boss – was Kurt Vonnegut. Before I went into the Navy, I became Sports Editor and upon return to finish school after the War was made an Associate Editor responsible for a weekly column.

My first attempts at serious non-technical writing occurred at Iowa State in the 70's, where the germ of the idea for a book on my life in engineering, now published, entitled "On the Cutting Edge" was formed. But, it was not until my retirement from teaching at USC, brought upon by the strange phenomena of my forgetting simple words, like 'combustion' during lectures, or 'halyard' while sailing, that I started a daily routine of writing. "Get out of teaching while you're still ahead", I said to myself in 1996. Since then, in addition to sailing twice a week and attending the South Bay Writer's Workshop once a week, I have been writing. And, I've been helped:

I thank all my collaborators for their insights and the joys of recalling the old times. A noted author, BH Friedman, a Cornell classmate, has continually given me guidance and always reminds me to "keep your day job". One new friend and crewman, Mike Kerrigan, himself a writer and stringer, continually helped me both passively and actively. Another crew member and former Boss at TRW, Bob Walquist, gave great aid and comfort in demystifying my language usage. Paul DeJong of Ames, Iowa and Bob Cleland of Sedona, Arizona contributed their wonderful cartoon drawings. And, of course, Patti, my dear wife of 50 years, has read and positively commented on every page. She has been especially helpful in telling me when I get too technical or give more detail than she wants to know. Finally, my 'Writer's Workshop' group, themselves being both would-be or published authors, have been very helpful in making suggestions that turned dull stories into bright ones.

The book is dedicated to my wife, our children and grandchildren, my extended Brodsky family of whom I am presently the patriarch, and all our friends who have made life so interesting and such a ball!

visit CORNELLSUN.ORG and CORNELLSUN.COM

The Cornell Alumni Sun

MARCH 2005 ■ ITHACA, NEW YORK ● EIGHT PAGES

Vonnegut, Schaap to Headline Events Celebrating Sun's 125th Anniversary

By LARRY ARNOLD '88
Alumni Sun Editor

When you hit 125, one birthday party just won't do.

The Cornell Daily Sun Alumni Association and the student staff of The Cornell Daily Sun are planning celebrations in New York City and Ithaca this September to commemorate the 125th anniversary of America's oldest continuously independent and daily college newspaper.

The New York City event, a dinner banquet on Saturday, Sept. 17, will feature novelist Kurt Vonnegut '44, the celebrated author of *Slaughterhouse Five*, *Breakfast of Champions* and many other works. He was a Sun columnist, assistant managing editor and associate editor during his years at Cornell.

Vonnegut's speech at The Sun's traditional end-of-year banquet in 1980 is one of the best-remembered tributes ever delivered to the newspaper. (An excerpt: "I was happiest when I was all alone — and it was very late

Back at The Sun again. *Kurt Vonnegut '44, former columnist and associate editor, will help celebrate The Sun's anniversary.*

at night, and I was walking up the hill after leaving helped to put The Sun to bed.") To brush up on your Vonnegutia between now and September, check out his official Web site, www.vonnegut.com, and the unauthorized but thorough www.vonnegutweb.com.

Vonnegut will be just one of several expected special guests. Other speakers will offer their recollections of The Sun over the decades. The banquet will be held at the Cornell Club in Manhattan.

The celebration in Ithaca will take place a week later, on Saturday Sept. 24, and feature Emmy Award-winning ESPN correspondent Jeremy Schaap '91, who served as a Sun sportswriter, sports editor and senior editor, continuing the Sun legacy created by his father, the late Dick Schaap '55.

All alumni and friends of The Sun through the years are invited to attend either event, or both. Details will be announced later this year.

See VONNEGUT page 7

A Talk With The Sun's First Female Editor in Chief

When female Cornellians win election as editor in chief of The Cornell Daily Sun — a regular occurrence these days — they carry on the legacy of Guinevere Griest '44.

In 1943, Griest became the first female editor in chief in the 63-year history of The Sun. The same tumultuous event that led to her barrier-breaking promotion — World War II, which

drew young men into military training and service — also motivated her historic term. Griest had a chance to write just one editorial before The Sun finally gave in to circumstances and suspended operations until after the war.

That editorial, excerpted in *A Century at Cornell* by Daniel Margulis '75 and John Schroeder '74, expressed an optimistic view

about The Sun's future that, sadly, proved unrealistic:

"We are taking over the reins of Ithaca's Only Morning Newspaper at one of the most critical periods in its history. In 1918 the exigencies of war caused a temporary setting of The Sun for the first and only time in its history. Though the war we fight today reduces that struggle to the stature of a mere

pre-view, circumstances have happily allowed us to keep our heads safely above the horizon, if below the zenith attained in the past."

For the final months of her time at Cornell, Griest served as editor of the Cornell Bulletin, a once-weekly fill-in for The Sun published mainly by former Sun

See EDITOR page 2

Kurt was my first boss at the Sun; he was an associate editor. His boss, the editor in chief was my fraternity brother, Miller Harris. Gwen succeeded him before I went off to war; leaving as wartime sports editor.

X

PREFACE

I'm a Pennsylvanian. Early on, I learned about Pilgrims, starting with William Penn. Pilgrims came here not only to escape oppression but also to find a nurturing clime – an environment where you were free to express your opinions, to live in freedom without fear, and to ply your trade in peace. Well, like they say about Democracy, it may not be perfect here, but it's the best we have. But certainly not the best we could hope for.

In this book of stories, you will see the Pilgrim and his friends dealing with equal amounts of joy and adversity, and never – or almost never – afraid to take on the powers-that-be. You may not agree with all the opinions expressed herein – but you will learn how an outsider –a minority in religion, ethnicity, politics, and thinking – copes in a mystical world of WASPS, evangelicals, right-wingers, and republicans. If you don't like what you read, write a "Letter to the Editor" or avail yourselves of a local Small Claims Court!

I've always been a story teller and, now, I'm a really old story teller. Consequently, I have lots of stories to tell. In this book, I've selected eight categories of life's adventures and built a Chapter around each. The eight chapters contain stories that have remained fresh in my memory because of my inveterate lifetime habit of saving letters, newspaper clippings and work memos. Many of them expose the foibles of a perverse world which suffers fools who like to tilt at windmills and fight injustice at all levels. Many of the annals are funny or quirky and, I think, make for enjoyable reading. My tongue is many times in my cheek. The serious tracts are for you to muse about. The opinions are always my own and are always controversial.

The reason I have so many stories has to do with the diversity of my life experience. The tales told cover the span from after my Bar Mitzvah, into college at Cornell, into the Navy in WW2, working as a hot jazz musician in Greenwich Village, attending grad school and getting a ScD at NYU, working on the atomic bomb in New Mexico, on guided missiles in Pomona, California, and finally getting into 'space' in California, France and Israel, and into teaching at UCLA, Iowa State University and, 3540 km away from the corn belt, the University of Southern California. Then – on retirement - I began writing.

The initial chapter has to do with the struggles of my friends in the world of commerce; all fortunately ending with triumphs over adversity. Next comes a serious chapter in which I unload against the right wing conspiracy and all its accoutrements. Only a few of you will agree with my thinking, and I salute those who do! Chapter 3 tells of the difficulties of changing careers from engineer to author – and leaves the question of my success still in limbo. The fourth Chapter documents my life-long struggles through military and civil law mazes, while the fifth brings you stories from my Writer's Workshop – my support group in this new career. What follows, in the sixth Chapter, are stories and 'Letters to the Editor', Op-Ed pieces, and letters I sent while my dander was up or I was busy saving the world. The next-to-last Chapter is all about sailing – and a love of the ocean that I've had for a lifetime. The final stories all come from post retirement days and describe adventures that have occurred outside of my writing 'office hours'.

Originally, this book consisted of two volumes. On advice from a friend, I have culled the pertinent theme stories which I felt were most appropriate. But, as I proof-read this volume, I realized that there are still many stories that I have left to tell, both about the past and about things that happened yesterday. I hope I will have the time to tell them!

Chapter 1

ANNALS OF MERCHANDIZING

- **SCRAP THE NORMANDIE (~1948-1953)**
- **ANY ICE TODAY, LADY? (~ 1951)**
- **FLXIBLE FLYER (~ 1971-2)**
- **THE ROCKET SCIENTIST (1974-1998)**
- **THE CLASS FAILURE (1982)**
- **THE WING OF THE CENTURY (2004)**

These are stories that illustrate facets of the human condition when involved in matters of commerce and trade. The first four have to do with business adventures of and with dear friends; then follows a heart-rending story from my 40th high school reunion; and, finally, the inspirational story of the couple who invented hang gliding.

In summary, however, it's all merchandizing, as best illustrated by the following parable: *Two beggars, each with a cup for donations in hand, were sitting on a bench in front of the great cathedral in Mexico City. Each wore a chain necklace; one with a Cross pendant and the other with a Star of David pendant. There was a continuous flux of donations into the cup of the man with the Cross; and none to the other.*

A passing priest, taking pity, addressed the man with the Star of David: "Son, don't you realize that you are in Catholic country? You really should not expect any donations." "Thank you, Father," the man said, "I understand what you are telling me". As the Padre moved away, he then leaned over to his companion and said, "Moishe, looks who's telling us about marketing!"

SCRAP THE NORMANDIE

I have a lifelong college friend who is an established and respected author with over 25 published novels, biographies, monographs, plays and stories to his credit. Although none of his work to date could be classified in the 'best seller' category, he is nevertheless, through the circumstances of his publishing revenue and inheritance, living a good life. He now maintains quarters in mid-town Manhattan and the Hamptons, and has found time in his life to attend worldclass writer's conferences in Iowa and Cassis, to name two.

How he managed to elevate himself to the modern state of being very 'comfortable', as the really well-to-do are wont to describe themselves, is a 'local boy makes good' saga for our times. This part of my parable (you will see later why I use this warning word) forms half of the story; The other half, 100% true to the best of my knowledge, is a vivid illustration of capitalism, with all of its risks and rainbow ends, at its dynamic best. It concerns the scrapping of the former French luxury liner, the Normandie.

After WWII began, the Normandie was converted into a troop carrier and served valiantly by shuttling GIs from the US to England in preparation for D-Day. Tragically, while in dock in New York harbor, it caught fire, rolled over on its side suffering some structural damage, and partially sank into the mud of the Hudson River's bottom. An early attempt was made to refloat it by repairing the hull damage and welding it water tight, and then attempting to pump it up with air. This approach didn't work and the poor ship continued to lay low as a ward of the city, tying up an important commercial pier, seemingly forever. The government, stuck with the docking fee of an undesirable and expensive tenant, periodically sent out invitations to bid on salvage rights, but there were no war-time takers. The Normandie was hopelessly sinking further and further into the mud, and nobody knew how to economically raise and dispose of it, or scrap it in-situ.

The SS Normandie, renamed USS Lafayette when converted to a troop carrier by The US Navy lies capsized after a disastrous fire

CAREER

Owners:	Compagnie Générale Transatlantique
Builders:	Penhoët, Saint Nazaire, France
Laid down:	January 26 1931
Launched:	October 29, 1932
Christened:	October 29, 1932
Maiden voyage:	May 29, 1935
Fate:	Caught fire, capsized at Pier 88 in the New York Passenger Ship Terminal in New York City in 1942; wreck remained on site throughout WWII, and was sold for scrap on October 3rd 1946

The family of one of my boyhood Philadelphia friends owned a very large scrap yard, readily accessible to the Hudson, on the Raritan River in New Jersey. The Yard recognized the great financial potential of scrapping the Normandie, with its wealth of non-ferrous metals, copper, brass, bronze, lead, etc. to go along with the huge steel tonnage. After the war was over, they hired an engineering firm that had developed specialized recovery techniques for the Navy, to study the overall problem of salvaging the Normandie. When it appeared that this outfit had found a feasible, but very risky, solution, which they estimated would cost a million dollars – a lot of money in those days - the scrapyard made an uncontested – and very low -bid for the salvage rights and were cheerfully given the award. They recognized that the gamble was akin to shooting craps, but the winner's stake would be immense.

The hired Engineers had come up with a brilliant, but never before tried, solution. Using the recently developed capability of shaping thin polystyrene sheets into balloon-like shapes, they proposed floating the ship by having divers inflate ten of thousands of such balloons inside the stricken vessel until it lifted itself out of the mud. Thence, it would be towed by tug boats to the scrap yard. The subsequent operation, which took over a year, was one of the most impressive engineering feats of its time, and was a complete success. A few years later, the revenue from the scrapping operation amounted to over 13 million dollars.

In 2006, I told this story to Bob Cleland of Sedona, Arizona.
He missed the spelling of 'Claster' – but otherwise got it right!

Rather than letting this newly acquired fortune burn a hole in their pockets, they joined forces with their Tishman cousins who were major players in the post-war skyscraper building boom in New York City in financing the erection of new four and five star hotels. Around this time, a year after I had finished, my writer friend completed his war-interrupted education at Cornell: I had earlier received an engineering degree and was at grad school on the GI Bill, and he, on graduation sporting an English Lit. degree, had not a whit of an idea of how to make an immediate living from his writing. His fate was soon settled after a discussion with his builder Uncles, who were the above-described partici-pants in the ongoing building frenzy.

They, knowing his artistic bent, asked him to take on the specific job of furnishing each of their many hotel rooms, just being and soon-to-be completed, with original art work done by local artists. He zestfully took on his assignment and immediately became the patron saint to the struggling but uniquely talented artist colony of the greater New York community. The job was such that he not only had the opportunity to 'discover' new talent, but also allowed him time to start his writing career in earnest. It was a sweet set-up!

Among his new found acquaintances were the struggling artists Jackson Pollock and his wife, Lee Krasner. My friend and his wife became socially friendly with the Pollock's;

so much so that they named their first born, "Jackson". From time to time, in the period before the art world 'found' them, the Pollock's gifted my friends with several of their works. Of course, at that time these treasures had no significant value. My friend and his wife greatly admired these gifts and displayed them on the walls of their Brownstone or, as the numbers grew, stored them for rotation. By now, I think you can readily see why they later moved from the rich to the '*comfortable*' category.

Ordinarily, this would be the end of the story, which for all of my post-college life I thought was completely true, or at least only a bit apocryphal. I sent my first version of this story, which named names, to my friend for his approval. I got back a somewhat scolding letter, which said, in part, "-------. The piece you wrote has nothing to do with me or anyone in my family, so of course I don't want you to use my name. I suspect the Normandie may be about one of your fellow Philadelphians. ---------".

What do I know for sure? I know the Normandie story is true, for I did get it from the horse's mouth. I know the art story, for my writer friend told me directly about this part of his life. What I don't know is how many Pollock's, if any, my friend has; but can understand his reluctance to admit to any because of possible tax ramifications. I also am not completely sure of the scrap yard - builder familial link-up which ties the stories together. Even if not 100% true, and these are really two independent tales, I think they make a hell of a story – parable or not!

The Artist at work using his inimitable technique

ANY ICE TODAY, LADY?*

In mid-1951, I was promoted to a Division Head job in the research branch of the burgeoning atomic bomb development laboratory then called Sandia Corporation (now Sandia National Laboratory). Sandia, in Albuquerque, was responsible for the incorporation of the atomic warheads developed at the nearby Los Alamos Scientific Laboratory into production A-Bombs; the testing program that proved they would work; and to find out how much damage they could be expected to do. When I had first arrived there in late '49, I was about the 700th employee of an outfit destined to number in the thousands. Most of the technical people were PhD physicists. They had been lured to the wild west by bonus-type salaries and a one month vacation per year guarantee.

Dr. Ken E., a garrulous, extroverted Texan became my new boss. He was a one of the pioneering group of scientists who had migrated from the Applied Physics Laboratory of the Johns Hopkins University to help found Sandia. Like his APL compatriots, he was an expert in proximity fuzing and firing of missile warheads; a critical skill needed in the A-Bomb business. Because of a commonality of interests and relaxed attitudes, he took a fatherly interest in me technically, and our families soon became socially friendly.

Ken and his elegant wife Jewell had an interesting and probably lucrative hobby. They bought old southwest-style adobe houses that were in a state of disrepair and fixed them up into top modern operational condition. Often, they furnished them beautifully applying Jewell's keen artistic feel and antique hunter's zeal. Then, they either sold or rented them. The houses they worked on generally were in Tijeras Canyon; the lovely valley area through which Route 66/Central Avenue - wound between the Sandia and Manzano ranges on its way East from Albuquerque to Tucumcari and thence Amarillo.

Although the Erickson's were about 10 years older than wife #1 and I, we got along well together. They shared our interest in horses and enjoyed our political activity. We both reserved the weekends for house projects. One Saturday morning when I was heavily engrossed with fence building and was particularly grubby looking and unshaved, Ken drove up in his pick-up. "Son ", he said, "C'mon and give me a hand getting an ice box for our housing project". Like for me, and many others in our generation, the word "refrigerator" never took hold - nor does it today - and I knew exactly what he was looking for.

---

*For the Title's derivation, see the Author's *Songs My Mother Never Sang to Me*. In the Chapter on College songs, you will find that this comes from the University of Pennsylvania's football fight song. It was sung after every touchdown: "—Any ice today, lady? No! Giddyap!"

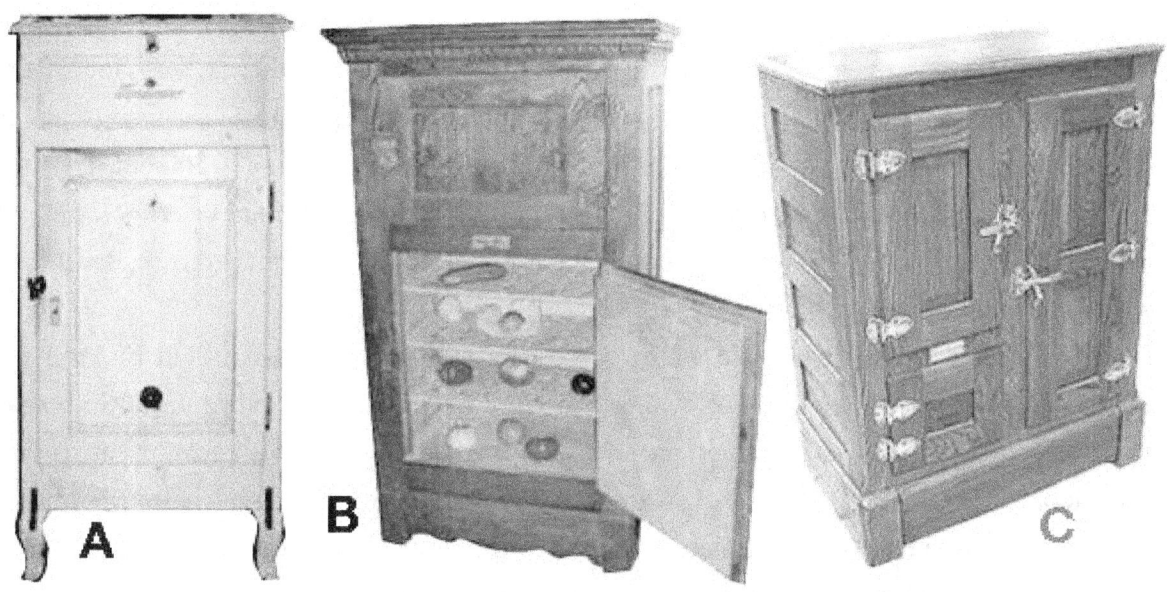

For those of you who never had the pleasure, this is what old fashioned ice boxes looked like. A block of ice was usually delivered twice daily to the back porch from a horse-drawn cart. In the summer, the Ice Man would give the kids shavings to suck on. Ken, of course, sought the newer electrified version—but still an 'ice box'.

I hopped into the pick-up, glad to be relieved of the dirty work with the posthole digger. Ken looked even grubbier than I, down to his ever lovin' cowboy boots. "I've been shorin' up a dog-goned root cellar", he apologized. We drove off looking for the second hand appliance shop on Lomas Avenue that we both knew about. There were at least 30 'ice boxes' of all shapes and sizes strewn around the outdoor lot, and we started looking at the "good" ones.

Eyeing us suspiciously, the proprietor came up and asked us what we were looking for. Ken said, "A pretty good large ice box for my house, - that's not too expensive". The proprietor allowed that he had two that might fill the bill. One, which he said he wouldn't guarantee, but thought would fill the bill, was $30. The other cost $65 but, he said after again carefully looking at us over his spectacles, "You probably can't afford it." Without cracking a smile, Ken said, "My, that's a mighty good looking ice box - how about $55 cash?" The deal was consummated.

FLXIBLE FLYER

My friend Howard lived a charmed life in the 20th century. His drama was one of epic highs and lows. Early on, he learned well the ancient adage, "The Customer is always Right", but in this story we will see that his enthusiasm for his new assignment may have clouded his normally better judgment. But, who knew that his potential customer's loyalty and satisfaction with an incumbent supplier would supersede a solemn promise, and lead to a monumental career downturn.

We became friends when we were co-workers at Aerojet in Azusa and El Monte, in L.A. County. We both worked on rockets that were fired essentially straight up into space and spent 5-6 minutes in the true space environment before falling back to earth. They were called 'Sounding Rockets'. Howard was the prototype of a blond-haired Brooklyn-born savvy go-getter. He was a hard driver, acerbic, and very knowledgeable with hardware. He co-invented and developed a self-contained pre-flight-programmed control system which pointed instruments at stars or other heavenly bodies once the sounding rocket arrived into outer space. He developed potential customers in France and NATO who were interested in using his rocket pointing control system on their scientific sounding rockets.

As a result, he was asked to take up residence in Paris and work with the Europeans; incorporating his control system into their sounding rockets. As time went by, he was promoted to be head of Aerojet's European Operations. Almost four successful years later, he and his family decided they wanted to come home. In 1969, Howard nominated me to the Aerojet corporate moguls as his replacement, which did happen; while he negotiated for a new job back in the USA. After a spell of Aerojet jobs, he landed on both feet as the well-paid Vice-President of International Sales of Rohr Manufacturing Corporation in Chula Vista, just south of San Diego. The job came with all the accoutrements and perks of high office. The family celebrated by buying a lovely house, somewhat beyond their means, in La Jolla, hard by the beach near Scripp's Pier. He was immediately handed a tough first 'do-or-die' business acquisition assignment.

Rohr had just bought the 'Avis' of U.S. bus manufacturer's, a trouble-wracked outfit called "Flxible". Its previous owner had been unable to make it grow or fix all the nagging problems that caused unpredictable breakdowns that made it bus brand name #2. Howard's assignment was to lead a proposal effort aimed at selling at least 600 improved design Flxible buses to the city of Caracas, Venezuela.

It turned out that the city depended on an ancient fleet of around 1200 Mercedes Benz vehicles, many first purchased pre-WW1. Somehow the city kept them operational by utilizing the shear genius of South American mechanics who seem to have a monopoly on such skills. But, now, they were finally beginning to show their age and were to be replaced, en toto. Because the city wanted to encourage bids from others than Mercedes to keep the price down by encouraging competition, Caracas promised an unprejudiced open competition and assured bidders that under no circumstances would Mercedes get more than half of the order.

Heritage

(from Wikipedia)

The world's first motorised bus was built in Germany by Karl Benz in 1895, some years before Gottlieb Daimler also started to build and sell buses in Germany as well. By 1898 both Karl Benz and Gottlieb Daimler, then rivals, were exporting their buses to Wales and England. Soon Daimler products were sold in the British Empire in a partnership with the British company Milnes. Milnes-Daimler developed a double-decker in 1902 and provided a bus for the first motorised bus service in the United Kingdom the following year. Though the company met success in selling buses throughout the British Empire, the partnership between Daimler and Milnes had to be undone due to the First World War. Due to economic hardships in the early 1900s, Daimler Motoren Gesellschaft and Benz & Cie. merged into one company in 1926, two years after both companies signed an agreement of mutual interest. Thus, Daimler-Benz AG (also known as Mercedes-Benz) was formed. In the next year, the company presented its first combined bus range. By that time emphasis was given to diesel engines (as opposed to petrol engines) for commercial vehicles

---

We saw Howard during Rohr's hectic redesign/proposal period in the early '70s. He came to Ames, Iowa, where we were then living, to visit the Sunstrand Corporation plant there. At their Iowa facility near us, they made very fancy automatic gear shifts that smoothly powered most of the new behemoth trucks through about 27 gear ratios. He quickly found out that their product was much too expensive, making him revert to a less expensive General Motors-supplied system for the Rohr/Flxible bid.

A couple of months later, with the requisite 20 proposal copies in hand, he flew down to Venezuela to deliver the package the next morning. He truly believed he had a winner, knowing that his job was on the line if he didn't make the sale. By much cajolery and sleight-of-hand, he had whittled Rohr's bid down to a barely profitable margin. He figured that would be a good business move, since a win would establish Flxible as a world-wide bus competitor, and would also energize the interest in their buses in the US.

A Flxible bus –from WIKIPEDIA- the 'AVIS' of U.S. buses.
They folded in 1996.Greyhound buses were simply better.

He was met at the airport serving Caracas by an Agent that he had hired to get him through the government red tape. As they drove into town, Howard got his first look at the glory of the ancient Mercedes buses. He immediately noticed that the rear exit doors of the old clunkers were behind the rear tires. Knowing that his soon to-be-proffered design had the rear door ahead of the rear tires, he asked the Agent why the Mercedes design might be preferred.

The Agent replied, "Senor, just look at the buses as they come to a passenger loading kiosk. Notice that they really don't come to a full stop. People just jump off the back platform and jump on in front. Experience has shown that too many people would be run over if the rear exit was not behind the wheels." Sure enough, as he paid more attention as they drove further into the center of town to his hotel, he took in the scene and noted the veracity of the Agent's words. The buses would slow down, to about 1-2 miles per hour, as they drove up to the loading area. There was a mad scramble to get on or off the bus. Old women and children simply couldn't play.

Howard took this in apace; gulped; and had the agent organize an all night rework and reprint session, wherein he changed the design to move the rear exit aft of the wheels. By dragging the right expert artisans away from their TVs and out of their beds and urging them upward and onward, he developed, duplicated, and inserted replacement pages replete with intricate re-drawings and skilled new renderings. By the next morning, the 20 revised proposal copies were ready to officially turn in, apparently no worse for wear.

A few weeks later, with no further explanation, Caracas announced that Mercedes had been awarded the contract for all 1200 buses, and Rohr suggested that Howard might wish to retire. Shortly after that, Rohr sold Flxible to Grumman Aircraft, who had no better luck peddling the product; finally giving up.

That he again managed to land even more solidly on his feet after this debacle is a tribute to the man, and the subject of the next even more harrowing success story which follows. The lesson here, I guess, is not only that a good man is hard to find, but to also raise a caution in bidding: A good incumbent is hard to unseat!

THE ROCKET SCIENTIST

When, after 14 years of working its way through the lower court system, the Supreme Court of the United States finally ruled in his favor, the flavor of his victory was anticlimatic. My friend Howard shrugged, and although he could, he decided not to counterattack. A few years later, he sold the business and was able to comfortably live out his life with bittersweet memories of the struggle.

All through the 90's, you could not help but notice the continuing activity at all of the nation's gasoline service stations. They were either replacing their underground storage tanks or shutting down because such replacement was simply not financially viable. Howard, my friend and former co-worker at Aerojet, found a way to take advantage of this refurbishment, and it soon made him a millionaire.

Howard was a true rocket scientist. Unlike me, who understood rockets mostly from a theoretical standpoint, he had really gotten down and dirty with them. He knew their innards, had tweaked and loaded them, and had been involved with many firings at many exotic places. When he was deposed from his job as International Vice-President of Sales of Rohr Manufacturing, he found a way to apply his knowledge of rocket technology for fun and profit, albeit mixed with grief.

But, this success did not occur overnight. As he left Rohr to seek other pastures, he had a family and a big La Jolla home mortgage to concern him. During his earlier stay in Europe, while he managed Aerojet's European Operations in Paris, he had saved a tidy sum. This accumulation being the result of his good salary with many financial perks, plus not having to pay income tax on his U.S.-furnished salary; as was the rule for long-term émigrés. However, his cache was finite. He needed to find a business to invest in to make a good living.

After rummaging around a few months, he found a manufacturing company in a nearby town to the north of La Jolla doing a business he liked and knew something about. Not only was it for sale, but it was also breaking even with no on-site owner supervision. He studied the business and soon had an idea, born of his rocket experience, that he felt sure was worth a fortune. He went for it!

The company he bought in the early '70s, which I shall call 'Moore Manufacturing', was an old line fabricator of steel gasoline and petrochemical tanks, such as were buried under every gas station. Most of these tanks, no matter who made them, were beginning to develop slow leaks which were polluting underground water resources throughout the country. The Environmental Protection Agency had taken note of this deterioration and had postulated the need for corrosion-resistant tanks post haste. They allowed 10 years for replacement, or else.

The Underwriters Laboratory (UL), a very powerful oversee organization which approves the rules governing the manufacturing of all such tanks, decreed that henceforth all new tanks must be double-walled and instrumented with leak alarms; and all the old tanks replaced within the cited period. These time-limited new dictates opened the door for Howard to produce the figurative 'better mouse trap' and scoop the world!

He really was! He was co-inventor of a payload pointing system for a rocket that took pictures from near space looking up or down to Earth

Drawing from experience gained during our earlier days at Aerojet, a major manufacturer of liquid rocket engines and solid rocket motors, he recalled the new way that cases for large diameter rocket motors were now being made by wrapping strips of resin-impregnated fiberglass materials around a dummy form called a mandrel and curing them in an oven. Often, a very thin steel liner would be used as the recipient of the fiber wraps. Such 'composite' (a word coined to describe this new way of fabricating tanks) cases were stronger than steel-only cases and a lot lighter in weight. Moreover, since they were impervious to the long term storage of volatile rocket propellants, they would be highly compatible with the considerably less corrosive petrochemicals.

Advised by a friend who had run the case production at Aerojet, he devised a way to make double-walled composite tankage using a process that would be considerably less expensive than double-walled anti-corrosion-coated steel tanks - which no one really knew how to build anyway. He also developed an accepted method to test for corrosion resistance and included a built-in alarm system to detect leaks. But, a major roadblock stood in his way: the Underwriter's Lab manufacturing code – the so-called "Boiler Code" - simply did not allow composite materials for the tanks they inspected, insured, and sprinkled with holy water.

ASME Boiler & Pressure Vessel Code

The New 2004 Edition of the ASME Boiler & Pressure Vessel Code (BPVC) contains thousands of pages of new code, standards, and figures. The 2004 edition includes Section II-D, which has been separated into Customary and Metric volumes, and Section XII Rules for Construction and Continued Service of Transport Tanks, which is a new section that may soon be referenced by the Department of Transportation. ASME BPVC is an internationally recognized code for the latest rules of safety for design, fabrication, maintenance and inspection of boilers and pressure vessels, power producing machines and associated subsystems, and nuclear power plant components. IHS is pleased to provide you with the Boiler Code at reduced 2004 pricing and the addenda and interpretations are available at no additional charge!

He needed to assure the UL that his design was satisfactory and cause them to change their Code to allow his design. He managed to get himself appointed a member of the governing committee. He also hired a structures Professor from San Diego State University to make sufficient stress analyses and materials analyses with the purpose of coercing the UL Governing Committee to rewrite the Code to allow composite tankage. Howard and his expert witness took several runs at the UL powers-that-be and finally convinced them of the rightness of his cause. By the time this was done, he had a production line in gear and sales force on the road. With a better, and at that time, the only 'mousetrap', he rapidly became a millionaire. A true American success story, only . . . .

One of the biggest of the old time tank suppliers took Moore and Howard to court, claiming he unlawfully used chicanery and inside influence to get the Code changed; essentially putting the old timers temporarily out of business until they could develop new technology on their own. This move signaled the start of a 14 year court struggle that, ping-pong -like, bounced back and forth in the lower court system with this - side, that - side decisions followed by appeals to ever higher level courts.

His side lost the second round of appeals. The subsequent judgment action forced Howard to seek the protection of the bankruptcy court, rather than post a 4.5 million dollar bond pending his next appeal. This move protected both his company and his family fortune, but did not alleviate the personal grief it wreaked. The court actions, of course, made millions for the lawyers involved.

Finally, the case made it to the Supreme Court. After their deliberation, Howard won the final complete victory. The long court battle was over. For a while, he contemplated going after his tormentors in the courts on grounds of false persecution. But, during the long struggle, he managed to keep Moore going at a good profit and set up his children for life. He decided to chalk it up to experience, though I'm sure he still has dreams of sweet revenge. But - as they say - a bird in the hand . . . "

THE CLASS FAILURE

I flew to my 40th Central High School reunion, our first such affair since graduation in January, 1942, without my wife. So – unlike my former classmates at our all-boys school who had stayed in Philadelphia all their lives and brought their spouses to the affair – I could cover a lot of ground. I didn't need to introduce the 'little woman' to one and all, and stand by while the wives also caught up on their lives. Except for a few life-long friends like rock-ribbed Republican 'Obe' O., Editor and Publisher of the Arlington Press, Washington, DC's, afternoon paper; and fellow engineer, Dr. Hubert F, I hadn't seen my classmates since our graduation right after the start of the war.

All the 177th Class 'rich and famous' were there: Over 85 out of a class of around 130, with 13 war casualties. There was #1 in the class (I was #3 or #4), Buddy S, the well-known Time/Life correspondent; and the beloved and noted Yale Prof, Dr. Abe Alvin F.; the still acerbic Dr. H. Leon B., the noted medical researcher; and my former near neighbor in Germantown, Jo S., the World Bank whiz; plus a host of successful businessmen, lawyers and doctors. As I schmoozed with them, I became exceedingly pleased and proud of the life accomplishments of my former compatriots. I was glad that I had taken the time to make the long journey especially since, after the death of my Mother a few years earlier, I had few compelling reasons to return to the city of my youth.

Central High has always been listed among the top 20 high schools in the nation and, after Boston Latin, is the second oldest. I flew into Philadelphia from my California home in Hermosa Beach armed with my Yearbook. During the flight, I studied the pictures, trying mightily to put the right names to the sea of boyish faces. I mentally groaned that very recently, coeds had forced their way into attendance. This despite the long time existence of the very excellent 'separate but equal' Girl's High. Think of it! No longer the freedom to go unshaven; to tell dirty jokes out loud and fart in the classroom!

When I got to the meeting site, I was given a name badge with my graduation picture on it. Naturally, like my old skinny self, very few were recognizable in the reality of antiquity. Worse, Dan K., the suave dark complected guy who had rightfully been voted "Best Looking" had turned into a fat blob, his stomach sagging over his belt!

As I bobbed and weaved though the crowd, catching up in thumbnail conversations, I remarked to a classmate how impressed I was about *his* career and about the notable successes of all of our classmates. "Yeh", he said, "except for one guy that I just talked to – I

The CENTRALIZER

Vol. XXXVIII   Central High School, Philadelphia, January 12, 1942   No. 10

Courtmen Beat Roxboro, 28-17, In League Opener

By Murray Firestone

...ferocious Mirror quintet brought back the "Injun killin'" days, when they invaded the Roxborough' lanes and administered a 28-17 scalping to the house club last Friday, as Bob Vasoli and Wilmer Harris were the ring-leaders as the Mirrors sounded the victory bell in their opening league counter.

The Crimson and Gold drew first blood, as Bob Vasoli dropped first in his five field goals in time of two charity tosses, giving him twelve points. The Mirror lead was short-lived, however, as Al Rams knotted the count at side-court, set shot. But Fischermen came back on pointers by Vasoli and Harris were never headed thereafter.

The second period found scoring equalled at both, and tallied five markers. The C.H.S. scoring featured corner stabs Vasoli and Fenster, and a looney set shot by the redoubtable Rus. The Elgins' cut the Mirror edge to 14-10 at intermission a field goal by Matt "Moon" lembeski and a rebound shot Charley Smith, the 6'4" center. The Fischermen, out to score the game a rout, bombarded basket for 8 points in the third period, while holding the opposition to a meager 3. The highlights of this period were two classes from the far corner by Robert Vasoli, who was having one of his big "on" days, proceeded to pepper the rim.

Continued on Page Three

First Aid Training Given in Special Class

About 160 Central boys are being trained daily after school in special first aid classes so they may assist teachers in halls in the event of air raids render first aid whenever necessary.

The course consists of lectures given by Mr. Morl, Mr. Petlo, Mr. Barno. Students in the classes are learning the rudimentary principles of treatments concerning bandaging, bleeding, burns, sprains, artificial respiration, carrying, and the treatment for shock, hysteria and unconsciousness.

Although the course is designed primarily to co-operate with the Civilian Defense Program, the boys will have sufficient knowledge from it to give treatment in case of automobile accidents, drowning, and athletic injuries.

With deep regret Central students learned, last week, of the death of Leonard Claghorn, of the 180th Class, who passed away during the Christmas holidays, following an emergency appendicitis operation.

Boys to be Wardens In Air Raid Drills

177th Holds Senior Prom, Prepares for Graduation

Pin, Record Book Appear; Final Day is Jan. 21

Wednesday, January 21, is the final undergraduate day at Central for members of the 177th Class. When the class marches out after the senior farewell in the afternoon, it will have completed the last day of its four-year stay at Central.

Two days later, the seniors will reconvene at Kugler's Restaurant for the traditional evening banquet, and four days after the banquet, the commencement will be held Tuesday evening, January 27.

To complete another chapter in the history of the class, the Record Book will be distributed today, and is expected to adhere to the excellent standards set by previous graduating classes. Max Chervin, Herman J. Obermayer, and Arthur D. Silk, all of whom obtained their journalistic experience on the "Centralizer" are the "bigwigs" of the yearbook staff.

The banquet, the commencement, will be held Tuesday evening, January...

To complete another chapter in the history of the class, the Record Book will be distributed today, and is expected to adhere to the excellent standards set by previous graduating classes. Max Chervin, Herman J. Obermayer, and Arthur D. Silk, all of whom obtained their journalistic experience on the "Centralizer" are the "bigwigs" of the yearbook staff for remembrance of the occasion.

"Crusaders" Highlight Dance at Curtis Hall

The boys looked handsome, the girls looked stunning, the hall looked beautifully decorated, and faculty members looked on as the 177th Class passed another great milestone in its history by holding the Senior Prom at Curtis Arboretum last Friday night.

Bob Brodsky and his Prom Committee thought that by selecting a site in the Glenshaw Point district, the money saved would enable them to get a better band than is usually present at the semi-annual function, and their opinions were well upheld by the "Royal Crusaders" who provided some of the best music, "solid 'n' sweet", that has been heard at any Central prom.

More than 125 couples attended this final social affair of the class, with all the girls being given some small gifts as they entered, for remembrance of the occasion.

Sport Awards Given In Athletic Assembly

To reward their efforts in representing Central in athletics during the fall season, 108 members of the football, soccer, and cross-country teams received letters and certificates in last Wednesday's semi-annual athletic assembly.

With Mr. Otto J. Fischer acting as master of ceremonies, each coach presented a token certificate to the captain of his team.

S. A. to Organize Student Monitors For Service Here

Student Monitors, who volunteered for war service in the school, will be organized under a plan passed by Student Council last week.

Four committees are to be formed in charge of Morale, Conservation, First Aid, and Army.

Elections This Week

Our 177th graduating class ended our CHS careers in January, 1942, a few weeks after Pearl Harbor. I was 16, thus not yet subject to the draft.

---

forget his name – who said he had just "lost his job and had no prospects". I felt badly about this, and we commiserated sadly. I felt a knot of pity in my gut at this news. We both agreed that at our present age, 57 or 58, this was indeed a catastrophe.

Sometime later, still working the crowd, I finally ran into a true old friend of my youth. "Stan, how the hell are you? You look great!" "Bob", he grinned, "I am great, but unfortunately I have just lost my job and I have no prospects". "Oh", suspecting a rat, he being the first class failure encountered, "tell me about it". His story unfolded:

After the war, Stan finished up at Penn, and went right on to the Wharton School for his MBA. He went to work on Wall Street for 10 very successful years, but really didn't like many aspects of what he described as a cut throat, ulcer-inducing business. He took a chance and bought a franchise – the first one granted in New York City – from an outfit called McDonald's. He quit the Street to run it full time, and shortly thereafter bought a second franchise.

"Bob", he said, "Just last week I sold both shops and some other holdings for 18 million dollars. Now I don't have a job; have no prospects; and don't know what to do!"

THE WING OF THE CENTURY: FRANK ROGALLO'S TRIUMPH

The modern sport of hang gliding is unquestionably the child of the fertile imagination and ingenuity of Frank Rogallo and his wife, Gertrude. His invention, first called the 'Rogallo Wing' and now generically dubbed 'paraglider', provided a safe, economical, and easily constructed and transported device that has delighted adherents and opened up new vistas in sport. It created a new recreational field that continues to burgeon. Alas, for the Rogallo's – since he invented the device while working for NASA – it did not bring the millions that were rightfully due to them. But, I know for a fact that Rog died a happy man, secure in the knowledge that he had made an indelible impression on the 20th century.

Their success story could stop right here and the Rogallo's would still be heroes, but there is much more to be told about other applications of the basic design. These alternatives were entirely unforeseen by anyone except 'Rog' himself. His initial design of the late '40s had no rigid members. It was intended to be an improvement on the basic parachute in that it provided considerable lift and thus was highly maneuverable, thus permitting a large landing footprint. By 1968, this concept was applied to the final recovery of NASA's so-called 'flying bath-tub' space rescue and return vehicle.

An early Rogallo wing paraglider

But, Rog had other thoughts about his baby. He foresaw its possible use as a high lift orbital reentry configuration with unassisted landing ability. He spoke about astronautics applications of his wing in a talk he gave in the early 60's. I recently found a copy of this talk that he gave me amongst my souvenirs and it, along with other found Rogallo relics, galvanized me to write this piece.

The lift of the reentry return vehicle was too low to permit a low speed landing. Thus, the Rogallo paraglider was introduced into the program. It was again considered in the '90s when NASA revived the space station Crew Return Vehicle idea.

PARAWINGS FOR ASTRONAUTICS

Francis M. Rogallo[*]

In previous talks I have found that people are interested in the history of this concept. I will therefore begin with a review of the history under two headings - Pre-Sputnik I and Post-Sputnik I. I will then very briefly discuss parawing applications, advantages, configurations, structures, and materials, and then show you a film of the flight of several parawing vehicles that we thought had some interest relative to astronautics.

PARAWING HISTORY BEFORE SPUTNIK I

Although parawing history on earth may have begun with the pterodactyl 150 million years ago, and Leonardo DaVinci is credited with some proposals for using such wings in manned flight about 500 years ago, I would like to skip to 1945 when I began a serious and con-

Around the same time, NASA Langley Research Center, where Frank worked, put out a request for proposal which would apply his principles to an inflated parawing that would reenter the atmosphere at about 5000 mph after inflation and separation from the Aerobee sounding rocket. It was on this project, IMP (Inflatable Micrometeoroid Paraglider), which my company won as a result of the proposal effort I led, that I first met Rog and was converted forever into parawing nirvana.

The IMP program flight test achieved its goals, and led me to make, in 1963, a successful proposal to the Air Force for the initial development of a reentry paraglider to rescue a crewperson from an orbiting space station. This program was called FIRST (Fabrication of Inflatable Reentry Structures for Test). The idea caught the public's imagination and was written up in TIME magazine in the Feb. 1, 1963 issue. Rog was very excited by both of these projects and continued to root us on. Multi-passenger versions were proposed in 1964, and again in the '90s for the International Space Station.

Artist's rendition of IMP. The Aerobee nose cone in which it
was packed is shown being released at beginning of reentry.

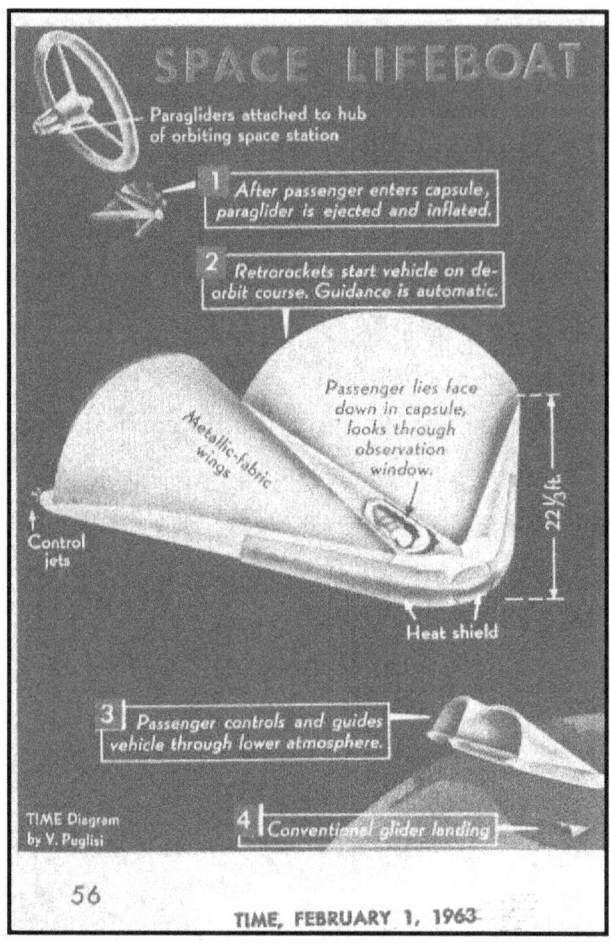

The FIRST system, with crew member in prone position. Inflation s by Nitrogen supplied by a hose/tether from the space station

As the Apollo program progressed in the mid-'60s and the Air Force contemplated its MOL (Manned Orbiting Laboratory) program, other applications of the Rogallo wing concept were proposed. The most pertinent was its use in the recovery of first and second stage boosters of the Saturn size. Instead of parachute/ocean recovery - and encouraged by NASA/ Marshall Space Flight Center - we proposed using parawing attachments to bring back the spent boosters to the launch area. And, we proposed to the Air Force an unmanned version of FIRST to return payloads from the MOL to Earth. Neither concept came to fruition.

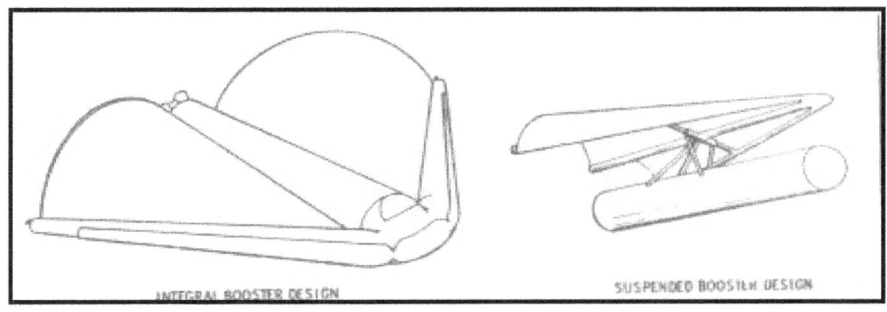

Two proposed schemes to return boosters 'home'. A two 200 foot diameter balloon set-up, with netting to 'catch' the boosters completed the picture. The integral design (left) was inflated; the right hand design collapsible.

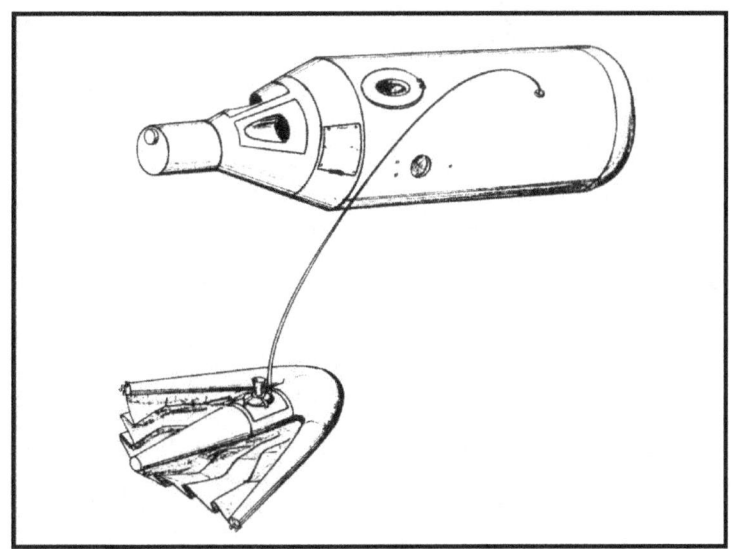

Small payload package returns were visualized.
Several might be dispatched during a mission

Obviously, the '60s were a time of great hope and zeal in all aerospace ventures, and Rog – one of truly early aerospace engineering graduates (Stanford, 1935) stayed active long enough to see many of his dreams realized. In 1971 – a bit after he retired – he sent me the note below, along with the picture of an early Rogallo wing in flight shown earlier. He was a great pioneer and, fortunately, reminders of him continue to joyously fill the air.

17 Milford Rd.
Newport News, Va, 23601
April 13, 1971

Dear Bob,

I received your note and the enclosed information of March 31, and I was happy to fill out the ATAA form recommending you for Fellow Grade.

Since retirement I have spent much time at Kitty Hawk, N.C., where we have a beach cottage. We would like to build a retirement home there, including a private aeronautical research station.

Best wishes to my friends at Aerojet.

Sincerely,
Roy

He did!

Chapter 2
ANNALS OF MORALITY

- **CREDO OF A GOD-FEARING ATHEIST**
- **A RETORT BY A FRIEND**
- **DOES THE POPE REALLY UNDERSTAND?**
- **WHAT ABOUT PUBLIC PRAYER?**
- **THE BEAUTY OF TENURE**
- **ON ABORTION**
- **WOMEN**
- **BINDLESTIFFED**
- **THE NEW ATHEIAGNOS WEEK HOLIDAY**
- **PEACE AT LAST IN THE MIDDLE EAST**
- **MORE PLEDGING**

October 24, 1972

Dear Folks,

I'm sure that the Bright Angel Retirement Home has thanked you and the many others who have made gifts to the Home that have brought so much pleasure and comfort to us residents.

But I wish to thank you personally from the bottom of my heart because I am the recipient of the little portable radio which you gave me. I listen to it constantly while I am awake. I have never had a radio of my very own since I came to the Home to live. Everything is nice here and they take wonderful care of us. There are two of us in each room. My roommate is Martha Jones. She is 87 and I am 83.

Martha has had a radio of her own since I came here ten years ago. She kept it so low I could never hear the programs. When I asked her to turn it up so I could hear she wouldn't do it. Bless her, she is a sweet soul and I suppose she can't help being that way.

Last week she dropped her radio and it broke into so many pieces that it cannot be repaired. Last night I was listening to the evening services of the First Methodist Church and the beautiful hymns that I love so well. Martha asked me to turn it up so she could hear, so naturally I told her to go fuck herself.

Again, thanking you, I am,

Gladys Gardiner

I found the above letter amongst my souvenirs. I know not from whence it came.

CREDO OF A GOD-FEARING ATHEIST

I've been a closet atheist for over 65 years. I suspect that there are lots of others like me throughout the world. We have chosen anonymity to avoid society's slings and arrows - figurative and literal. To my mind the only notable latter-day avowed atheist was the recently late Madalyn Murray O'Hair - who was apparently 'silenced' by true believers. Why 'come out' now? Only in my twilight years do I dare cross the line from passive atheism to a slightly more active role. At this point, it doesn't much matter which virulent disease, including intolerance, gets to me first.

It takes a certain amount of guts mixed with foolhardiness to ascribe to this unpopular position - especially these days. A combination of the militant religious rightists; religious fanatics of all sects; the violence-inclined among the religious anti-abortionists; the white supremacist Christ-aligned militias abetted by NRA zealots; and the remnants of the Klan, both singly and in concert; as well zealous Islamists, strike a certain amount of terror and trepidation in those who vocally oppose them. The venom of these extremists might well be turned against such heretics, such as me, and their families, who blaspheme their peculiar brand of morality. Their native hatred in this country evolves from their avowed purpose of actively safeguarding and watch guarding obsolete puritanical views that long ago formed the ideological foundation of our country.

Somewhere between my Bar Mitzvah at 13 and my confirmation at 16, I began giving a lot of thought to religion, politics, and social mores. I started reading serious books - Thomas Wolfe, Dos Passos, Veblen, and yes, the Old and New Testaments. They caused me to start thinking about religion and its impact on the world. I also took more interest in the beliefs of my parents and friends. Only a very few of the latter had any real feeling about religion, and none went to Hebrew School two times a week after high school, as I did. Despite losing my older sister to leukemia when she was 18, a cataclysm that often drives people into the bosom of the church, my parents seldom went to synagogue for other than for the high holy days. In fact, on Yom Kippur - a day of atonement and fasting, my father was known to sneak around the block from our Schul to an Italian deli for a pick-me-up. Still, since they belonged to a conservative synagogue, they did insist that I become Bar Mitzvahed and Confirmed, and attend Hebrew school.

By Confirmation, I had clearly turned into an agnostic. I felt no need for the concept of a God. I believed that each person is responsible for his or her own actions and must bear the responsibility for them. I believed that each person is a god-like creature and can certainly know right from wrong. I saw the beauty of the Golden Rule. At the same time, I began to recognize the reality of religion being the 'opiate of the masses' a la Karl Marx. But, I could not yet take the final jump to atheism since, in my heart of hearts, I still feared the inevitable lightning bolt. I dared not vocalize these feelings, even to my friends, lest I be called a Communist or, worse, a traitor to Judaism.

Confirmation Service

Congregation Adath Jeshurun

Broad and Diamond Streets
Philadelphia, Pa.

Sunday, June 1, 1941
Shabuoth, 5701

Program .... Shirley ... Adele ..

Psalm 1 (Hebrew) .... Renate R. Hirsch
Psalm 1 (English) .... Suzanne H. Wolf
The Heavenly Light (Meyerhardt) ..... Carolyn Irma Esterson
Charlene Elizabeth Apfelbaum ....msioff
.... By Parents
Psalm 121 (Hebrew) .... Robert Fox Brodsky
..... to Class .... Elizabeth M. Levinson
Closing Prayer ....
Blessing of Confirmants .... Rabbi Max D. Klein
Presentation of Certificates ....

Confirmation Reception

A joint reception will be given for the confirmants, their parents and friends in the auditorium of the Synagogue, under the auspices of the Women's Association, tonight, Sunday, June 1 from 8.00 to 10.30 o'clock.
The Congregation is cordially invited to attend.

Already an agnostic, I nevertheless was dutifully confirmed and indeed enjoyed the social interactions with girls as a relief from my all-boys high school. Note that I presented the class address!

Gradually, however, as my godless life went on with reasonable progress and a modicum of success, the searing danger of the thunderbolt subsided. I finally evolved mentally to the state in which I remained for most of my adult life, until I wrote the first draft of this piece a few years ago: a full blooded, but non-vocal 'God-fearing' atheist. It has never been difficult for me to reconcile being ethnically Jewish, yet having no religion. Nor do I think my non-belief is or was a ploy to escape being Jewish - and thus more like the great majority of my peers. In the child raising days of my marriages, both my wives and I agonized about rearing our four children without God or religion. We held firm in our beliefs. Now, our kids tell us that they did not suffer or feel 'left out' and, indeed, are very happy about having one less concern in their lives.

What I do regret, however, is that I never succeeded in imbuing in my children the pride and delight of being Jewish - a feeling that continues to grow in me, despite my equally strong objections to the religious aspects. Thus, four living persons have been lost to Judaism - to the greater benefit of mankind, I hope. Nevertheless, it was a hard tradeoff, and one I won't disclose or discuss with my orthodox cousin Susan and her husband in Haifa - for fear of losing their friendship. As for me, I have never hesitated admitting to being Jewish or being an atheist to anyone who asked. I just never saw fit to advertise either condition. I have greatly admired the few active atheists I have known or heard about - but from afar. I maintain the nagging feeling that as soon as you take up the battle, you are only becoming a proponent of another 'religion'. I think maybe that is why so many people are innate but undeclared atheists. Perhaps we are truly a silent majority?

At this point, my dislike of organized religion is laced with contempt for the many hypocrites who preach but do not listen! I believe that many of the troubles in the world stem from the pontifications, baffling didos and inconsistencies, and 'learned' pronouncements and interpretations of the disciples. I believe that much that is evil in the world - past and present - can be hung on the door of organized religion. The wars, famines, inquisitions, holocausts, pillages, slavery, burnings, acts of terror and looting are the scars of failed credos. All the prejudice, racism, anti-Semitism, anti-anything can be squarely blamed on zealots who, in the name of their diety, wish to impose their tenets on all others. All this evil has arisen from the teachings of the overly pious - and will continue until we are either released from the tyranny of religion or the faithful really begin to take all of its basic teachings seriously, not just the ones that are convenient.

As I muse about religion, I am awed by the power of the mind and its ingenuity in making an almost coherent ethos out of whole cloth. The fantastic fabric of beliefs and rules of morality that man has devised to keep the masses under control and to shore up and justify his belief in the unproven, speaks volumes about the magnificence of human mental ability. This cathedral has been erected because man is unwilling to take responsibility for his individual actions or face a futureless death. Religion is the house of cards that man has devised to assuage his conscience about the commission of unthinkable deeds and to attempt to circumvent the inevitability of death.

But think of the fabulous concepts that have launched hundreds of thousands of weekly sermons for over two thousand years: the concepts of a single god, and its derivative Father/Son/Holy Ghost triumvirate; the very necessary life–after-death immortality; a heaven and a hell with their angels and devils, saints and sinners; the separation of "soul" from body; a child of virgin birth and his resurrection; the ascension to heaven on a white horse; a chosen people, creationism and its friend, Intelligent Design, and the host of other equally fanciful and mind-boggling ideas.

These concepts all arose to fill to satisfy man's craving to find a reason for existence (i.e., unwillingness to recognize a crapshoot) and an understanding of how it all began (not content to agree that after God got it all started, he died). On the positive side and to its everlasting credit, Religion, 'for them that needs it', relieves the fear of death and nothingness, fills a need to believe in something if one does not believe in one's self, supplies a routing for prayer, precludes the fear of free choice, and fulfills a need to belong - in a majority position. These beliefs are the rock upon which many lives are anchored. Atheism can never fill this void for those who will never accept the scientific explanations of our universe and how it operates.

The perpetuators of the status quo of this fabric are the clergy, who wish to maintain mind control and shepherd their flock into their version of heaven; the politicians who use religion to maintain control of the streets; the parents who want to control their kids and to have them live comfortably with their neighbors and friends; the choirs and accessories who make their living from religion; and bigots of all kinds who use religion to explain their anomalies. Man has paid a terrible price for the luxury of having religion! And, so have we atheists! Try to put yourself into the mind frame of a true unbeliever. Can you begin to imagine the Alice-in-Wonderland world in which we live?

Contrast the living reality with the way the world should be if religion really worked. Look at the wonderful truths, concepts, ideas and artifacts that have evolved from religion: the superlative Golden Rule, the mostly reasonable ten commandments; the equally logical dietary law ideas; the beautiful hymns, gospel songs, and psalms; the magnificent edifices and artistic creations; and perhaps even the very concept of freedom. A magical theory, which in many cases, is accompanied by poor or mystical application.

Why hasn't organized religion worked? I think that deep down, most sense the ethereal nature of their chosen religion, and therefore realize that its teachings are not immutable.

These deep seated doubts must extend even to the zealous. They leave room for much individual and group interpretation of the 'true word of the Lord', and thus open the door to the atrocities that the world has and is witnessing in the name of religion. What it gets down to is the "holier than thou" attitude which permits the extremists to believe that they are acting on mankind's behalf by forcibly imposing their beliefs on the unwashed. Such are the things that witch trials and burning at stake were made of, and now appear in a more modern, more mass destructive form.

Do I have doubts myself? Am I, too, a zealot? I don't think so - at least up to now. I have kidded with my wife and friends that on my death bed, I will want a priest and a rabbi in attendance to copper my bets. But, in truth, I have no fear of death since I have led a good worthwhile life and know that my immortality will last only through my childrens' and grandchildrens' and surviving friends' lives. I dislike dissing the religion of my forefathers, but I cannot honestly see my race being universally better or worse than the others. Extremists abound and do not allow all into heaven. Religion, purported to be able to move mountains, in reality merely allows its minions to look the other way when their precepts are being ravaged.

I have become an activist now by documenting the feelings I have built up over much of my lifetime. I don't necessarily condone this activism. It might better have been written by someone willing to pick up the O'Hare legacy and crusading with more wisdom, and inspiration than I can muster. I have no stomach for picking up O'Hare's crusade.

I have unburdened myself and that is enough for me at this time.

To vividly illustrate the true nature of the practicing atheist's ethical problem, and to avoid loosing the aura of evil that saturates the times and places we live in, I shall not submit this piece for print other than to include it in this book. This is to assure that I and my family will be relatively safe from the crazies in the white sheets and white collars, and the abortion clinic zanies, since the readership of my book will not be widespread, and certainly not read by fringe folks. The irony, of course is that I - a grown man living in the land of the free - have to genuinely fear the backlash that could come from segments of the WASPish world with which I have lived, so far, in quiet silent harmony for all of my days.

Is there any hope that organized religion will rise to do as they say? I think not - not as long as there are livings to be made, kingdoms to be perpetuated, and human fears to be conquered. With this tract, I have made peace and stated my case. I will now sit and wait for the assassin's bullet, the cross burning on the lawn, or some such assault against me or my family - delivered with God's blessing by some pious soul who does not care to have his beliefs derided or questioned.

God – a peek

A RETORT BY A FRIEND

The minute I documented my thoughts on atheism (lower case 'a' to assure that it is not considered as just another religion), I automatically forfeited my rights as one of God's chosen people. But, what the hay! I asked myself for what He had chosen them? A tradition of discrimination and hatred passed down through the ages and culminating, but not ending, in the Holocaust? A fear of Dreyfus-like accusations? The right to be depicted as long-nosed Shylocks? And, a coterie of humiliations, Temple desecrations and character assassin-ations that have dogged our footsteps for time immemorial? The final irony is that even though I have abandoned Him and one of his favorite religions (presumably?), the 'stigma' of being Jewish will follow me and mine to our graves. None the less, I take great pride in being an ethnic Jew, and would choose no other ethnicity if given a choice.

Shylock and his daughter in the play,
"Merchant of Venice" by Will Shakespeare.
He was usually depicted in caricature with a
prominent nose, and remains a
symbol of anti-Semitism

Having completed my "coming out of the closet" essay draft, *CREDO OF A GOD-FEARING ATHEIST*, I sent it for review to a friend whom I admire and respect even though, God bless him, he is a rock bound conservative Republican (capital 'R', but the capitalization of this wretched word wrenches my guts) and a M.O.T. (Member of the Tribe). We have been friends since third grade. He is a noted journalist, having been editor and publisher of a major newspaper. In a return letter, he sent me a thoughtful reply, which I feel represents an erudite opposing viewpoint not clouded by mysticism. I will excerpt from it:

"As I have gotten older, I have become progressively more disillusioned with secular solutions and explanations for life's dilemmas. (As I read your piece, I was not sure that you were not more of a secularist than an atheist) (Note: I'm not sure what this means?)

In our short lives, we have seen men walk on the moon, babies conceived in petri dishes, and hearts and livers successfully transplanted. Technology has substantially answered many of the questions that historically drove men to religion; where do we come from, where are we going, why do the stars twinkle?

But neither technology nor secular results of central planning have been able to explain the randomness of good health, good brains, success, etc. When you become reconciled to the fact that there is no rational explanation for the distribution of life's blessing and curses, it becomes inevitable that you embrace religion in some format. I have no trouble embracing religion. I find no other satisfactory answer.

(The above is a key paragraph in his letter. It is one which I find very troubling, and will comment on it later.) The letter continues:

As to not imposing on my children, my beliefs: I am convinced you do children a disservice when you profess to be value neutral. This applies to the moral standards of being alive, as well as to embracing religion. I did not – and do not – expect all of my children to embrace my religious beliefs, or to share them. I believe I had an obligation – and still do – to present them what I believe is best. If it is unsatisfactory, they should reject it, but at least I do not sway. I have gone through 72+ years, and I don't have any convictions about which I feel strongly enough to want to pass them on to the next generation. I believe it is part of my duty to tell them intellectually, theologically, socially what I believe to be wheat and what I believe to be chaff.

As to being Jewish: I enjoy being part of a band of brothers. I find succor in the notion that I am part of a tradition which goes back almost 3000 years (note: I would have said nearing 6000). When I go into a synagogue in a foreign country where I do not speak the language, but I hear them say the Shema or singing 'Ain Kehlohanu', I am thrilled that I am part of a tradition that transcends all national ones (note, I expect that Catholics evince the same sense of oneness when the service is in Latin). I am part of a tradition which has made the world a better place to live in."

As with my question on the paragraph above which I previously promised to comment on, I question my friend's last sentence. Has organized religion really made the world a better place to live? I think not. As I pointed out in my "CREDO", I see religion's inter- and intra- jealousies as the root of most of the world's conflicts and cruelties.

I am pleased with his next to last paragraph. It sort of leaves me 'off the hook' on my lifelong concern that my wife and I did not do right, religiously, by our children. I take comfort in that!

But it is the questioned paragraph that really bothers me. Why should "the randomness of good health, good brains, success, etc." be credited top a deity? Why is it necessary to have rational or scientific answers for all of the world's still unanswered questions? This is the nub of religiosity – the reason a deity is needed by many. Why won't people see existence as a 'crapshoot' –a true life example of 'Chaos' Theory. Darwin understood this many years ago, but his proven theory is so abhorrent to many that Creationism, now being disguised as "Intelligent Design", continues to have a burgeoning number of followers. Many of these are the same people that play the tables at Las Vegas and pray to God for luck.

DOES THE POPE REALLY UNDERSTAND?

"Religious Freedom" was the watchword that brought the Pilgrims to the new world, and remains as one of our supposed beacons bringing immigrants here from all corners of the world. But is there religious freedom in a country that suppresses, and indeed condones the actions of extremists who look on those of us who are professed atheists as an anathema to take murderous action against? Is there religious (or any other kind of) freedom when sects of organized religion, led chiefly by men, deign to tell women what they can and can not do with their own bodies? Is there religious freedom when the Pope attempts to reconcile his church with reality and is attacked by his own minions for his 'liberalism'. Let me cite an example of the latter problem:

A few years ago, an article written by Larry B. Stammer in the *LA Times* noted that the then Pope had not only legitimized Darwin's theory of evolution, but also improved on it by adding the 'scientifically proven' (my causticism, not the Pope's words) concept of 'soul'. I will quote from the article, which was headlined, *"Evolution Is More Than a Theory, Pope Tells Scientists"*:

"Pope John Paul II, ----------, said this week that Charles Darwin's theory of evolution is 'more than a hypothesis'

While endorsing evolution at a meeting in Rome of the Pontifical Academy of Sciences, the Pope said believers must continue to acknowledge God as the creator of all things, and to understand that humans have soul in addition to a physical side.

The Pope's brief words are likely to trouble fundamentalist Christians, who believe in the literal truth of the Genesis creation story – that God created the earth in seven 24 hour days and that humans were created independently of other creatures. ----------------

The pope's statement comes as some in the religious right in the United states have been attempting to force public schools to teach creationism as well as evolution, which they belittle as 'just a theory'. ----------------"

The Pope's findings were not taken as infallible by all his people. In fact he was labeled as 'senile'. In his '*Column Right*' in the October 29, 1996, issue of the *LA Times,* Cal Thomas, that bastion of great conservative thinking, headlined his bit, "The Misguided Evolution of the Pope" with subtitle, '*If man is not a unique creation of God, he is of no greater value than any other living thing*', thereby definitively confirming the extant pecking order in the animal kingdom. The column forthrightly commences:

"Pope John Paul II, who courageously stood against the tyranny of Soviet communism, has succumbed in his declining years to the tyranny of evolutionary scientists who claim we are related to monkeys. (note, I believe that they also claim we are related to

those horrid looking Neanderthals*). However the Catholic Church spins this one, many will be led to believe that Science is God and the ultimate determiner of our origins. Was there a scientist present at the beginning?"*

The Maestro himself, from his Web site blog, 2007

Now, there's an erudite, pertinent, zinger if there ever was one! Later in his column he rightly expresses a small part of the evolutionary theory, cleverly (?) smeared with the mysticism that I have been railing against:

*"Evolutionary scientists have been anything but humble in their attempt to replace the Jewish and Christian high view of man. Their lower view claims that we are material and energy shaped by pure chance in a random (*note: and presumably illogical?*) universe with no creator, no purpose, no destiny, and no hope. God asks the ultimate question of Job that ought to be asked of evolutionary science: 'Where were you when I laid the earth's foundation? Tell me, if you understand. Who marked off its dimensions? Surely you know! Who stretched out a measuring line across it? On what were its footings set, or who laid its cornerstone, while the morning stars sang together and all the angels shouted for joy."*

Fortunately, there are some folks who have either ignored or rebutted such drivel and misinformation. In the Saturday, December 16, 2000 issue of the *LA Times* (Section B), Bernadette Murphy, in a Book Review column entitled, " Themes From Thinkers Who Are Not Believers", reviews a book entitled, *"ATHEISM- A Reader"* edited by S.T. Joshi (Prometheus Books). In it, she writes:

"What is the elusive ingredient intrinsic to religious faith? According to "Atheism: A Reader", a collection of essays that spans the last three centuries to provide an atheistic critique of religion, belief may simply be a knee-jerk reaction to the existential horror of life, and religion itself little more than a sham designed to prey on human fear and supers-

tition." (note: Wow! That 'horror of life' phrase makes me want to resign from the atheist corps!)--------------

"Bertrand Russell forcefully disputes the idea of God's existence based on the first-cause argument. According to Russell, the supposition that, because the world exists, a Creator must also exist is a flawed argument not unlike the story of the elephant and the tortoise: 'A certain Hindu thinker believed the earth rested on an elephant. When asked what the elephant rested on, he replied that it rested on a tortoise. When asked what the tortoise rested upon, he said, 'I am tired of this. Suppose we change the subject.' Russell equates believers' inability to provide hard scientific proof of their faith with the same kind of subject-switching, using emotionalism and vague sentiment to replace facts."

The Popemobile

The Popemobile provides a bullet-proof shelter for his highness. But who would want to take his life? A fellow Catholic who is a staunch creationist? A follower of some other religion not believing in the Golden Rule? It is a true puzzle-ment!

While the above elephant-tortoise parable answers some of Cal's questions, what is really going on here? Does the Pope really understand the implications of his infallibility? Does he realize that in adding the factor of 'soul' into Darwin's theory, he has moved from the scientific to the mystical?

Does the screaming left hand column-first page headline of the (Good) Friday, April 13, 2001, LA *Times: "Doubting the Story of Exodus"* - '*Many scholars have quietly concluded that the epic of Moses never happened, and even Jewish clerics are raising questions. Others think it combines myth, cultural memories and kernels of truth*', mean that the bible can not be taken literally? If so, when does it stop? Is the fabric ripping? Will the circle stay unbroken?

WHAT ABOUT PUBLIC PRAYER?

On two occasions, once in 1992 and the last in 2000, I felt the need to take a stand on the issue of public prayer. In neither case was I successful, except for letting off of some steam. The first issue had to do with our Pledge of Allegiance to the flag, and the correspondence below is self-explanatory:

Aug 21 1992

Ramona Ripston, Director
ACLU of So. Cal.

Dear Ramona:

   The purpose of this letter is to ask the ACLU to consider undertaking an unpopular, but challenging cause, using me (if no one better is apparent) as the plaintIff. I am a long-time member of the ACLU. I am galvanized into action as a result of an article which lately appeared in a San Pedro city newsletter, which discussed the history of The Pledge Of Allegiance.

   Since the mid- fifties when it mysteriously appeared (I recall no great debate) I have had the appended phrase "under God" stuffed down my craw. I somehow feel un-American when I omit the phrase as I always do during the symbolic recantation. I think my civil rights are being abrogated by a country that apparently only gives lip service to the separation of church and state. I would like to seek action – i.e. a court opinion - on the legality of having religious folks impress their beliefs on all and sundry. Prayer in school is not permitted- so why prayer or imprecation at public events?

   I hope you will consider my plea not frivolous – albeit windmill tilting - and agree to join the fight on what I believe to be an important "family value" issue. However, I cannot but believe that perhaps this battle may have been fought and lost.

   Very truly yours,

   Dr RF Brodsky
   PS: I would appreciate your sending a copy of this to the National organization.

   Soon after, I received the following return:

ACLU FOUNDATION
OF SOUTHERN CALIFORNIA

August 27, 1992

Dr. RF Brodsky
401 2nd Street
Hermosa Beach, California 90254

Dear Dr. Brodsky:

Thank you for your letter of August 21, 1992. Although I am fully sympathetic to the complaint you raise, unfortunately the issues have been litigated and lost.

You reason that, if prayer in school is not permitted, then why is prayer pervasive at public events. I must tell you that when the Supreme Court upheld the ban on school prayer at graduations this year, we were all pleasantly shocked, not just surprised. Eight years ago, the Supreme Court upheld the practice of prayers at the opening of legislative sessions. The Court distinguished its ruling in that case based on a ubiquitous historic practice that predated the Constitution. Most of us thought that case would a stepping-off point for restricting prayer in school. But that has not turned out to be the case. The Court draws a line between "impressionable" youth and adults who can simply walk away from the prayer.

While the ACLU does not support that distinction, it is unlikely we can reverse the legislative prayer case with this Court. At the same time, that does not mean that we do not intend to continue to try and restrict the alignment of religion with public function, in this society, Whenever we believe we stand a reasonable possibility of winning such a challenge -- or at least not making significantly worse law -- we will continue to fight for what you aptly describe as an important "family value." To that end, we won a good decision from the California Supreme Court invalidating graduation prayers. We also won a good decision from the federal courts directing the County of San Bernardino to divest itself of a Christian theme park, Desert Christ Park, which it owned and operated. We will continue to press this issue.

I thank you for taking the time to share your concern with me. Please stay "galvanized". Even if we can't advance, at least we may be able to hold them where they are for now.

Most sincerely,
Ramona Ripston
Executive Director

Apparently I was not sedated by this news, and went back to the drawing board:

Aug 31, 1992

Romona Ripston, Exec. Director
ACLU Foundation of So Cal
1616 Beverly Blvd
PO Box 26907
LA, CA 90026-9938

Dear Ramona:

I thank you for your prompt reply to my letter of Aug 21, which questioned the constitutionality of the 1954-inserted phrase" under God" in our pledge of allegiance to the flag (i.e,; the Republic) However, I was not satisfied with your answer, and thus must again take up the cudgel:

You said, "the issues have been litigated and lost". It was not clear whether it was the specific issue of the constitutionality of the "under God" phrase that had been considered, since you discussed at length the related, but completely different (in my mind), issue of public prayer. If this specific issue has indeed been tried and lost, then I will fold my tent realizing the difficulty of a fair review with the presently constituted Supreme Court.

If this is not the case, then I rush to point out that the specific issue is whether our country officially acknowledges that our affairs are indeed being carried out under the official aegis of God, and that our country is subservient to his will and benevolence. I believe that this is just what this addition to the pledge implies. This does not appear to be a constitutional position, and thus could become a true cause celebre for ACLU consideration. Please edify me- and, as before, honor my request to send my correspondence to ACLU national headquarters (or send me their address).

Very truly yours,

The prompt reply noted sorrow in that I wasn't satisfied with the previous reply, but "There is simply nothing we can do." I was referred to the National Office if I wanted to persist. I threw in the towel, and the beast in me did not again arise until July 2000. Again, it was a matter of public prayer, but now on a local city basis:

We had been living peacefully in the sleepy bedroom community part of greater Redondo Beach (the other, inland, part of Redondo is somewhat industrialized, featuring my old alma mater, aerospace giant TRW) for several years, and could not help but notice the quirkiness of the governing City Council. They appeared to be a highly Waspish 'Good Old Boys' club, who continually were at war with any constituents or appointees who did not go along with their ideas. This attitude has recently cost the city burghers a fortune in a law suit pay-off brought on by the Council's questionable dismissal of a City Manager who only wanted to manage without a lot of their help.

The case in point, however, commenced when a 'rogue' columnist in the very conservative *South Bay Daily Breeze* noted that the City Council was persisting in the practice of calling upon padres with very specific religious axes to grind, i.e. often invoking the aid of Jesus Christ and / or the Trinity, to kick off their council meetings. Their thinking is that public prayer is a privilege maintained for Christians only. Most others cities who still were holding on to the practice of prayer before such pow-wows were using non-denominational prayers (of course, to the chagrin of atheists and agnostics). The resulting flurry of articles and Letters to the Editor about this practice led me to write:

July 14, 2000

Mayor Greg Hill and City Councilpersons
City of Redondo Beach

Dear Mayor and Council:

By now, it should be clear to you that the reason you have heard few if any complaints about the religious aspects of your council meetings is because very few people were aware of the practice. Most of us have been brought up believing fervently in the separation of church and state, which - as I suspect you all know – comes with our Constitution. I find it hard to believe that my City did not abandon this practice when other cities in the South Bay (and all over the country) did so.

I feel I am speaking for all minority and especially atheist constituents who feel that a prayer has no part in the business of running the city unless we are in a " Spahn and Sain and pray for rain" situation. I know I am speaking for myself and my wife, and she is neither minority nor atheist.

Very truly yours,

cc: ACLU of So. Cal.

I never heard back from the Mayor, and the Council persists in this practice to this date, despite a recent election whose results any fool could interpret as indicating restlessness by the troops (alas, the Mayor ran unopposed). In fact, a recent article by Leslie Simmons in the *Breeze* noted in its banner, "Burbank prayer ruled constitutionally wrong," followed by, "A judge Thursday barred religious prayer from being said at the beginning of

Burbank City Council meetings, after finding that an invocation last year mentioning Jesus Christ violated the first amendment. -------". A portion of my July 14 letter to the Mayor was repeated in the rogue columnists' commentary ("Commotion over RB prayer doesn't want to go away", July 31, 2000), among others, including a genuine "Born Again", who had similarly complained. The ACLU, in the meantime, had replied thusly:

July 18, 2000

Dr. R.F. Brodsky
110 the Village, #410
Redondo Beach, Ca. 90277

Dear Dr. Brodsky:

Thank you for your letter to Ramona Ripston, which she referred to me.

The ACLU is currently litigating a similar case against the Palo Verde Unified School District (Bacus v. Palo Verde USD), which opens each board meeting with an explicitly sectarian prayer that ends, "In Jesus' name we pray."

The case is now on appeal to the 9th Circuit Court of Appeals; a ruling in our favor would greatly strengthen arguments to end sectarian prayer in other settings, including city council meetings. We have received complaints from other cities in Southern California about this practice. Assuming we are successful, once we have a ruling in the Bacus case we can inform these cities that their practice is unconstitutional and must be ended.

Thank you for bringing this to our attention.

Sincerely,

Elizabeth Schroeder
Associate Director

Despite the fact that the Burbank ruling, as well as an anticipated favorable ruling in the Palo Verde case, probably will settle the local issue, I fear for the national sanctity of the separation of church and state. Apparently this battle has to be fought on every battleground, every day, and vigilance vs. the religious right continually maintained.

Quotations: (via 'Googling' under 'Public Prayer')

- *"Americans are being denied the right to express their religious speech in the public square." Ralph Reed, Christian Coalition.*

- *"Public schools can neither foster religion nor preclude it. Our public schools must treat religion with fairness and respect and vigorously protect religious expression as well as the freedom of conscience of all other students. In so doing our public schools reaffirm the First Amendment and enrich the lives of their students". Secretary of Education Richard W. Riley June 1998*

- *"A Congress that allows God to be banned from our schools while our schools can teach about cults, Hitler and even devil worship is wrong, out of touch, and needs some common sense." Rep. James Traficant, (D-OH) 1999-APR-27.*

- *"There is no such source and cause of strife, quarrel, fights, malignant opposition, persecution, and war, and all evil in the state, as religion. Let it once enter our civil affairs, our government would soon be destroyed. Let it once enter our common schools, they would be destroyed." Supreme Court of Wisconsin, Weiss v. District Board, 1890-MAR-18.*

- *"A union of government and religion tends to destroy government and degrade religion." Supreme Court Justice Hugo Black, Engel v. Vitale, (1962)*

- *"School sponsorship of a religious message is impermissible because it sends the ancillary message to members of the audience who are nonadherents that they are outsiders, not full members of the political community, and an accompanying message to adherents that they are insiders, favored members of the political community", U.S. Supreme Court ruling, Santa Fe v. Doe, (2000).*

THE BEAUTY OF TENURE

The battle over whether university Tenure is an essential blessing or the work of the devil remains a topic of vital interest on the campus. For me, the question was highlighted by the somewhat outre series of events that occurred in the '70s:

Those who wish to abolish or qualify Tenure cite the lack of incentive to continue a vigorous research and teaching program following its award (e.g.: see http://www.aaup.org/postten.htm). They point to a few Professors who clearly began 'coasting' through their careers once having achieved Tenure. Their zeal to conduct research and to seek improvement types of sabbaticals may have diminished significantly compared to their valiant 'publish or perish' efforts exerted while struggling to achieve permanency. Tenure is a 'for life' commitment and can only be revoked if a grievous sin, e.g. such as improper relations with a student, can be rigorously proven. Tenure is generally considered a 'free ride', a sinecure, through a career; cancelable only if the specialty position being filled is dropped from the curriculum. This seldom happens, but could occur if an entire academic course of study is eliminated.

Academic tenure is primarily intended to guarantee the right to <u>academic freedom</u>: it protects respected teachers and researchers when they dissent from prevailing opinion, openly disagree with authorities of any sort, or spend time on unfashionable topics. Thus academic tenure is similar to the lifetime tenure that protects some judges from external pressure. Without job security, the scholarly community as a whole might favor "safe" lines of inquiry. Tenure makes original ideas more likely to arise, by giving scholars the intellectual autonomy to investigate the problems and solutions about which they are most passionate, and to report their honest conclusions. (from WIKIPEDIA)

I have been aware of the intricacies of dealing with college faculties for well over 30 years. For a period of 9 years, I was an engineering Department Head at a large mid-Western university. When I replaced my Department's beloved multi-year Head, I inherited a too-large faculty which did include one or two tenured faculty members that anti-Tenure adherents would call 'deadwood' and would consequently consider as candidates for dismissal. I arrived on the scene at a time of engineering recession, when the undergraduate student population of my Department had dropped from a high of over 500 to a number like 200 and still diminishing, in a period of two years. The extant faculty was geared up based on the larger population.

The first thing I had to do was to 'lay off' several of the young and very promising untenured, and consequently unprotected, faculty; having, by long established academic 'law', to retain the tenured faculty, some of whom who did not conduct research programs or have PhD degrees. But, I soon found out that these so-called 'deadwood' professors were excellent undergraduate teachers, and loved to teach. I also soon found out that there really is no such thing as 'deadwood' faculty. I learned that the outstanding feature of all professors, whether they are really good teachers or not, is a tremendous pride in what they are doing.

But the basic justification for maintaining tenure was clearly demonstrated a few years into my term of office. My memory of the episode was recently refreshed when I visited my former, and now retired, Dean and personal friend, who is the main protagonist of this story. He was able to clear up some of my recollections about the tumultuous events that focused around him in the 70's:

My Dean was, and is, as fair and honorable a person as I have ever known. He made no bones about his sincere beliefs. He was a rock bound Baptist and a staunch believer in Creationism. He taught Sunday School at his church and, after his retirement, continued teaching at nearby Faith Baptist Bible College. If he had any overt prejudices, he never exhibited them to me – an outlander to the mid-West and an ethnic Jew – or to anyone else, to my knowledge. He assiduously separated university business from his religious beliefs. In my mind, his actions always set the highest standards of what I think the Judeo-Christian ethic represents in theory. However, in a recent correspondence, a now-retired member of my faculty who was on hand during the excitement provocatively wrote,

" ---- and that he did a very good job of matching his religious convictions with his administrative convictions. Actually I often wondered if he wasn't being hypocritical in his matching of those convictions. I was never able to visualize in my own mind how a person with his religious convictions could really make a separation between religion and administration.--. "

The maelstrom that descended on the Dean's head started innocently enough. An article in the school newspaper revealed that while giving a talk to a college Bible Study group, a member of the Liberal Arts faculty averred his ability to very clearly see "auras" around certain favored people's heads. The assertions in this article started a brou-ha-ha on the campus that lasted for weeks. My Dean was inevitably drawn into the fray. Because of his reputation as a true believer, the Dean, probably being baited, was asked by a reporter if he thought that such an outrageous assertion was cause for the professor's dismissal. In his reply, he reaffirmed his credo not only in free speech, but also in all beliefs including the theory of origins, Creationism. This was duly reported upon in the widely distributed paper, and fused a further storm of "Letters to the Editor", Engineering faculty meeting verbal barb exchanges, and overt specially-called zealot meetings. In particular, one rash Engineering faculty member challenged the Dean repeatedly, loudly, and disparagingly, and called for him to resign – saying that such beliefs were not consistent and, indeed, were inimical to the engineering mystique. In my opinion, this faculty member's persistent actions went beyond the pale of decency and, were it not for Tenure, clearly made him subject to immediate canning, along with button and epaulet ripping, by any reasonable semi-vindictive boss (especially if I had been running the show). But, I frankly doubt if my Dean would have done this, even if it were in his power. Such a move would not be compatible with his morality. Instead, in a May 8, 1979 memo distributed to the Faculty of the College of Engineering, he wrote:

"-----. Recent publicity may have generated some confusion regarding my views relative to the teaching of theories of origins in the public classroom. I would like to clarify my position.

First, as an administrator I wholeheartedly support academic freedom both in concept and practice. In the classroom this means an instructor should have the liberty to teach subject matter pertinent to the course with as few restrictions as possible. The only restrictions are general good taste, sensitivity, and First Amendment concerns with regard to race, creed or religion. In controversial subjects, the instructor has the right to present all sides of an issue and the right to have a personal conviction regarding the subject material. I do not support legislation that would require the instructor to take a particular position or to advocate an issue with which he or she does not concur. -----

Secondly, my name has been improperly used, without my permission or approval, in publicity and news reports identifying me with the University Bible Study. I am in no way connected with the Bible Study group and have serious reservations about some of its activities.

As your Dean, I view it of utmost importance that neither I nor my title be used by any group to reflect adversely on the College of Engineering and its distinguished faculty. I make every effort to administer the College of Engineering without mixing personal views with administrative action. Should you want to discuss personal beliefs with me, however, please feel free to do so. I would be pleased to visit with you at any time. In any case, I want to avoid misunderstanding and misrepresentation."

The memory of this somewhat bizarre episode lingers on in my mind and, I imagine, the minds of my colleagues at the university. It was a unique and startling example for all of us of the value of Tenure. For no matter what evils it may also carry with it, it fully protects the right of free, unafraid, unfettered speech – our most precious liberty.

I had a certain amount of trouble staying awake at the dean's department heads' meetings. Paul Dejong, the artist, got my (cornet) instrument wrong, but my attitude right.

ON ABORTION

Personally, I'm over the reproductive age, and my children are also too old to be vitally concerned with the problem, so my interest in the abortion debate is cerebral, rather than emotional. For some years, I have watched with both *amusement* and then *chagrin* while Males (mostly but, alas, joined by women of fervor and/or of deep seated or church-driven religious and mystical beliefs) have tried to legislate what Females can and cannot do with their bodies. It reminds me of a parent stroking a daughter on her forehead and saying, "Father knows best".

What hasn't *amused* me is that women have let this happen to them, surrendering their rights of citizenship to the strong silent type men who can't shake the ancient idea that women are chattel. Where is the widespread female righteous indignation? Where are their votes against these retro Neanderthals?

I ceased to be amused and philosophical about the situation when the kooks started bombing abortion clinics and threatening Doctors under a cloak of piety. I finally had enough after a fatal bombing episode, and my solution to the problem, which I knew could never be settled peacefully, appeared as my 'Letter to the Editor' of the LA Times on Jan. 18, 1995:

Abortion Clinic Violence

There is a simple way to immediately end the intractable strife between the pro- choice (or laissez-faire) and anti-abortion factions: Have the government approve the "morning-after"abortion pill (after all, 50 million Frenchmen can't be wrong!) and insist that it be made widely and economically available in a great variety of venues. The widespread availability will preclude the shooting up and/or arson/bombing of the distributors, and cause the pro-lifers to give even more stress to their very effective (and very nonviolent) TV and ad campaigns.

R.F. Brodsky, Hermosa Beach

In my naïve mind, this simple step would settle the issue of violence since the kooks could not possibly bomb every outlet where the pill would be available. But the pro-lifers did not abandon their crusade even in the certainty that the pill will eventually become as available as Viagra, or more so. They succeeded in delaying federal approval of RU 486 until September 28, 2000, and it must still be Doctor-prescribed (though presumably 'on demand', just like the now-famous blue Viagra pill). And, the battle still continues here in the USA.

There is no such threat of violence or indeed is the pill and abortion an issue in other civilized countries. Here, in the good old U.S. of A., however, nothing is certain except abortion and taxes. I recently got a money/support-seeking letter addressed to "Dear Friend of Woman's Rights" from The Feminist Majority Foundation warning that the new administration may put the distribution of the pill "in jeopardy". Even more ominous was this article in the April 28, 2001 issue of the Des Moines Register.

Lawmakers push to ban abortion pill at colleges

By LYNN OKAMOTO and KATE KOMPAS
REGISTER STAFF WRITERS

Thirty-one legislators in the Iowa House are trying to prevent the Iowa State University student health center from offering the so-called abortion pill to university students.

Dr. Marc Shulman, chief of staff at the center, said earlier this week that the pill, also called RU-486 or mifepristone, may be available to students as early as next fall. The action still must be approved by the health center's advisory committee and top ISU administrators.

2001

LEGISLATURE

State Rep. Barbara Finch, an Ames Republican, said Friday that she wants to ensure the abortion pill isn't made available at ISU or any other state university in Iowa.

Thus, it looks like battles will joined in every state and the argument, aping the Middle East stalemate, will drag on and on. Of course, the pill will soon be available on every street corner in Tia Juana and Juarez and a profitable overseas non-prescription mail order business will also evolve to serve those not bordering on Mexico. But, the 'true believers' will fight on, with violence if they can find a new target, ever anxious to tell everyone how they should live their lives – and their cause will continue to be served by politicians who find a pro-life stance to be of financial and/or political benefit.

Another quixotic episode in this drama is being acted out today. U.S. drug companies who produce the RU-486 pill are now charging prohibitive prices, making it just as expensive as an old fashioned surgical or chemical abortion. And the abortion Doctors, who now can legally can prescribe the pill, would just as soon do the procedure at which they are skilled, since it earns them more money than a mere consult for a written prescription. But I'm sure the righteous will continue to fight on, even in the face of inevitability! They are resourceful and clever but, alas, the rogues in their numbers do not believe in the effectiveness of their otherwise excellent, in my opinion, non-violent campaign of offering alternatives. They will continue to be vicious until sensibility, in the form of clear unambiguous laws* and directives, wins the day.

---

* In August, '07, the FDA finally cleared the sale of the pill at pharmacies. Of course all pharmacies may not offer them.

WOMEN

I can't get over how dumb some – but not all - women are! Somehow, most women relish their role of second hand citizenry and sexual objects that men cleverly relegated them to hundreds of years ago and, through various devilishly shrewd doctrinal devices, have managed to maintain. Most women remain oblivious to their state of chattelry, and many who are so aware actually enjoy their situation, being convinced – via religious or 'Family Value' hype – that this is the way it was meant to be. True, there are a few pioneering type women who have fought the good fight through the ages – but they have either been ridiculed, burned at stake, bewitched, bruised by the glass ceiling, or made to mysteriously 'disappear', a la Madalyn Murray O'Hair. Clearly, the great majority of ladies have been and continue to be duped, world-wide – AND THEY SIMPLY DON'T KNOW WHAT'S GOING ON!

A typical lady – unveiled and disarmed

I first became aware of the reality of the situation when the Equal Rights Amendment was defeated by a coalition of fanatical women led by Phyllis Schlafly, aided and abetted, I am ashamed to say, by my nutty but lovable black sheep cousin Alyse. Under the guise of saving the sanctity of womanhood and the home, and cheered on by powerful men who never have cared to see women attain the status of independent beings, they managed to defeat a measure which, in the United States at least would have been a major move towards feminine equality and independence. But, the defeat of the ERA only permits the continued subservience of women to men, albeit some bones have been thrown their way by a few political appointments and elections, plus CEO recognition for an elite few. The defeat of the ERA was a right wing – Organized Religion triumph. And do the multitude of women who were in favor of the passage of the ERA rise up? No, most remain docile and continue to vote Republican. THE LADIES SIMPLY DO NOT KNOW WHAT'S GOING ON!

All over the world, women are being brain-washed to accept polygamy and/or to eschew birth control devices and consider abortion as a venal sin. In the United States, polygamy in the Mormon Church is certainly frowned upon of late, but there is still a wink of the eye present. In the Muslim world, multiple wives for those who can afford them are the norm. In the third world, the countries are too impoverished to teach about and distribute birth control devices. Only in China is there a sensible pro-feminine birth control policy, although female babies are not celebrated. But, it is in the so-called civilized world where the massive subversion of woman-kind really takes place. The reason as to why this has happened is apparent. In countries where more cheap labor is needed and where organized religions wish to increase, or at least maintain, their membership numbers, women have been relegated to the role of producing children as fast as they can. The blame for this state of affairs rests squarely on the major religions, particularly the Catholic and Muslim faiths. In their beliefs that their way is the right and only way, they win by dint of sheer numbers. Thus they either uphold polygamy, 'right to life', 'abstinence' instead of birth control education, oppose the easy distribution of the 'morning-after' pill, urge the boycott or shoot up of abortion clinics, and continue to champion the denigrated Russian-Roulette rhythm method of birth control. All such stratagems continue to enslave women. AND THE LADIES DON'T KNOW WHAT'S GOING ON!

To get a clearer view of the enormity of the extremes that men have driven women to, look at the ads in the fashion magazines to see the latest quirky garbs in *Elle, Vanity Fair,* etc. that are being peddled. Men designers have made caricatures of women. Look at the bathing suit issue of *Sports Illustrated* for the latest in beach wear. Then, for comparison, look at what men have forced women to wear in most Muslim societies. What a contrast! Men have also led women to believe that they are responsible for the upbringing of the children and the proper management of the household – even these days when many American, Asian and European women work full time jobs. How can they compete in the market place when they also have to rear babies? AND THEY SIMPLY DON'T KNOW WHAT'S GOING ON!

One "Christian Mother" in an early March, 2002, issue of the *LA Times* cried out after years of faithful drudgery at family raising:

"I rebelled. I reincorporated four letter words into my educated vocabulary. I returned part-time to my profession. I scrimped to purchase a 'pre-owned' Volkswagen Rabbit. I hired a cleaning lady, enrolled in ballet classes at the local college and resumed reading fiction. I had awakened to the impossibility of my own expectations. I did not dump my faith, just switched churches. However, throughout my epiphany and ensuing choices, I had the luxury of not being mentally ill or suffering post - partum depression. I was just very, very angry – at myself for trying to live someone else's definition of Christian mother, at my husband for being a bystander and at our church for not providing praise, offering grace or permitting diversity".

Yes, here was a woman who was at last beginning to get it – BUT SHE STILL DOESN'T KNOW EVERYTHING THAT'S GOING ON!

I've saved the best (worst?) for last – the matter of women having a much more difficult time separating LOVE from SEX, thus leaving themselves at the mercy of men who generally have a better and crasser handle on the concept. Unmarried women tend to consider each new male acquaintance as a potential life partner, while men look on a new candidate as a potential piece of ass – only later considering a more lasting relationship if the sex is good. Many women are not aware of the very strong sex drive that lives within the typical male. This is a drive that is so strong as to make men do unethical and foolish things – which many women do have the good sense to use for entrapment purposes. Women simply have no idea how truly remarkable is the sensation brought on by oral sex, even if done amateurishly. Recent events illustrate that such reveries could possibly bring down an empire, but failed to do so because the male 'judges', although jealous, were understanding and admiring. But this has nothing to do with romance or love, even though women might like to think differently. Here, again, unless more women figure out how to beat or tie men in the love/sex game, they are doomed to despair. AND MOST OF THEM STILL DO NOT KNOW WHAT'S GOING ON!

I realize that in making these disclosures, I am being traitorous to my gender. Men have known these things for many years of course, but naturally have remained mute for fear of upsetting the status quo and missing out on some nookie. I can do this now because I am past the age of caring and not the subject of vengeance, at least on this topic. I can disclose these self-evident truths since my wife of many years, though she may be loathe to admit it, REALLY DOES KNOW WHAT'S GOING ON, and hates it!

A pix from the year Brazil beat Turkey for the 'coupe du monde' *in futbol*

BINDLESTIFFED

These – post September 11, 2001 – days are trying times for your run-of-the-mill pious Americans and Judeo-Christian type folks all over the world. Now, I'm <u>not</u> talking about the extremists at the far end of the spectrum: they have no trouble with <u>their</u> God. They know exactly what HE is doing and are generally happy with the results of HIS work. The God of Jerry Falwell has clearly and unambiguously shown his wrath on Americans who abide with homosexuals, abortionists, misogynists, and 'pre-verts' of all callings. Like-wise, the Allah of the fanatic Muslims has made a clarion call for a Jihad against those who support Israel. In both of these extreme cases, no ambiguity exists.

The problem lies with the God of the 'good' religious masses: The God of the Chris-tians all the way from the mild Unitarians to the disciplined Catholics and Baptists; the God of the Reformed, Conservative, Orthodox and the ultra-Orthodox Jews; and the God of the Muslims of the several extant sects. Before September 11, this Judeo-Christian tri-umvirate considered themselves to be a monotheistic society. The Muslims were pleased to include Abraham and Isaac and Jesus as major players in their company, along with their main-man, Allah. The Christians agreed that the 'One-God' that the Jews had discovered was also their God, albeit they supplied him with some help that the Jews wouldn't warm up to. But it <u>was</u> a MONOTHEISTC society, and encompassed quite a huge number of people, although it remains true that there are untold millions of other folks who, heavens to Betsy!, have no God at all, or question whether there is a God, or seek their solace in other mostly Asia or African - based deities or otherwise mystical figures. September 11 did not disturb <u>their</u> equilibrium or belief system!

Truly, it is the pious religious middle ground masses that now must face up to their beliefs about their personal God. They must ask whose side is this God on? How could God let such terrible or wonderful events happen to the 'innocent flocks'? Does God know what HE is doing? Does HE care? Does he favor the Arab terrorists or the Jewish terror-ists? Is HE on our side? – or theirs? Did HE personally design the individual fate of those killed in the World Trade Center or the non-partisan civilians killed in Afghanistan? These are heavy questions, and deserve the thoughtful attention of millions of Friday, Saturday and Sunday sermoneers for many years to come.

Will they make it clear in their explanations of what has happened that these three ma-jor religions, albeit sharing one God, are really the products of mankind's interpretations. Each has painstakingly built a house of cards replete with laws and mores, some good,

56

some nonsensical in light of today's society. Will they have the guts to ask the basic question of whether there is a God and the corollary – is a God really necessary? I doubt it. More likely, to keep the machine going, they will dictate three Gods, all related through divine provenance?

What we have left in the wake of the unholy destruction is a world that looks like this: The Muslims, deep down and no matter how truly religious, will always want Israel to disappear into the sea and will be enemies to anyone or to any state that supports Israel; The United States will eventually come to understand that the only sure way to 100% return to the peace and serenity we used to know is to abandon Israel, and there may be enough 'righteous citizens' to someday, in the not-to-distant future, cause this to happen; and the American Jews, like me, will keep sending money to Israel because we know it may be the only place, the true Homeland, where we can retreat to when the world, and the USA in particular, once again chooses to turn against God's "Chosen People".

THE BELOW FROM <GOD.COM> -; MAKING ONE THINK IT MAY NOT BE CUT AND DRIED. QUESTION 4 IS A REAL POSER!

There are over six billion people in this world and each person has his or her own thoughts about God. How can a person know for sure what He is really like?
At some point in your life, you may have some of the following questions:

- Does God exist?
- Is there a heaven and hell?
- If so, how does one go to heaven?
- Why are there so many religions and which one is right?
- Is the Bible really true?
- Why is Israel a focal point in history?

THE NEW ATHEIAGNOS HOLIDAY WEEK

Isn't it about time that we atheists and agnostics have our own holiday? After all, the pious world celebrates Christmas, Hanukah, Kwanzaa, Ramadan with great zest and ceremony – and the populace accepts these ritual holidays as a matter of natural fact. We, on the other hand, in our self imposed closets, have no joyous period in which to demonstrate that there are viable alternatives – AND, believe it or not, that there are a lot of us. This state of un-holy status-quo clearly deserves to be re-examined!

But what can we do? How can we make our advocates jubilant without becoming just another organized religion? Speaking for my branch of non-belief, the hard core atheists – we live in fear of advertising our non-belief lest such professions of non-faith become commercially organized. An obvious case in point is the widespread commercialization surrounding the birthday of J. Christ.

Thus, we cannot broadcast from the highest mountain tops our non-belief in a super deity with all the accoutrements, traditions, beautiful and inspiring music, scriptures and fables that accompany Him or Her.

In my youth, we called this a 'Hanukah Bush'.
Clearly atheists need an equally impressive symbol

"A" as in Atheist means 'without', not 'anti'. We are not anti-God; we just don't believe there is such an essence. We have no way of explaining to religious folks of any degree, from strict Catholicism to laissez faire Unitarians, our awe of the vast fabric that organized religion has woven around their beliefs. We cannot tell them about our skepticism of the pure skein of yarn that human beings have created out of equally pure empty space, none of which can withstand examination by the scientific method. Or, with the futile attempts that are continually made to reconcile science with religious fancy. We simply cannot accept these premises on the basis of faith alone.

We could tell 'the others' that we have no need for a concept as ethereal as a living God. We could tell them to face up to their mortality and give up on the idea that there is a life beyond this one. We could ask them to recognize, by the perversity of random events, that there is no deity who has a grand plan for each and every living being. Or one to whom we can pray to with the hope of getting a satisfactory outcome every time. We can refer them to chaos theory, which – as applied to us humans – teaches that life is basically a crapshoot. Some die young – some live a long life – Allah be praised!

Then, we could tell them of the indignity we religious minorities suffered when the world made us pledge allegiances; made us say daily prayers in school to 'keep up with one's classmates', made us not speak up for fear of scorn or rejection or physical harm, and continues to oppress us with 'holier-than-thou' righteousness.

The best we can hope for is that our peers do not make laws or conditions which will force us to move to more tolerant climes. We can abide by 'In God We Trust" on our currency – but that's a concession. We can only hope against hope that in the USA our judicial system will indeed eventually separate church from state; and that the term, "Under God", will be dropped from the pledge of allegiance in a country supposedly founded on the principles of freedom FROM religion as well as freedom OF religion.

We are asked to – and do – honor, as good neighbors should, such concepts as a virgin birth, a resurrection, a giving of ten commandments, an ascent to heaven on horseback, a Devil, and Saints and Sinners, even though such theories do not stand the test of investigation. We are asked to be pleased and grateful when true believers state that they will say a prayer for us. But to believe in such man-conceived concepts is beyond our pale of understanding. We hope that the Creationists will continue to fight a losing battle, and another Scopes trial will not occur.

Nevertheless, we are surrounded by presumably vast multitudes who do accept the whole megilla and, what's worse, threaten – in some cases – to burn at stake infidels such as we. That's probably the real reason we dare not be more vocal about our non-beliefs. We are scared! We are intimidated. In fact, I use the term 'non-belief' rather than state positively that our beliefs do not require a deity and the bevy of accoutrements, out of such fright. Catch 22 – you can't run a campaign based on non-beliefs. We are self-made eunuchs!

Well, what CAN we do? I propose that we initiate the AtheiAgnos Week – a joyous period devoted to the study of the philosophy of our own patron Saint Agnos. It should occur annually as the third week of December. During this week, fasting will take the place of lunch, and each night, before dinner, a paragraph of text from the sacred writings of the late martyred Madalyn Murray O'Hair will be intoned. The week will be dedicated to small children, who will receive presents from Saint Agnos; one for each of the seven nights of the holiday. These presents will emanate from inside the seven life-sized paper mache (rich folks might prefer more substantial gilded) statuettes of Ste. A. Prior to dinner, today's statuette will be decorated with baubles and tinsel and lights, in preparation for the after dinner gift extraction frenzy. The proletarian version of the statuettes will sell for $15 each and their yearly production will be the basis for a huge kick in the economy. Now isn't that a pretty picture? Doesn't it proudly raise us up to the level of the great religious sects that abound. Isn't the world a better place?

To make the new holiday whole, we need to compose both beautiful songs to rival "Silent Night" and the myriad of the other evergreens; and we could also develop suitable 'fight songs'. The latter could be along the lines of the vigorous Judeo-Christian oldie but goodie, "The Game was played on Sunday", but sung in Swahili:

"The game was played on Sunday,
in heaven's own backyard.
With Jesus playing fullback and Moses playing guard.
Oh, the angels in the grandstand,
Oh, Lord, how they did yell.
When Jesus scored a touchdown
Against the boys from Hell!
(chorus)
Stay with God! Stay with God!
Jesus to the one yard line,
Moses doing God-damn fine

Stay with God! Stay with God!
Jesus knock 'em, Moses sock 'em
Stay with God!"

So, Atheists (there, I used a capital 'A') and Agnostics unite! Let's hear it for AtheiAgnos Week. Let's come out of the closet and yes, alas, admit that we are now an organized religion and stand ready to take the heat. Let's all be like a member of my Writers Workshop group who proudly proclaimed, "I'm a lapsed Unitarian!"

THE COMPETITION THIS YEAR

December 2007

6 - St. Nicholas Day (International)

8 - Bodhi Day - Buddha's Enlightenment (Buddhist)

12 - Virgin of Guadalupe (Mexico)

13 - Santa Lucia Day (Sweden)

16-25 - Las Posadas (Mexico)

20 - Eid al-adha (Islamic, Muslim)

25 - Christmas (Christian, Roman Catholic, International)

26 - Boxing Day (Canada, United Kingdom)

16-24 - Hanukkah (Jewish)

26 - Jan 1 - Kwanzaa (African-American)

PEACE AT LAST IN THE MIDDLE EAST

A few years ago, while visiting our son who lives near Worcester, Mass., we drove by an outdoor storage yard which garaged many semi-rig trailers. One such, nearest the street, was a custom job that featured a conventional back door attained by walking up a railed ramp. It also had a series of windows on the sides. It was labeled with large black lettering "Mobile Chapel". Its function was obvious – to bring the word of the Lord to those communities not blessed with their own facilities. Like a heaven-inspired miracle, a solution to the Palestinian's problem of gainful employment immediately came to mind. It was truly an epiphany!

Ah, yes, my friends and fellow worshippers, the "MOBILE MOSQUE" (pat. pending) is the answer! In many not primarily Muslim outposts, Los Angeles being a prime example, there is a paucity of Mosques, and this lack is likewise reflected in other reasonably civilized countries throughout the world. So, let's put the jobless Palestinians, who now have nothing better to do than make bombs and blow themselves and others up, to work building an endless supply of "MOBILE MOSQUES" (pat. pending). In one fell swoop, we solve the problem of full employment in the fledgling state of Palestine, thus reducing their dependence on seeking employment in the state of Israel. This, in turn should allow peace to return to that blighted area and allow all of us to sleep better.

I say 'endless supply' for I have the certainty that many more will be needed to replace the ones that are blown up next to kindergartens and other strategic buildings after services are over.

From an 'Ad' I Found Googling 'Chapel On Wheels'. The 'Ad' Includes a Moving Picture

Church on Wheels specializes in portable staging, seating, sound and lighting equipment, and all types of support and transportation equipment for mobile churches.

We have been in business for over 35 years, and have a loyal following in churches, malls, hotels, convention centers, professional sports franchises & movie theaters. We have built on our business by providing our customers what they need.

We offer a large selection of Portable Stage, Seating, Backdrops, Folding tables, skirting and backdrops, raffle and drawing equipment, speaker's lecterns, and much more... Even if you don't need a pre-loaded trailer, we can provide you with any of the components listed.

If there is something that you may be looking for on this site, but don't see it, please call us at 800.270.7982, or email us. We will help you locate it or manufacture it for you.

See why you should purchase your trailer through us.
See why OUR transportation carts are so much better.

MORE PLEDGING

In 2002, a remarkable court ruling in California, instigated by a divorced parent whose daughter, now under the guardianship of her Mother, objected to the 'under God" clause in the Pledge of Allegiance, came to pass. A high State court ruled unconstitutional the 'new' wording to the original non-sectarian Pledge, which was added by Congress during the Eisenhower administration. The ruling caused such a furor that the 'cease and desist' order made by the court to apply in California was held in abeyance for review and ruling by a Federal appeals court. Their decision was scheduled to be made in 2003.

This event was adjudged as one of the major happenings in 2002 by an *L.A. Times* staff writer in an 'end-of-the-year' summation, and prompted my equally prompt

"LETTER TO THE EDITOR
Dear Sirs:

In her Friday, Dec. 17, 2002 column, "Reflections on 2002: Courts", Anna Gorman noted that a major point of national concern was the question of the constitutional legality of the inclusion of the words "under God' in our Pledge of Allegiance.

No matter what the forthcoming court decision on this issue may be, now is the time for United States' citizenry to consider the basic morality that guides the country they live in, and inform their law makers on their finding re this issue. The United States was founded on the basis of permitting religious freedom for all. I presume that this includes the right to have no religion at all, and all other shades of credos ranging from atheism, agnosticism and all the way to far right religious fanaticism.

But, apparently I presume incorrectly, for the religious folks have somehow managed to infuse the phrase "under God" into the national psyche. In doing so, the supposed religious freedom that our forefathers sought has been disregarded for many citizens – and their numbers are huge, albeit for the most part silenced by fear of symbolic cross burnings on their lawn. Their idea of 'God' may be quite different from the Judeo-Christian one, to whom this imprecation is presumably made.

To make matters more complicated, it has become increasingly clear that the former monotheistic God we thought we knew no longer exists. Whose God is it that the Pledge addresses? Is it to the Christian God, who suffers pedophile priests and 'family planning' murderers? Is it to the Hebrew God, who presided over the holocaust and now assists his 'chosen people' by making Israel a paradise to dwell in? Is it to the Muslim God, who apparently, with the silent approbation of his followers, sanctions jihads and terrorism. Or, is it to the essential God, that many non-formal-religious folk believe watches over us all and spreads the good and bad evenly, and perhaps arbitrarily, throughout his flock. Maybe we should recite 'under Gods' to cover all the bases? It is a puzzlement!

The citizens must decide – not by majority rule; not by judicial decision; but by what's right for the country."

In their judgment of palatability, the Editors saw fit not to print my remarks. When the federal appeals Superior Court made its ruling in 2003, it supported the finding of the lower court. This created such a hue and cry in the ranks of the pious, that a further appeal to the highest court in the land was quickly mounted. Alas, the Supreme's, in their infinite wisdom shaded by a touch of cowardice, chose to dodge the bullet. They ruled that the original question had been raised by a person who did not have the proper standing since he was not the guardian of the complainant. So, at this point at the end of the Year of Our Lord, 2005, the issue still remains moot.

It is now up to the ACLU or some other publicly-spirited entity to find another person to press the issue. The final outcome – obviously many years away – will no doubt result in yet another defeat for the holy warriors who will never understand the ingredients of a true Democracy and can not comprehend a society that seeks an even-handed treatment of all its constituents. We'll be back!

Chapter 3
ANNALS OF AUTHORSHIP

- **THE HARD LIFE OF A POET**
- **THE HARD LIFE OF A WRITER**
- **THE HARD LIFE OF AN AUTHOR, NO.s 1 & 2**
- **WITH FRIENDS LIKE THESE**
- **VHAT! VEE LOST?**

As far back as I can remember, I liked to write. I was always involved in school Bulletins and Newsletters, but really became serious about writing in High School. Here, my friend Obe, who was Editor, urged me to work on the "Dipper" ('Dips the Dirt'), our class paper. At Cornell, in my freshman year, I tried out for the Cornell Daily Sun, and successively was a reporter, a night editor, Sports Editor, and finally, Associate Editor. In the latter position, in my senior year, I wrote a twice-a-week column meant to be humorous, and it often was. In my Freshman and sophomore year, the Associate Editor of the Sun, my boss, was no less than Kurt Vonnegut, and he and the Editor, Miller Harris, and the business manager, J. Basil Abbink (from whom, when I wanted to be funny, I used the 'R. Fox Brodsky' signature which I reserved for special occasions) all helped to turn me into a fair - to- middlin' newspaper man and headline writer.

I made my first attempts at non-technical writing at Iowa State in the 70's, where the germ of the idea for what has evolved into "On the Cutting Edge" which includes stories about my life in engineering and teaching. I did not start writing in earnest, however, until my retirement from teaching at USC in 1996; hastened by the strange 'senior moment' phenomena of my forgetting simple words; like 'combustion' during lectures, or 'halyard' while sailing. "Get out while you're still ahead", I said to myself – and I did. Since then, in addition to sailing twice a week and attending the South Bay Writer's Workshop once a week, I have kept busy writing.

The five stories in this chapter depict my struggle to achieve fame and publication in what must be considered my 'second' career. Wish me luck!

THE HARD LIFE OF A POET

It seemed innocent enough at first; who would have thought that it would lead to my utter devastation. It arrived in August, 2000 in the form of a letter from 'The International Library of Poetry (poetry.com) and, in part, said:

"Dear Poet,

The International Library of Poetry is currently reviewing poems for one of its forthcoming anthologies – and if you should submit a poem for consideration, there is an excellent chance that you could soon see your work in print!" The letter went on to describe the many monetary prizes that were to be awarded, the entry procedures, a description of their beautiful anthologies of "artists of considerable talent", and included the sentence, "You don't need to be a professional poet to enter or win our competition."

That did it for me! It so happens that I had recently completed my first attempt at poetry since grade school, and had produced an epic entitled, "End as a Man". You shall see this epic at the end of this story after you have been properly prepared and forewarned. It is of a geriatric sexual nature, and should not be read by pre- or post- menstrual women lest it lead to their utter disillusionment. I had previously dispatched it hopefully to the *New Yorker*, but got the same 'Dear John' letter that they normally send me for my doomed short story non-fiction submittals. But, here, I saw a last chance for poet immortality, or at least a chance to partially catch up to my cousin Susan, in Haifa, who gets her poetry regularly published in legitimate editions. I sent it off, and promptly forgot about it, until I got the letter which marked the beginning of yet another 'cause celebre', the totality of which is described in my following letter of Sept. 14. '00:

"Vanessa Hairfield, Ass't. Editor
The International Library of Poetry
1 Poetry Plaza
Owings Mills, MD 21117

Dear Vanessa:

I was Crushed, Overwhelmed, Chagrined by your letter of September 6, '00 informing me that you had a change of heart about the promised publication of my beautiful, poignant and soul baring first poem, " End as A Man". You stated, "Although your poem is well written (ed. note: I did take the trouble to exquisitely rhyme 'Viagra' with 'Niagara'), we sincerely regret that we will be unable to feature it either on our website or in our an-

thologies (ed. note: or, I presume, as an 'entered' candidate for the several promised monetary prizes, "to be determined in August (!) 2000). Once your poem went on to further review, we found that it did not meet standards established by our Senior Editorial Board. ------"

The reason that I was crushed, overwhelmed and chagrined by the above is because it completely contradicted your earlier glorious advisory of August 22, '00, which said in part:

"Dear Robert,

After carefully reading (ed. note: the 'proof' had two major mistakes that I corrected in my return reply, in which I also indicated that I was not going to place a $49.95 order for the Anthology in which my poem was to appear, nor would I send $25 for a bio to appear in that same book) and discussing your poem, our Selection Committee has certified your poem as a semi-finalist in our North American Open Poetry Contest. Your poem will automatically be entered into the final competition held in August 2000. As a semi-finalist, you now have an excellent chance of winning one of the 104 cash or gift prizes - - including the $1000.00 grand prize. You may even win the $10,000.00 annual grand prize! - - -

Before going any further, Robert, let me make one thing clear . . . your poem was selected for publication, and as a contest semi-finalist, on the basis of your unique (ed. note: ah, yes!) talent and artistic vision. We believe it will add to the importance and appeal of this edition. IN THIS REGARD, YOU ARE UNDER NO OBLIGATION WHATSOEVER TO SUBMIT AN ENTRY FEE, ANY SUBSIDY PAYMENT, OR TO MAKE ANY PURCHASE OF ANY KIND. - - -."

Now, Vanessa, even to a naif such as I, the above has all the appurtenances of a bookselling extortion scam worthy of being brought to the attention of the Federal Trade Commission, which I fully intend to do if my grievances are not redressed quickly. In any case, you have supplied me with a wonderful story to chronologically complete my chapter, "Annals of Authorship", to appear in my new book, "A Pilgrim Muddles Through".

This publication you can not prevent - the damage has already been done, and you have earned the suspicion. But you can redress my grievance by publishing my anguished poem which, I assure you, will be the star of the issue, even though not Dickinsonian in tenor. And, if you don't believe I'm serious, I refer you to my chapter, "Annals of Law" which covers my highly successful and financially rewarding tilts at the windmills of wrong-doers.

Yours, in Poetry"

Having received no answer as of November 9, I did send off the following letter (with the afterthought message on her copy, *"Vanessa, Hell hath no fury like a poet scorned!"* written in the margin):

"November 10, 2000

Federal Trade Commission
ATTN; CRC
600 Pennsylvania Ave., NW
Wash. DC 20580

Dear Sirs:

    I request that you investigate an outfit which I believe is using the mails to defraud, in a manner akin to the Ed McMahon/ Dick Clark scam. I believe the attachments enclosed will self-indict the "International Library of Poetry" for running a bait-and-switch operation to the detriment of struggling poets (and, in my case, against very senior citizens-Shame on them!).
    The letter I wrote to Ms. Fairfield - to date ignored - pretty well explains the scam. The other enclosures further serve to document my grievance.
    I hope you will see the righteousness of my case, and will deal with them as severely as you dealt with the Publisher's Clearing House scoundrels. After all, all I personally asked for was for them to publish my poem as they said they would.
    Thank you for your consideration,"

I had yet to hear from the FTC on this matter when Vanessa did finally reply, on November 14, 2000, as follows:

"I am writing in response to the letter I received concerning your poem, "End as a Man". As it states in our rules we can chose (sic) to not publish a poem at any time. Your poem, "End as a Man" cannot be published because of its graphic nature. This is a family orientated business and your poem contained such phases (sic) as "may help masturbation", and "when you want to hump" which are not suitable for children. I am very sorry for any trouble this may have caused, but if you submit a new poem, or edit the graphic material out of "End as a Man" we will be happy to publish it. I am also sorry that I did not respond to a letter you sent, but I did not receive that letter and therefore could not answer. Once again, I am sorry for any inconvenience and I look forward to receiving your new poem. Sincerely,"

I could not wait to get off the following reply, the very same day:

"Ref: VIP#2346371
Dear Vanessa:

    There are several things puzzling about your above referenced letter of Nov. 14, 2000; but I appreciate your concern about my 'inconvenience'.

1) You say you are sorry that you did not respond to my only other letter to you of Sept. 14, but, "I did not receive that letter and therefore could not answer". What letter, pray tell, did your Nov. 14 missive answer then?

2) You say that my poem cannot be published because of its graphic nature. Well, it had the same graphic nature when you first received it and apparently, from your acceptance letter, said you were going to publish. Since you sent me a galley proof of the poem, albeit bollixed up (however, they got the 'dirty' words right!), <u>somebody </u>must have read it and decided that it was 'fit to print'. That somebody, if not you, should be talked to by a Dutch Uncle.

I have trouble with disallowing poetry that 'tells it like it is'. You are making a case that all poets are effete. Were he alive, Robert Frost, for one, would disagree with this characterization. Now if you had thrown out my poem because it was lousy poetry (It was, after all, my first serious attempt in the media; and certainly does not come up the high standards set by my Poet Laureate cousin, Joseph) I could understand, although I did miss the small print that said you had the right to not publish even after you did accept it. Rather, it still looks to me that you are not entering my poem in the contest or printing it simply because I did not order the Anthology in which it would have appeared, nor take up the $25 bio-printing offer.

Lest you think I am mean and vindictive, I will not send a copy of this to the FTC since they are apparently not following up on my first letter. I will, however, honor you with a copy of my story which will appear in my next book in its "Annals of Authorship" chapter. Enjoy!
 Very truly yours, "

As I wrote this in mid December, 2000, I of course could not tell you if there were any winners here. The FTC did write to thank me for pointing out the action – but promised nothing. I can, however, give you the golden words of my poem; so long as you promise to keep them from the eyes of the innocent and impressionable who, according to Vanessa, cannot stomach 'naughty' words, even though they may be written in the finest interest of ART!

END AS A MAN

Baloney! Your testosterone's low",
    said my primary care physician, omnisciently.
But my heart doctor, who's from Niagara,
    advised, "Don't take Viagra- you'll blow
a gasket and end up in a casket."

Nevertheless, I took the dare, without a care.
    But the result was unnerving!
Instead of an erection, - only dejection,
    And this after a double serving!

My urologist said, "In view of this,
    Your options are few:
Instead of Viagra, try praying at Agra. If that doesn't work,
you can resume the "pump", when you want to hump,
or suffer an injection to achieve an erection.

Or, finally, an implant operation may help masturbation,
    but may not give your wife jubilation."
Oh, what to do to get a last screw?
    I leave it to your imagination.

THE HARD LIFE OF A WRITER

I hit paydirt! In the hopes of finding both a publisher for my books and/or a literary agent, I subscribed to *WRITER'S DIGEST*. Its January 2001 edition had a lead article which attracted my attention, since I had amassed a large backlog of unpublished non–fiction short stories and simply did not have the time or persistence to peddle them individually. My long-range game plan was to place them in what was then conceived of as a two volume set, "A Pilgrim Muddles Through".

The article was entitled, "The 50 Best Places to get Published Online". I decided to try the top two, rated '79' and '78.5', respectively. The rating system had to do with 16 criteria, such as, Number of Manuscripts Purchased; Pay Rates; Response Time; etc. I got off two e-mails, both with the same message, and in accordance with their suggested query protocol. As I wrote this story, I had yet to hear from #79, but 'T.H. Wong', listed as Editor of *AUTHOR ONLINE,* did respond as will unfold in the following saga, wherein the names and addresses have been altered to protect the innocent, namely me, from ensuing civil or criminal action:

Subj: Stories?
Date: 12/14/00
To: submission@Learnalot.com

Dear T.H. I found out about you from the Jan 2001 issue of Writer's Digest, and went to your web site. The latter was not particularly helpful in telling me what kind of stuff you were looking for. Let me give you two options (the third being "no thanks", of course):

One story, meant to be amusing, concerns my entering a poem into a 'contest'; having it accepted for inclusion in an anthology ($49.95); and then being rejected as not fit for family reading. The beautiful poem, "End as a Man" is about Viagra, and to make sure you grasp its inherent class, I have cleverly rhymed it with Niagara.

The second story, "Great Aerospace Events of the 20th Century" is a serious effort to name the most important advances in the last 100 years.

Both stories are around 2000 words, and can be sent via e-mail. Please let me know if you want to see more. I have had several (~8) non-fiction short stories published in the last two years.

Dr./Prof. (USC) RF Brodsky *rfoxbro@aol.com*

Within the hour, I got a triggering response, which only later I learned was a preprogrammed automatic one entitled, *"Confirmation from Author Online"* and signed by, *"Eds."* Subsequently, in a fit of pique engendered by a second quirky reply, I deleted both this reply and the later one, so I can only paraphrase their contents. This one essentially said that they would consider my "submission" and not to bother them until they answered. This inane robotic message energized my immediate reply:

Subj: Re: Confirmation from Author Online
Date: 12/14/00
To: submission@Learnalot.com

Dear Eds.: You answered the wrong question! I didn't submit anything. I asked you if you cared for me to submit one or two stories. Please READ your mail and instruct me properly. Best regards, rfoxbro@aol.com

Again, remarkably, the Eds. answer came swiftly back, chiding me severely for trying to tell them how to run their business and suggesting that I buy a copy of their magazine to see about their interests. Since this didn't seem unreasonable, even though I had originally only asked them a simple question, I put my tail between my legs, and wrote:

Subj: I surrender dear
Date: 12/15/00
To: submission@Learnalot.com

Dear Eds: I give up! You win the battle of snideness. All I did was ask a simple question (see below). Your rating of 78.5 in the Writer's Digest apparently did not account for callousness or for the fact that struggling young writers can't afford your magazine without a retainer. It would have been easier for me to have sent you the two stories without asking if you might be interested. The results would have been the same. Ciao rfoxbro

At this point, never realizing then that this was the stuff that great stories are made of, and with my blood pressure noticeably rising, I deleted the Eds. answers. Ah, too soon, for I then received the following very straightforward message. This time it came directly from T.H. himself from his own private e-mail address:

Subj: Re: I surrender dear
Date: 12/15/00 6:58:05 PM Pacific Standard Time
From: goodfellow@yahoo.com (T.H. Wong)
To: Rfoxbro@aol.com

No one's trying to be snide, "Rfoxbro"; however, your command that I READ your letter and "instruct" you "properly" required an answer you could understand AND be instructed by: If you'd actually read Author Online, you would have read an article by me recently which dealt with "Editorial Pet Peeves." One of those "Pet Peeves" dealt with let-

ters from "struggling writers" which begin, "Dear Eds," or "To Whom It May Concern," et cetera. I should have added that editors--of whatever magazine--do NOT like to be told what to do by "struggling writers" who may have received an automatically generated email response to their "query," which is precisely what you received. Your letter was cocky and insulting. My response was not at all "callous," and certainly didn't deserve your "snide" response. Editors, Sir or Madam, are not your enemies, do not like to be lectured by you on how they should conduct business, and actually DO like to read promising manuscripts. If you have a promising manuscript, by all means, send it along. As I'm reading it, I will definitely overlook your attitude, which needs some attention.

T.H. Wong
Editor, Author Online

Thus chastised, I hastened to respectfully get off the next volley:

Subj: Re: I surrender dear
Date: 12/16/00
To: goodfellow@yahoo.com

Dear Mr. Wong. I sue for peace! I have many (so far unpublished) stories. Below is a recent funny one, which I hope you will like. It features my touching poem, "End as a Man". Previously, I queried if you might be interested in an historical essay, "Great Aerospace Events of the 20th Century". In general, my stories are either whimsical or semi-technical historical. I don't know what you may like and would appreciate a hint. I don't have time (I am 76) to both read your magazine and continue writing. If you see any merit in the below, I shall send more with the slightest encouragement. Regards   Bob Brodsky <rfoxbro@aol.com>:

"RFBrodsky, Dec 2000   ~1800 words

THE HARD LIFE OF A POET

It seemed innocent enough at first; who would have thought that it would lead to my utter devastation. It arrived in August, 2000 in the form of a letter from 'The International Library of Poetry (poetry.com) and, in part, said:

"Dear Poet,

The International Library of Poetry is currently reviewing poems for one of its forthcoming anthologies - and if you should submit a poem for consideration, there is an excellent chance that you could soon see your work in print!" The letter went on to describe the *many monetary prizes that were to be awarded, the entry procedures, a description of their beautiful anthologies of "artists of considerable talent", and included the sentence, "You don't need to be a professional poet to enter or win our competition." Etc., etc. ------------"*

Shortly thereafter, I received joyous and entirely unexpected news (for I was sure that even Mr. Wong could not rise above his chagrin to recognize a true work of art, and that I would be forever on his "A' shit list). But, Mr. Wong obviously had been touched by my struggles as a lyric poet:

Subj: Re: I surrender dear
Date: 12/16/00 10:42:27 AM Pacific Standard Time
From: goodfellow@yahoo.com (T.H. Wong)
To: Rfoxbro@aol.com

Dear Bob Brodsky,

Well, you know what?--I like this very much, not only because it's lively
and readable, and tells an interesting story, but because it slams Poesydot.Com, one of the Net's leading scam sites. So I'll offer you 7 cents a word for First North American Serial Rights and publish the piece in mid-January. If you can supply cwendell@oneida.com with the following info, we can get the contract out to you (Oh, if you can also send the manuscript as a Word attachment, please, to the same email address, that would be very helpful; before sending, please put all commas and periods inside quotes to save "cwendell" unnecessary editing):

Your home address
Your social security number
The title of your article
Your rate of pay (7 cents a word)
Your home phone number (optional)

Thanks very much, Mr. Brodsky. I look forward to hearing from you.

Best,

T.H. Wong
Editor, Author Online

P.S. We'll have to run a disclaimer with the piece that you bear full responsibility for it in case Poesydot.Com gets upset.

Greatly elated that I might add significantly to the fortune I have already earned for my writing in year 2000, I hastened to reply with this worried note:

Subj: Wunaful, Wunaful!
Date: 12/16/00
To: goodfellow@yahoo.com

Dear T.H.:

I am amazed at the alacrity of your responses!!

Although I am used to more recompense (e.g., AIR & SPACE gives me $0.85 per word), I will gladly accept your offer with one proviso. I did send the story to the NEW YORKER, a magazine I would dearly love to break into. I am quite sure that I will get the usual 'Dear John' on my submittal - but would like to give them preference in the very long shot

chance that they would buy it. Can you wait a few weeks - or go ahead for February instead, giving me a right to pull it by the end of January?

By the way, my wife says if you publish it, don't mention her name (or, she says, mine either, tho I am proud of my work).

In reviewing our recent correspondence, I believe that it, per se, has the makings of a good and funny story which reveals us both as the pompous asses that we may indeed be. I intend to write this story and will give you first crack - or first demurrer- at it (although I see it as funny, not mean). In the interest of full and accurate documentation, I would like to ask you for a favor. In a fit of pique, I irrevocably deleted your first two messages to me: the first was the now apparent "form" letter (don't call us, we'll call you); and the other was your advice to read the magazine. Could you please resend these, if you still have them?

Since you liked my story, maybe I should send you a chapter from my new in-the-works book: the "Annals of an Outraged Citizen" chapter for example, for you to pick through for stories you may like? Would there be any problem of your having published one or more of my stories, which would later appear in my book (so long as you were given credit?) But, I still don't know what you are interested in.

REGARDS (I will follow up with <cwendel> as soon as you advise me on the NEW YORKER problem.), Bob

I didn't know then how this episode would eventually turn out, but either way I knew I would be a winner. I would either accept the filthy lucre or turn the event into a story. Subsequently, I did get my usual "Dear John" from the NEW YORKER (I figure my writing is too sophisticated for them and my poem to lurid for their gentle appetites). But, I decided to forego the 7 cents per word reward, since it really wouldn't pay the rent.

THE HARD LIFE OF AN AUTHOR, #1

My daughter, Bette, is an award winning book designer. My son Bobby, also of Santa Fe, is the proprietor of the Rabbit Art Works and is a nationally known ceramist. They both agreed to lend their talents to help me convince potential publishers that they should publish at least the first book of a then completed trilogy of volumes that describe some highlights of my career in the high-tech aerospace field. This book was entitled, "Atom Bomb Stories" and covered my New Mexico adventures in the atom bomb business as it was starting up in the late '40s. In the stories told therein were included all the snafus and excitement that came with the development of six new Atomic bombs as they were being added to our growing arsenal inventory. We'll leave it up to you to decide if my children's participation in this effort may have been a big mistake.

Having read and liked the draft, Bette suggested that she would make a 'treatment' to show a publisher what the book could look like. She had just had great success with her latest book, which was formatted to look like a note book in which pictures and text were 'pasted' in – a scrap book, so to speak, including the imprint of mock binder coils in a basically square layout. This is the technique she proposed for "Atom Bomb Stories" treatment. For the cover, she selected a copy of a brightly colored tile that son Bobby had made. It depicted a child's notion of an in-flight rocket belching flame against a starry back ground. In the back roads of our great country, typical Santa Fe-ans, while in pow–wow around their primitive campfires – like to think of this as an expression of 'Art'. The 'treatment', thus brightly covered, then went on to include a Preface, Table of Contents, and one exemplary chapter about a key Atom Bomb test in the Pacific.

On the suggestion of a friend, I wrote a query letter on August 9, 2004 to the Editor, R. Poarch, of the vaunted Smithsonian Press, believing his interests included things semi-scientific. I explained that I had recently completed a trilogy, entitled "The World in a Jug", which tells first-hand historical stories of the major events in aerospace world as the nuclear, missile, and space ages unfolded during the period 1944 to the present. I briefly described the contents of the 3 Volumes and, among the several mandatory enclosures noted that I had included a short illustrative 'treatment' of the first Volume, "Atom Bomb Stories", as it would be done by my daughter, Bette, the special projects art editor for the *NEW MEXICO* magazine.

After a while, the following very surprising answer appeared:

September 21, 2004

Dear Dr. Brodsky,

Thank you for your recent query about publishing with Smithsonian Books, which Robert Poarch passed along to me. We appreciate your interest in our press.

Unfortunately the books you propose aren't appropriate for our list. They appear to be aimed at children and young adults, and we publish serious adult nonfiction. I wish you the best of luck finding a publisher to work with.

Sincerely,
Mary Lou S.
Assistant Editor

Bette's Proposed Cover

Somewhat angrily, I fired back my best shot:

"October 4, 2004

Mary Lou S., Assistant Editor
Smithsonian Books

Dear Mary Lou:

I am outraged by your 'Dear John' letter of Sept. 21 (copy included). You obviously do not follow the old saw, "Do not judge a book by its cover". It is equally obvious that you were put off to not read a single word once you saw the 'treatment' of the cover; concocted by my daughter, a prize winning book designer who is Special Projects Art Director of the New Mexico Magazine and which utilized a colorful, albeit puerile tile made by my son, a nationally known (Rabbit Art Works) ceramist, also of Santa Fe. BUT- to tell me that a book called "Atom Bomb Stories" is "aimed at children and young adults" is truly a gaffe of the nth degree! What fun for die kinder! I can, with some confidence, assure you that my books' contents are 'serious adult nonfiction' works – just down your alley.

Thus, I am giving you a chance to recoup. I have enclosed the complete text of "Atom Bomb Stories" for re-evaluation before you send me a proper and analytical 'Dear John' with enough sincerity to make me believe that you really gave it a look. I think you owe me that. I do thank you, however, for implying that the proffered cover 'treatment' was perhaps misleading.

Note that the text contains only about half of the illustrations that I intend to include. Note also that if by some miracle you should actually like what I consider to be an update on "USA" (are you old enough to know Dos Passos?), I am prepared to forward the other two books of the trilogy to you.

Very Sincerely,
Dr. RF Brodsky"

Dead silence ensued, as I thought it might. Finally, at the end of my tether and now really provoked by Mary Lou's intransigence, I fired off the following book-publishing killer to her Editor:

"Nov 9, 2004
Dear Mr. P:

It has been over a month since I sent (Oct. 4) a letter to Mary Lou S. bitterly complaining that she had frivolously "Dear John'ed" me on a submission you routed to her following my original letter to you of August 9. I pointed out to her that she obviously did not read a word of the material I sent. She instead noted (Sept.21) that my 'great fun book' entitled "Atom Bomb Stories", "appears to be aimed at children and young adults, and we publish serious adult nonfiction".

Rather than disclose her gaffe to you directly, I wrote her back enclosing the complete text of the book in the hope that she might atone. But, to date, I have not heard word one. Naturally, by now, I suspect your organization, including yourself after reading this, is so poisoned that I do not expect an encouraging reply to my original query. I do however expect a letter from someone in your House noting that she has at least read some of the book before sending a new "Dear John" statement. I also expect you may want to exhort her to be more careful.

Wishing her, as she wished me, "the best of luck finding a publisher to work with", I am

Dr. RF Brodsky
Prof. of Astronautics (ret.)
Univ. of Southern California"

Not too long later – the mails being painfully slow and apparently carefully checked for deadly anthrax emanations, as noted below - a reasonable but confusing apologetic letter from Mary Lou arrived:

November 18, 2004

Dear Dr. Brodsky,

I am writing in response to your letter of October 4, 2004, which I only recently received due to delays in the mail system in Washington, DC that we've been dealing with ever since the anthrax attacks a few years ago. I'm very sorry that you were "outraged" by my letter regarding your submission. To be completely frank, we receive a large number of submissions, and since we have a small staff, we do not have time to thoroughly read every proposal that is submitted to us, especially those that are unsolicited. If after a quick skim of the material, it appears that a proposal is not a good fit for our list, we will return it to the author with a note such as the one that I sent you. We simply do not have the time to write an analytical response to every proposal that we decline. It's the same way in most publishing houses.

In your case, it turned out that, as you noted in your Oct. 4 letter, the design concept, which, if I recall correctly, looked very much like a picture book for young audiences, did not reflect the serious nature of the text. The brevity of the story also contributed to my impression; the vast majority of the books that we publish are 200+ pages long. Upon look-

ing at the material again, I see that my judgment was hasty, and I apologize. The writing is clearly aimed at an adult reader.

However, I am still going to have to decline to publish your books. Unfortunately, shortly after I wrote to you in September, the Smithsonian decided to close its book operation as of January 2005. So, we are not able to take on any new projects.

Again, I do wish you luck finding a publisher for your trilogy.
Sincerely,

It is still not clear to me whether publishing my book would have been the straw that broke the Smithsonian Press's back, or that the 'treatment' was not 200 pages long. The complete manuscript I sent her was clearly at least that number, less the many illustrations pending. This whole saga, however, clearly demonstrates the difficulties an over-the-hill author faces. It makes one wonder if the coward's way out – self-publishing – might not be the best answer.

THE HARD LIFE OF AN AUTHOR, #2

As I was nearing completion of my book about my life adventures in the engineering and teaching trades, I began my search in earnest for a Literary Agent to represent me. As noted earlier, my Santa Fe daughter, an expert in book design, prepared a slick 'treatment' of the first trilogy volume, then entitled "Atom Bomb Stories". We both felt that we might hit upon a single publisher or a joint-effort between her magazine combined with the Museum of New Mexico Press and/or the University of New Mexico Press. Simultaneously, I also started a correspondence with the Literary Agent of a long-time friend who, with her help, had published two semi-technical books.

Frank Joseph Malina (October 2, 1912 in Brenham, Texas- November 9, 1981 in Boulogne Billancourt (France) was an American aeronautical engineer and painter, especially known for becoming both a pioneer in the art world and the realm of scientific engineering. His father came from Bohemia. His formal education began with a degree in mechanical engineering from Texas A&M University in 1934. (Wikipedia)

It soon developed that 'Justine M'., who lived in Aix en Provence in southern France, and I had much in common. Her father-in-law was one of the founders of Aerojet, and I had made his acquaintance when we lived in Paris suburb Neuilly sur Seine and he in nearby Boulogne sur Seine. Moreover, her husband was a nuclear physicist, so she obviously knew well the genre in which I was writing. I sent her the material she desired, and had great hopes that she would take me on as a client. But, as the title of this piece suggests, I still have not come to grips with the realities of writing for a living. After several weeks of email fencing around, this cryptic but true analysis arrived:

"Subj: some thoughts.
Date: 6/6/04 8:45:44 AM Pacific Daylight Time
From: Justine@Justinesworld.com (Justine M.)
To: Rfoxbro@aol.com

Hello there:

The good news is I do think there is excellent material here for the public -- the challenging news is that I do not think they will 'buy' it in its present form - other than those who are New Mexico history buffs and those who were themselves involved - too small an audience I fear to help you to find a publisher easily.

What is lacking from the writings I've read so far is a very strong "need to know and why does it matter?" What's the relevance of all this to-day -- politically, militarily even - morally etc., etc. - to you as you were living it ... looking back as you are able to now.... This would all help hook in people today....

You do not really touch on that in what I have read...

What you have here are a series of 'yarns' relevant to a more sophisticated reader who has an interest in 'anything space' related - but the characters are very one dimensional in your writing -- so it's hard to be caught up in the tales because of that... and yet I know they must have been many fascinating individuals; but somehow, that does not yet come through in what I've read so far. You do not enable people to understand the many layers of your own personality; there are only hints....

However, it will not work at all for younger people - meaning those in their late teens and early 20's - because - alas- very few will immediately focus on the relevance or the interest to them today.

You are very modest and do not go nearly enough into your own thoughts - more on all the actions - which really gives the stories an interesting 'diary feel' to them - but without the emotional pull and the deep thinking that no doubt you did experience over all those important and very exciting years.... the stories risk to not sustain the reader's interest.

I think you would have a reasonable chance of 'selling' this to a New Mexico based publishing company that specializes in covering local history etc... But in order for that to be a good chance, you would need to do a fair bit of re-writing to the Preface and some to the Introduction. You would also need to write the competition information very differently before submitting.

From reading what you've sent me, you have really had a fascinating life - full of adventure and an extraordinary chance to be part of something that changed the world forever.

My best suggestion----

What you might consider, is taking all this material and writing a screen play from it... with a film in mind; then we could try to get it in front of someone like Tom Hanks who is a great space buff; and see how that goes.

This whole story begs for visual input - to give your story and all the characters the true depth and richness of texture that it and you - so obviously deserve.

I hope you do not mind my frankness, but life is very short - and I do not believe in 'coating' editorial input. You have worked very long and hard on a series of stories that encompass much of the passion of a big part of your life's work. It is very tough to write and I can see how much effort you have put into all this. I salute that effort and respect what it's taken to get this far.

If you decide to try to get a New Mexico publisher to take on the work, and you would like me to help you rewrite the preface etc., etc... please let me know and we will chat about how that might be done.

Kindest regards,
JUSTINE M."

I mulled this over for a few days; sent Justine a temporizing email also asking if she might be interested in seeing my then two volumes of "A Pilgrim Muddles Through"; discussed it with my wife and daughter; and then re-contacted a former Editor at a well know technical and semi-technical publishing house with whom I had had earlier correspondence. Three days later, my ruminations over, I sent my decision back to France, with a copy to daughter Bette:

Subj: My thoughts
Date: 6/8/04
To: Justine@Justinesworld.com

Justine:

Again let me thank you for the care you gave and the thought effort you made on my behalf. I have heard similar words from my Writer's
Workshop Group: "Lack of emotion!; What do YOU think?; Tell me about the people, etc. All these comments, and yours, are true. --BUT
You remember "The Media is the Message"? Well, the stuff I write has to do with the STORY, NOT the people, NOT my feelings, NOT how great thou art, NOT what my opinion is. I think my stories are interesting and illustrate how problems are made and solved - in a field of high technology. That's what I want to get across. Of course, I recognize that this limits my readership - but I still think there are many people in this world of an inquisitive nature that would enjoy them. I cite engineers, faculty, students, historians and science buffs - the same people who read Popular Science and Popular Mechanics.
So, both because I lack the time left to me and because I am bull headed, I do not want to undertake re-write. Moreover, I am probably writing for a few in my immediate family who might be interested and I do not need to write for a livelihood (Though I would hope that my Daughter who will someday inherit my several (so far) books could make some money off of them).

I plan to take the following course of action: My Daughter will try the New Mexico people for ATOM BOMB STORIES publication. If we have success there, I'll come back to you again for a re-think about the trilogy. I am also going to try an editor I know at Wiley and will again see if my technical society is interested in publishing. I'll keep you informed.It is frustrating to have so many stories to tell, most of which could individually find a home in one magazine or another. I just don't have the savvy or inclination to peddle them in lieu of continuing to write.

I am sure you got my earlier mail about my 2 volume "A Pilgrim Muddles Through" books and I await a show of interest for that. My other two books are music books and I'm guessing they may not be down your alley.

Regards   Bob

An Editor at John Wiley and Sons had previously looked over what was then my first book and had liked the content, but wanted me to change it into a format where I was not the protagonist. Can you imagine an egotist like me doing so? But, nevertheless, using the argument espoused above, i.e. "The Story is the Message", I attempted to change her mind via email:

Dear Hana:

You may remember me from past correspondence. I was referred to you by Jim Harford. At that time, I had just about finished a book which compiled a number of individual engineering stories. You expressed some interest, but felt I might be a 'one-time-only' author. I have now 98% completed a trilogy, whose content is briefed on the attachment.

My work is intended to highlight some of the major engineering events and breakthroughs in the last century. It is NOT a memoir, but rather a telling of stories that are interconnected because I lived through them and participated in many of them. I do present the back ground surrounding the stories, but do not emphasize characters, emotions or, in most cases, opinions. The STORIES, not me, are the focus - and I think they are fascinating.

The audience for such books should be firstly Engineers from all over the world, especially those in the aerospace and related fields; faculty from colleges of Engineering and Science; aviation, space, and military buffs; military service and government people, particularly NASA employees; scientific and engineering Historians, members of many appropriate Technical Societies; and some laymen who are fans of aerospace developments. I can visualize an audience of perhaps 3-400,000, if properly exploited.

If you would like to explore further, tell me what you would like to see - anywhere from the three complete manuscripts in their present state, down to a special short 'treatment' of "Atom Bomb Stories" done by my daughter, a prize-winning book designer, who is Special Projects Editor for the NEW MEXICO magazine.

I believe that Jim Harford (jimharford@msn.com) will vouch for my authenticity.

Regards

Dr/Prof Robert F. (Bob) Brodsky, retired from TRW, Univ. of So. Cal., Aerojet-General, Iowa State University

Accordingly, I urged my daughter to plow the New Mexico fields since she knew many of the publishing people involved. I asked her send a copy of her 'treatment' to Wiley, and received the following from her in answer to the note that I had sent to France:

"Hi Dad - that's a good letter and I support you in your decision. Maybe it's just that it's my family you're talking about but I found the end of Atom Bomb Stories quite poignant. It reveals more about you than you might think - the fact that the bulk of the book is dedicated to the excitement of the work and that at the end the dissolution of your marriage came out of left field, along with your recognition that you were no longer an "open cock-pit person", is a human ending to a story about technology and problem solving. My feeling about the book is that it is a nice mix of Albuquerque history, an exciting time in space science, and the story of a family. That's how I intend to work it with UNM Press and MNM Press. I'm sending off the material to Hana L. today.
Love B"

So, I continue to have irons in the fire, but fear that the last resort of self-publishing might have to be faced by my daughter, who will inherit all my then unpublished manuscripts. I sure as hell won't self-publish! "If my stuff isn't good enough for 'real' publishers, Screw 'em!"

A couple of years later, frustrated by the bevy of 'Dear John's, I decided to go for "author subsidized" publication. The result - "On the Cutting Edge", Oct 2006, distributed by the University of Nebraska Press (see also AMAZON.COM). Sic Transit Gloria!

WITH FRIENDS LIKE THESE

We all get epiphanies; some we don't like – but they do act as a wake-up call. I got mine in October of 2002, after more than five years of hard labor writing the 'Great American Novel'. The thunderbolt came as the aftermath of digesting a critical letter from my college-and-life-long friend, a noted and well published author. I had sent my 13 page description of our recently completed summer Baltic Sea cruise to many of our friends and relatives, and had included him and his wife for what I thought would be their enjoyment and edification, and not – as I have previously done – for his literary evaluation. This travelogue was a nice off-hand description of our journey and was well received, or so I understood, until -----:

"October 14, 2002

Dear Bob,

I'm afraid that this will be cold comfort, but try to accept my continuing impatience.

At some point you must recognize that writing is not about itineraries. That's for travel agents. Good writing, including travel writing, must have a voice that's personal and that makes fresh original observations.

Read (or reread) Huckleberry Finn and Life on the Mississippi. They stand up as American writing at its best. If you want to go further, try Paul Fusseli's Abroad, which is a good book in itself and for the British travel writers it will lead you to. Or, for something more eccentric, Henri Michaux's A Barbarian in Asia. But for God's sake spare yourself and the rest of us more "Boating on the Baltic."

Basta,"

One of my Friend's Many Books – From AMAZON.com

Jackson Pollock: Energy Made Visible (Paperback)

by B. H. Friedman (Author) "On January 28, 1912, when Jackson Pollock was born in Cody, Wyo , nothing could have seemed less likely to his parents than that this..." (more)

Key Phrases: unframed space, greatest living painter, younger painters, New York, Jackson Pollock, East Hampton (more...)

I asked myself, "What's really going on here?" Had my friend finally given up on me as a writer or is he still sore at me for writing an earlier apocryphal story about him that he vigorously disputed? Although he never did find my writing monumental, he had lately begun to give me some small encouragement. True, he was the originator of the advice to me "to keep your day job", but I always wondered if there wasn't a tinge of jealousy there. Perhaps a subconscious rebellion to the thought that a late-comer, and an engineer to boot, could write so incisively? In any case, his words forced me to face up to what I was accomplishing by spending maybe three hours a day typing away, with never a writer's block to slow me down.

When I finished my first book, then called "An Engineer's Life" (now published as "On the Cutting Edge"), I tried to peddle it to both likely publishers and agents, with no success. I got the feeling that because of my 70-plus age, no one was willing to invest in a short track record author. Perhaps unrealistically, I had already decided not to 'self publish'; for two reasons: One, I have seen the huge amount of effort and time it takes to push a book, as a direct observation of the by-and-large successful activities of a member of my Writers Workshop. I'd much rather spend my time writing rather than seeking publication and sales. Two, I have a huge pride problem which says, "If it ain't good enough for a legitimate publisher, to hell with it! Maybe my kids will appreciate it."

Since I was well into writing this second book, "A Pilgrim Muddles Through", and had a good head start on my third, "Mouldy Figge Tales", I decided to hold off further publishing efforts until the third was near finished. Then, I would have a trilogy, "The World in a Jug", to spring on an unsuspecting public – all anxiously awaiting a true Great American Novel. Supplied with this imposing body of work, agents and publishers alike would no longer need to fear my early demise, especially when I have a fourth, "Songs My Mother Never Sang To Me" practically finished. Yep, that's my plan. The question now is am I really kidding myself?

I have received hints about the impact of my work from various sources other than my literary giant friend. My wife, who assiduously reads my stuff and likes my writing, staunchly says, "Who cares?" I rebut by saying that everyone should care, because I am documenting things that happened over the last 60 years of the 20th century. "Yeah, our kids and grandchildren will probably care", she ripostes. I have other fans in my Writers Workshop group. Most generally they like my light hearted pieces, but say I am pompous and professorial when taking stands on women, politics, energy, law, medicine and other less frivolous topics. And they purport to not at all understand my pieces on the old time jazz music in which I claim a certain expertise, though these are written in perfectly clear English.

There are other indications, both positive and negative. Although I have had several articles and short stories published in the last few years, only one has been for 'pay' - at 85 cents per word – while the other 'pay' offer, at 7 cents per word which I disdainfully turned down, was a story about my beautiful poem on Viagra. At her request, I sent my first book to an Editor of a prestigious semi-technical magazine run by the Smithsonian, who had paid me for the story cited above. I suggested that she might glean some more publishable stories from the book. She emailed back:

"Bob, your book is a gem. I loved it. And I read every word. How is the publishing going? I didn't find any excerptable sections at first glance, but I plan to go back over it with a keener eye." I emailed her for help or suggestions and got back, *"As regards to what? Potential publishers? Formatting? Alas, to both of those I have to say no. I'm useless in those areas."*

Wryly, my greatest artistic encouragement has come from the poetry sector. True, I am a novice in this field, but – as previously noted - my monumental work on Viagra spawned this honorific email in an attempt to lure me to an expensive annual bash:

Subj: You... Your Poetry... Bo Derek... Hollywood!
Date: 9/26/02 6:35:12 PM Pacific Daylight Time
From: Smichaels@poetry.com
To: rfoxbro@aol.com

Ladies and gentlemen, and fellow poets... It's now time to declare the winner of the largest cash prize ever awarded to an amateur poet.. Our Poet of the Year for 2002... and Grand Prize winner of $20,000 is...
Robert Brodsky!
We're familiar with your work Robert, and you know...it could happen just that way!

Dear Robert,
I would like to inform you of your nomination as 'Poet of the Year' for 2002, and to personally invite you to read your poetry at the single largest gathering of poets in history.--------

Viagra, triumphant at last! Naturally, I was pleased that my poetic talent had finally been recognized, but a damper on my euphoria arose when I found that all of those in my Group who subscribe to a magazine devoted to prose and poetry received a similar invitation.

On the other hand, I have sent several pieces to the *NEW YORKER* magazine, all routinely dismissed, and to other diverse publications, all returning with a "Dear John' in my SASE. Clearly, these were messages that I was aiming too high -but I wasn't ready or willing to lower my sights.

So I plowed on – not discouraged until the fatal letter from my friend arrived. What remains now is to regroup. I come to the sad conclusion that, while better than the average retired engineer/professor's writing, my work is not yet of the of the *NEW YORKER* class that I strive for, nor probably of *READERS DIGEST* acceptability. Alas, I am not going to suddenly burst upon the literary scene as the darling of the geriatric set, or of the larger audience for which I think I am writing. But, plod on I shall, for I enjoy writing and it keeps me off the streets. My boyish hopes of Hemingway-like adoration are now gone – reduced to ashes by one letter from a friend who has the guts to "tell it like it is"

WHY CHOOSE IUNIVERSE

With iUniverse, you can publish your book, your way—*today!* Our top-quality publishing, editorial and marketing services make it simple for writers just like you to quickly and affordably publish professional-looking books. Whether you want to make writing your career or you want to publish a book for family and friends, iUniverse makes it possible.

ONE OF MANY SELF PUBLISHING OUTFITS SEEN ON THE WEB

VHAT? VEE LOST?

"Did you see the Sunday TIMES 'PARADE' section?" asked Nina before we started the serious work of our Writer's Workshop group. Getting either a negative or no response, she doggedly produced a cut-out copy of the article and passed it around, while explaining that it called for entries into a "My Favorite Drive" contest. The text was limited too 100 words, double-spaced, and the award, not a stunner, was $100. But, as she pointed out, the 10 winners work would be viewed by a huge multi-million reader audience, since the PARADE supplement is a part of most Sunday newspapers throughout the country. I read that the winners, as judged by a distinguished panel, would be announced the following October, three months away.

When her reading turn came around, Nina gave us her entry – a lush paean concerning a drive through Colorado. Frankly, though descriptive and nicely written, I was not moved. I could see a thousand entries all describing their favorite scenery – all lush, frilly, and treacly. In fact, during the next week's session, when both Jodie and I read our entries, I found Jodie's to be more of the same but, as Jodie is a poet and a blithe spirit, her bit soared mightily with lushness and raised my blood sugar count at least fifty points.

In the week between meetings, I decided to give it a go, but to try for a different approach. With great pride and smugness, I read my entry – even though I was sure the group could not help me improve it. In fact, because it was so good, I was wary that they might try to sabotage my effort by trying to get me to pretty it up. It was exactly 100 words, every one of them being a concisely honed winner! Nevertheless, I gave them a shot at criticizing it – expecting a standing ovation – but instead getting some ill-advised nit picking. In my mind, it was perfect:

July 1, 2001

AN ENTRY TO

My Favorite Drive Contest
c/o Parade
PO Box 5099, Grand Central Station
New York, NY 10163-5099

SOLO

Over 60 years later, the memory of my all-time favorite drive remains crystal-clear. The day after my 16th birthday, I successfully won my driver's license and finally was ready to solo. As I headed down Wissahickon Avenue to begin my circuit, I felt a rush! I was exhilarated! I was Free! - a man among boys, as my friends still had only learner's permits. I was Mauri Rose, the famous Jewish Indy racer! I triumphantly returned, careful to park the car across the street so my Father could not see the damage caused by driving too close to a hydrant.

The first Sunday morning that we could finally relax after a two hectic trips, one East and the other to Germany – both affected by the September 11 World Trade Center assault, my wife and I settled back to read the Sunday papers in bed. I stumbled upon the results of the Favorite Drive contest, which I had completely forgotten about. Oddly, my name was not among the 10 finalists, nor were Nina's or Jodi's. That the latter's works were not included was merely a confirmation of my shrewd ability to detect a winner. That I was not at the head of the list was clearly a miscarriage of all that is good and true in this country of ours. Either the fix was in, or anti-semitism is more rife than I ever expected!

I didn't think too highly of the three 'Favorite Drives' that they printed. Number One spoke of the delights of driving north on Highway 21 in the western tip of Virginia:---- "A thin layer of angel hair surrounded the foothills that day.------ I didn't have a care in the world." The second was just as saccharine: "Sunlight filtering through the leaves checkers this road in summer. ------ because, you see, this is the road takes me home." Greg from Pennsylvania spoke of the wonders of urban life driving: " ----- just busy streets and brick row houses. --- I see a boy in dungarees and sneakers. I see myself." Andy Rooney-like, I empathized more with this one. It reminded me of Philadelphia, too. I would not have objected to its being rated somewhere in the last five.

They merely listed their other seven winners by name and location, and said that you could read their stuff on the web. I didn't bother, fearing an attack of acute hyperglycemia. I noted that three of the seven were Texans and figured that the influence of our valiant President was strong in literary circles. Significantly, there were no winners from California – a State now firmly entrenched in the right-wing press dog house.

INTERNATIONAL MOTORSPORTS HALL OF FAME

Mauri Rose

(1906-1981)

Born during 1906, in Columbus, Ohio, Rose became an engineer and race car driver who won Indy three times, 1941, 1947 and 1945. In the post-World War II era Rose was an engineer who happened to be a race driver too. His proudest accomplishment was not winning the Indy three times, but the invention of a device that allowed amputees to drive an automobile. Rose started driving race cars in 1927 on dirt tracks near Columbus. His first try at Indianapolis took place in 1933, when he was running a modified Studebaker. In 1934 he finished 2nd at Indy, and in 1936 he finished 4th at Indy but won the AAA National Championship. At Indy in 1939 he came in 5th, and finished 3rd in 1940. Rose's formula for success included careful planning and the best equipment. Rose liked to qualify on the first day and then return just to watch his opposition. After the 1951 Indy race Rose retired and moved to California.

Mauri Rose, Inducted 1994

Chapter 4

ANNALS OF LAW

- **BRIGS I HAVE KNOWN**
- **YOU CAN'T WIN 'EM ALL**
- **YOU NEVER MISS YOUR WATER**
- **TACKLING A GIANT**
- **A 'FINE' ROMANCE**

My career in courts of law, military and civilian, began innocently enough during the Great War, when I was a mere Seaman/First Class. From then on, starting in graduate school, the pace built up to a crescendo of vital cases as life went on. I have included a few of these legal skirmishes to illustrate how our justice system works for and against the oppressed.

The stories in this chapter depict one big victory and several small triumphs over evil forces. As you will see, I learned to cherish the combat, and win, at 'Small Claims" court procedures. Alas, on other occasions, also sketched below, defeats were sometimes snatched from the hands of victory:

BRIGS I HAVE KNOWN

One of the first things I did after I reported for nine months Radio Tech school duty at Navy Pier, a five minute trolley ride to Chicago's famous Loop, was to buy – for $5 – a spare 'black market' ID card. The sailor whose picture was on the card looked something like me, certainly a close enough resemblance for the perfunctory, if any, inspections that were made as one exited and returned to the base. By cutting out the upper left hand corner rivet which held the card together and by inserting a special pinkish 1/2 inch paper square centered at the rivet's center and then reassembling, I created a 'Ship's Company" card which allowed me base egress and ingress at any hour of any day. I had liberated the pink paper from the desk of my unit's unsuspecting Chief Petty Officer, Mr. Huish. Without jeopardizing the sanctity of my true ID card, I was now determined to see the 'world' while facing the rigors of the upcoming winter of 1944-45!

I took care to select the upper of three stacked bunks for my sack site, being sure the unit was against the bulkhead (i.e., Navy for 'wall'). I did this for two reasons; the most important one being that a bed-check, made nightly by a low rank petty officer who usually reached up on tip-toes to my tier and patted to make sure something was there, could only be made from one side. It was not hard to fool him by rolling up a blanket on the prober's finger tip side to approximate a warm body. The other reason was gratuitous. Those who selected units located in the more luxurious middle of the cavernous bunk house were often 'dropped' upon by sea gulls who regularly visited the normally open ceiling vents.

Thus began a career of carousing-learning which took advantage of my ability to get by with very little sleep for long stretches of time. Like meek, mild Clark Kent, I attended classes all day and managed to stay awake most of the time. Then, right after evening mess, off I went to enjoy that "Toddlin' Town" with all its amenities available to servicemen. As time went by, I managed to find the great hot jazz venues on Rush Street and the South Side, to discover the wonderful "Golden Dome" music bar featuring singing bartenders and their equally wonderful dirty songs, to finally get laid by a patriotic 'V'-girl, to find a lovely girl friend, to enter the local world of hot music via a record store owner and record maker, and - courtesy of the USO – get free tickets to all major sporting events. I also managed to get into trouble with the naval authorities.

Navy Pier as it looks to-day. It was originally built in 1916 to serve Lake Michigan freighters and provide transportation to other cities on the Great Lakes, as well as for recreational purposes.

In 1941, Navy Pier was converted to military use and was used throughout World War II. From 1946 to 1964, it was a college campus. After a lull in the 1970's and 1980's, Navy Pier was revitalized and, today, it is a multi-million dollar convention, cultural and recreation center and Chicago's most visited attraction.

Navy Pier

One Monday night, an overly suspicious bed-checker took the trouble to climb up to the third tier only to find a rolled-up blanket substituting for a real sailor. He put me on re-port and, next day, even though I explained that I had been unable to sleep and had gone to the smoking room, Chief Huish gave me 10 hours of extra duty and revoked my liberty privileges for the upcoming weekend. That Saturday afternoon, while I working off my time with a broom and dustpan, I was paged over the P.A. System informing me that I had a visitor and should report to the receiving area. Who was it but Harry Passon, a sincere nabob in the "Big Brothers" organization. He was the father of my last Philadelphia girl friend. I called his daughter, Dottie, my last pre-service inamorata, Darcy Passion – ah; Were it so! It turned out he had been recruited by my parents, who had heard of my diffi-culties in my earlier telephone call to them, to try to straighten me out. He asked me if I could join him for dinner that evening, and I jumped at the chance, bemused by the oppor-tunity to illegally ease out of my burdensome restriction.

I spiffed up in my dress blues, used my usual 'ship's company' ID for egress, and enjoyed an evening of good food and ironical lectures on how I should shape up and really join the war effort. I also learned that Miss Passion had taken up with a well-to-do 4-F and was probably lost to me forever. Just starting to seriously enjoy the action and sexual encounters that Chicago had to offer, I found my heart unbroken by this news. When I returned to the Pier, I resumed my extra duty chores and learned from my fellow sweepers that I had not been missed; and was actually given credit for all the time I supposedly was toiling away with my trusty swab! But, I clearly lost forever the opportunity of becoming a 'Big Brothers' poster boy.

I was enjoying my new found freedom and wanted to spread the joy to my fellow swabbies. One day, I saw a bundle of base 'passes' – chits that were used to award heads-up students for an occasional week day evening leave- on Chief Huish's desk and promptly purloined them and distributed them to my friends. The Chief, who lately had come to suspect, via scuttlebutt I suppose, that I had a way to get off the Pier whenever I wanted to, dressed me down, inspected my locker, and told me he had his eye on me. I had a very clever hiding place, in my shoe, for the errant ID card. I didn't sweat it.

But, disaster did finally strike a few happy months later, when an over - zealous bed - checker again climbed up to my level; and found no one there. My 'smoking' excuse was not accepted and I was up for a "Captain's Mast" – the lowest level Court Martial in the Naval justice hierarchy. "Three days bread and water, with half rations on the second day, plus 20 hours extra duty" was the solemn verdict. Missing only one day of school, I passed the time pleasantly in a makeshift cage constructed with fencing material. Apparently there was no need for a real brig in a school atmosphere. Its location was right by an open area main passageway, where everyone could see and talk to me. My friends supplied me with chocolate bars and cigarettes. At night, a mattress was thrown in, and if I pressed a buzzer, a guard would eventually appear to escort me to the head. The jail time went quickly and I was able to catch up on my school homework. But, it was a scary experience, and for the rest of my time at Navy Pier, I was much more vigilant and aware of which swabbie was going to get bed check duty – since, by now, most of the checkers were my friends and could care less if I was out on the town. The Chief, however, remained an enemy, and was glad when I finally left the Pier to save the world elsewhere.

Somehow I managed to stay out of trouble during my next three month assignment at NAS, Buckhead – in the suburbs of Atlanta, where I attended Link Trainer Instructor's school. On graduation I had an added qualification (S1/c, Sp.T/LT) to refresh Navy pilots on blind flying procedures. As I think about it, the rules there must have been very lax, for during that sojourn my Chicago girl friend came to visit for two weeks, and I spent a lot of social off-duty time with lovely-but-alas-sincerely-engaged petty officer 3rd class Mary Margaret Maureen McMichael, whom I eventually replaced as an instructor; to allow her to bravely take 'overseas' duty in Hawaii.

Mary Margeret Maureen 'Marty' McMichael –
"pin-up" pix circa 1945

My next joust with military law took place early in my next assignment as a combination Link Trainer Instructor, radar repairman, and airplane captain at NAS Otis Field. Here, at the edge of the huge army Camp Edwards near Falmouth on Cape Cod, the Navy had established CASU (Carrier Aircraft Service Unit) 26. Its purpose was to supply a mobile, air-liftable cadre of experts to revitalize wounded aircraft carriers, no matter where they were laid up. When not so employed, we updated equipment, like new-version F4-U fighters, and retrained pilots and crew who were being reassigned from the Atlantic theater, where the Navy was no longer needed, to Pacific theater action.

Events   (from the WEB: I think this may be the squadron that I attended to)

01 APR 1945:

Fighter Squadron Forty-Three (VF-43) had its beginnings on April 1, 1945, when Fighter Squadron Seventy Four A (VF-74A) was formed at NAS Otis Field, Camp Edwards, Massachusetts. The squadron was assigned to Carrier Air Group Seventy-Four (CVG-74) aboard the USS Midway, (CVB-41). They were flying the F4U Corsair during Midway's shakedown cruise in May 1947.

Nurnie, my boyhood Nanny, now 40, was finally to be married and asked me to act as the 'best man'. I received permission from Lt. Sullivan for a three day weekend pass to go by train to Philadelphia for the big event. The day before I was to start leave he rescinded the pass, for no apparent reason. I told no one my plans, but left the Lieutenant a note saying I was going AWOL and would return on Monday. It was a very happy family reunion, and I did indeed report back to duty by 7 a.m. Monday morning. Sully put me on report and a second Captain's Mast was scheduled. Here I got a rather harsh "6 days bread and water with full rations every other day" sentence, to be served in the local brig. This was a separate undistinguished building with about 10 cells, managed by a CPO assisted by 3 shifts of round-the-clock 3rd class petty officer guard sets. In the middle of the cell block was the Chief's well appointed private quarters.

My cell was roomy; 4 standard mattress size area, whose sole décor was a single mattress. There were bars leading to the aisle, solid walls on each side, and a partial barred window on the outside. Inserted into the window frame was a ¾" plywood sheet with many 1" holes drilled into it to allow ventilation. It was peaceful and comfortable, and allowed a lot of sack-out time. I soon made friends with my leading day guard, who escorted me to mess when such was on the schedule, or who dutifully served up my bread and water and accompanied me on head breaks. His name was Gomez, and his visage, dark, mean and foreboding, was typical of the famous Mexican bandit caricature. It turned out that he was one of the sweetest guys I've ever known, and we greatly enjoyed each other's company. But, he did look fierce and his scary persona was emphasized by the big '45 he carried in full view in a hip holster.

He knew that my friend, Sherwood Fox, would stealthily slip through the empty weedy field behind my window and poke contraband Baby Ruth candy bars and cigarettes through the holes, while quietly conversing for a spell, every evening around 5:30 – just as the sun was starting to set. Gomez told me he was going to pull a prank on Sherwood the day before my release – since I would be on full rations the last day and would not need the sustenance. As Sherwood and I started talking, Gomez slipped up behind him, '45 drawn, and barked, "Halt, who goes there? Hands up!" I saw Sherwood turn around to face his accuser and I know he turned snow white when he saw the apparition facing him. He explained to Gomez that he was merely talking to me and denied bringing contraband. Gomez said, "You dirty son –of –a -bitch, I don't believe you. Now, when I lower my gun, you get the hell out of here as fast as you can, and you better run a zig-zag course because I just may decide to shoot you. Go!" I watched as Sherwood hightailed it out, snaking with all his ability, while Gomez and I had a good laugh. Later, Sherwood told me that his heart had almost stopped when he was accosted and it wasn't until he calmed down that he realized he had been set up.

There were visiting hours every day, and my WAC lady friend stationed at adjacent Camp Edwards normally appeared to chat with me in the guarded lobby. Apparently, she was greatly admired by the Chief - as well she should have been, being a good looking, very well endowed fighting unit. Before her fourth expected visit, the Chief came by my cell and said, "Ski, you've been a model prisoner and I'm going to do something nice for you. When your Army friend comes today, I'm going to put you two in my quarters for the hourly visit". I thanked the Chief and looked forward to the privacy. I was surprised, when Gomez escorted us to Chief's room, to find the curtains drawn, the bed covers pulled suggestively down, a lamp at the side of the bed, a radio on, and a condom on the lamp table. I don't why we restrained ourselves as much as we did– it must have been a guilty sixth-sense. Gomez told me at lunch the last day that the Chief had a convenient peep hole into his bedroom.

A few months later, I had my final, and most serious, clash with the Navy. I was at the huge Naval installation on Hampton Roads in Norfolk, Virginia waiting for shipment to NAS Guantanamo Bay, Cuba, my first permanent overseas assignment, where I was to spend my last few months before my scheduled discharged date. The war was over. The ships for 'Gitmo' left every two weeks and I had just missed one. We had nothing to do but wait for the next ship, and were not allowed liberty. The day before we were to finally ship out, I took the blanket from my bunk and laid it down on a small grassy island in the sun and sacked out, while a crew of ship's company did a thorough floor sanding job on our quarters. I was peacefully dozing when awakened by a sharp kick to my ribs. "Sailor, you're on restricted grass and your ass better not be here on my next round", a huge Shore Patrolman growled. I told them both to go fuck themselves knowing full well that I would be gone the next day, and went back to sleep.

When they returned to rough me up, they demanded my ID card and told me to report at 5 p.m. at their police station. Naturally I gave them my fake ID card since I would have no need of it in 'Gitmo', and of course did not show up at the witching hour. The next day, ditty bag on my shoulder, in the midst of the mob on the wharf ready to embark, I heard an ominous, "There he is!" All of a sudden, I'm not on a ship to Cuba, but am the star of a Summary Court Martial, the next to highest court martial there is. And the sentence is again a stiff one; "Ten days, half rations every other day". Remembering my rather pleasant stay at Otis Field, I took my sentence bravely but, it turns out, unknowingly.

The brig at Norfolk consisted of a large number of electric fenced-in Quonset Huts, each holding 10 or 12 prisoners, with an armed Marine guard at the egress. I soon found out that I was caged in with the Navy's really serious criminal element and quickly had the fear of God instilled in me. I kept to my self and said nothing, determined to survive. The worst humiliation was if you needed to go to the head in the middle of the night. You had to fully dress, knock on the door until the guard deigned to open it, and respectfully say - to a PFC, mostly – "Sir, may I go to the head?" More often than not, the bastard would say, "Not now, try me later. Get back in your sack". Usually you could make it on the second try, since they were not outright heartless.

After what seemed an eternity, I got out of that hateful brig the day after the ship left for Guantanamo. A few days later, near the grassy patch, I chatted up a nice Wave Officer in Discharge Operations. She told me that since I was now within six months of my discharge date, I did not have to go to Cuba, and could request final duty at any Navy facility of my liking. I ended up my brilliant military career at the Philadelphia Naval Yard, and was home for dinner every night – a returning, about - to - be- Honorably-Discharged conquering hero, loaded with GI Bill credits and a modest "Zone of the Interior" medal merit badge!

There's another story of Navy justice that you should know about. One night at NAS Otis Field, I was assigned to a monthly guard duty stint, stationed – with rifle – on the perimeter of the air field. Guards were emplaced about 100 yards from each other and instructed to shout at intruders, "Halt, Who goes there?" Around 3 a.m., I heard what I thought was a shot and some yelling from a few stations away. When I reported back in at 5 a.m. at the end of my duty, I heard that a fellow guard had shot and killed an errant cow. In traditional Navy fashion following a killing, he had to pay for the price of a bullet and was granted a week's leave. It's a wonder that there weren't more bovine casualties!

YOU CAN'T WIN 'EM ALL!

I've been remarkably successful in most of my skirmishes with the law! Especially in my latter years, when I learned that small Claims court Judges would simply not rule against a person in their '70s, no matter how ridiculous the situation. However, all was not milk and honey. Herein I cite three strange and wonderful cases where the fates were against me:

In the early 60's, I left the Aerojet / Rheem plant in highly industrialized Downey and headed for home in Claremont just in time for the 5 o'clock rush hour. I passed through a major intersection on a yellow light and was promptly issued a citation. I was really burned, because it was simply impossible to go through this intersection on 'red'. At the designated time, I went to Downey, a good twenty miles from home, for my day in traffic court; determined to convince the Judge of the unfairness of the citation. However, the citing officer did not show – too embarrassed, I imagine, to make his case. The charge was dismissed. On the way home from my victorious court appearance, I passed a stop sign without actually coming to a full halt. I immediately was hailed and cited.

Then, there was the ridiculous Sunday morning incident on the beach at Newport. It was early, and my wife and I, alone on the vast sand beach, were sitting in the sun, listening to a Dodger game being broadcast from the East, and sipping beer from the nondescript paper cups we had cleverly brought along, keenly aware of the ban on beer drinking in that outstanding and God-fearing Orange County Republican (then, not so much now) community. A kid in a tee shirt with a 'Bud' beer logo came ambling along, whistling and carrying a football under his arm. With the whole beach at his disposal, we wondered why he came so close to us. After passing us, he about- faced and returned. He politely asked us "What are you drinking". "Why, beer, of course"! With that, he opened the football at a slit made at a seam and pulled out a badge indicating he was a storm trooper and wrote us a citation. When I checked, I found that the fine was an outrageous $75 each and naturally arranged for a court appearance before our vacation ended.

Even though these were the days before an 'entrapment' defense would have carried the day, the Judge reduced the total fine to a very satisfying $25. I had to leave my wife with the Bailiff, as a hostage, while I went to the bank for the cash they demanded ("No checks"). On Newport Avenue, I made an apparently illegal U-turn to get to the bank, and immediately was awarded with another citation.

I saved the saddest defeat for last, and it is with some sadness and bitterness that I recount this colossal miscarriage of justice, which not only took me down, but also sullied the otherwise lifetime perfect legal record of a dear friend. Towards the end of April, 1986, I visited my old stamping grounds in Ames, Iowa; there, in part, to give an inspirational lecture to a student group from my former Iowa State University Aerospace Engineering Department. The venue was a meeting room in a large motel on 13th Street, a four lane road near the Freeway ramp. During the course of the evening, I had the opportunity to quaff two beers in order to clear my throat prior to my talk. On the way back to the house of the friends whose car I had borrowed and whose bed and board my wife and I were enjoying, I was awarded an unjust speeding citation and subjected to a humiliating sobriety test, the latter probably due to the unmistakable smell of beer on my breath.

Shortly after our return to California, I received a note in the mail indicating that even though the officer had cited me with an incorrect code number, the charges still stood. This came from the Ames Assistant City Attorney, by whose unmistakable name I surmised to be the wife of a former University friend and colleague. My pulse quickened, for I recognized the chance the whole affair could be thrown out of court because of the incorrect citation. Thus, the Assistant City Attorney was rewarded for her forthrightness by my immediate dispatch of the letter below, which, as you will see, contained a remarkably generous offer. I made sure to send a copy to my very good friend and past partner in crime, the Senior Partner of a prestigious Ames law firm, in anticipation of a fomenting legal battle:

May 6, 1986
Dear Ms. R.

Although I thought that the Officer who cited me for speeding was extremely unfair, since I was in an overspeed condition for <u>only</u> a short time in an attempt to get by two cars - side by side on the 4 lane road and going at an interminably slow pace. I had intended to pay the fine, since I could not appear in Iowa to defend my position. Now, however, your note of April 28, apparently indicates that I was given an incorrect citation. If this was the case, I think we both know that you must quash the charge, since your case could not possibly stand up in court. I am asking my attorney in Ames to corroborate this assumption.

In short, I do not agree with your forwarded "motion to amend and order amending" whose apparent purpose it is to tidy up your dirty linen. While I await your decision, I want you to know some of the circumstances surrounding this unfortunate event:

- *I am a former long - time academic Department Head at ISU and was performing a service to my former Department that evening by speaking to many of their student body.*

- *At my extreme age, I was subjected to the indignities of a sobriety (!) test – and I, a person who anyone will tell you has one drink a month on the average! For this indignity and breach of my civil liberties alone the charge should be suppressed.*

However, I am not an unreasonable man. In return for your court accepting a gift of $33 to City of Ames, I would expect the incident to not be reported to the Great State of California where Auto Insurance rates are outrageous. This is what is known in Legal parlance as a compromise - since it may serve both our needs.

Please let me know your thoughts - remembering that if I was wrongly cited, fair legal practice demands that you eat it.
Very truly yours,

This brought an almost immediate riposte on City of Ames ("All American City, 1982-1983) stationary, with copies to Clerk of Court and the Senior Partner, Esq.:

May 8,1986

Dr. R. F. Brodsky
401 Second St.
Hermosa Beach, CA 90254

In re: WI) 001021 Traffic Citation

Dear Dr. Brodsky:

Thank you for your letter of May 6, 1986. Please be advised that the amended motion was a routine legal procedure to give you notice of the Ames Municipal Code section you were allegedly in violation of and which the police officer inadvertently forgot to write on the ticket. The amendment was done prior to the date on which you were scheduled to appear or pay the fine and approved by Judge Hronek.

It is my opinion and experience that an amendment of this nature does not prevent the case from "standing up in court". The fact that your insurance rates may be affected by a conviction for violating a traffic ordinance is not a situation unique to you. Every person issued a citation has those same concerns. It is my policy that I do not "compromise", as you put it, on speeding tickets. I believe that policy results in fair and equitable treatment for all persons, regardless of their occupation, age, driving record, or insurance rates.

Any person who feels that they are not guilty of the alleged violation is entitled to a trial before a judge. I realize that since you live in California it is probably not worth the time and money to come to Ames for a trial. As a possible solution, I am suggesting a "paper" trial. In such a situation, each party stipulates to the facts that would be testified to, were a trial to be held. This could be done through your attorney. However, I might caution that such a procedure requires that you waive your opportunity to cross-examine the City's witness, in this case the police officer who issued the citation.

Let me be clear that I do not intend to dismiss the ticket nor will I be willing to accept a gift of $33.00 on behalf of the City of Ames in return for not reporting the ticket to the state of California.
If you are interested in a trial on this matter, I suggest you contact your attorney or myself. Certainly if you have questions, please do not hesitate to contact me.

Sincerely

The Senior Partner Esq., apparently felt that a last conciliatory word was necessary, as he folded before what he must have felt were overwhelming forces. Joining in the fun, he wrote the following to the Asst. City Attorney:

May 13, 1986

Re: WD 001021 - Traffic Citation

Dear Ms. R.
*   I am writing to join the entertaining correspondence between Dr. Brodsky and your-self (now among the three of us).*

I have known Dr. Brodsky since the "Platonic Wars" and I can tell you that Dr. Brodsky is an iconoclast. His iconoclastic writing (on a scale of 10) is 8.3941(a). His literary skills do not always reveal the sterling attributes of one who teases the established system. (Although for the ten years (approximately) he lived in Ames he wrote several letters to the IRS and most of his letters revealed his iconoclastic nature brilliantly – in this regard I can give you the names and addresses of several leading citizens of Ames, [and surrounding areas] who can corroborate my statements about Dr. Brodsky's unique qualifications as an expert in the respected area of iconoclasm)

Now that the parenthetical statements have been disposed of (I have disposed of the paren-thetical statements), I submit it is accurate to conclude that:
(1) Dr. Brodsky's letter of May 6, 1986, adequately "stipulates" the facts surrounding the unfortunate incident that occurred in Ames, Story County, Iowa, on or about some spring day in April, 1986, and
(2) Dr. Brodsky presumes (and he fails to presume accurately - as is often the frailty of an iconoclast) that the penalty to be imposed upon him amounts to $33.00, including the works.

Therefore, I respectfully ask that you handle the paperwork accordingly. Inform me by letter, or by messenger, or otherwise, of the results, and I will personally deliver to you $33.00 in cash (U.S.).
Remaining an officer of the court and your friend, I am

Yours very truly,

On June 4th, The Senior Partner , in acknowledgement of the unfavorable judgment reproduced below, sent me the official news of our loss and indicated that he had paid the fine on my behalf:

IN THE IOWA DISTRICT COURT FOR STORY COUNTY, CITY OF AMES,

Plaintiff,   **Case No. WD 001021**

vs.

ROBERT F. BRODSKY, Defendant.

JUDGMENT ENTRY

The City of Ames and the Defendant, by counsel, submit a stipulation to the Court based upon the Defendant's correspondence to the Clerk of Court filed May 8, 1986. In that correspondence the Defendant admits that he was exceeding the speed limit as noted upon the citation and the Court notes that his stated reasons therefore fail to constitute a legal excuse.

IT IS THEREFORE ORDERED that the Defendant is adjudged guilty of excessive speed, 40 m.p.h, in a 30 m.p.h, zone in violation of Section 26.39(18), Ames Municipal Code. Defendant, by counsel having waived time, it is further ordered that the Defendant is fined $20.00 and a $3.00 surcharge and $10.00 costs, the total of $33.00 to be paid to the Clerk of Court, Fifth and Kellogg, Ames, Iowa, on or before June 20, 1986.
The Defendant is informed his appeal rights are pursuant to Rule 54, Iowa Rules of Criminal Procedure, bond on appeal $75.00.

THOMAS R. HRONEK
DISTRICT ASSOCIATE JUDGE

CC: City Attorney
The Senior Partner

Now I am sure that the Senior Partner, my former lawyer, the former Mayor of Ames, and a fellow Rotarian to boot, is an excellent advocate in his normal field of expertise. But clearly he was out of his element in this case, where street smarts and choice invective were obviously called for. I know now that the late Johnnie Cochran, of OJ Simpson trial fame, would have decimated the Assistant City Attorney in a court of law: "IF YO' AIN'T GOT THE RIGHT NUMBAH, YOU DON'T GET TO RHUMBA"!*

---

* For you latecomers who did not follow the notorious OJ Simpson trial, Johnnie's winning words were, "If the glove don't fit, you gotta acquit!"

YOU NEVER MISS YOUR WATER
('TIL YOUR WELL RUNS DRY)

After all the infighting, my day in court had finally arrived. The case of "Brodsky vs. the Board of Directors" was scheduled for the afternoon docket, and was called up by the Clerk around 2p.m., when the Judge, following a break, made his imperious reentry.

The judge immediately asked me, "How can you take anyone to court for cashing a check that you made out and signed?', and added, "I should, a priori, throw the case out and make you re-file!" "But, Your Honor", I replied, "I clearly wrote on the check that it was to cover an 'Illegal and Contested' fine". I did admit that I had probably worded my formal complaint poorly when I filed it, The Judge, of course, understood the justice that I was really seeking and asked the opposition whether they would agree to continue the trial rather than having me go through the whole start-up process again; this time with a correctly written charge. They acceded and the trial began - with me having first licks.

At this stage in my life, I was well versed in the ways of the law, having spent considerable time watching the sometimes brilliant but always misguided peccadillos of the sharks and Keystone Kops who had conducted the OJ opera. Although stage fright prevented me from being brilliant, I presented my case with some modicum of competence. I first tried to establish my solid no-flake senior citizen status by attempting to introduce my "Who's Who in America" write up. The Judge would have none of it, urging me to press on.

I then outlined the events that led up to my appearance in court as a champion of the multitudes of abased senior citizen swimmer-tenants who have ever been maligned by a vindictive Homeowners Association Board of Directors for 'dripping' in the lobbies and hallways of condominiums throughout these United States:

We had moved from our two-and-a-half-blocks inland town house in Hermosa Beach to a condo in nearby Redondo Beach in August, '95. We had made the move because we wanted to live right on the beach; to hear the sound of the surf and barking Sea Lions at night and, either with the help of a newly acquired tripod mounted telescope or with bare eye, see the ships at sea and the doll-babies on the beach right from our 5th floor patio balcony which overlooked the pool area. There were some sacrifices made in the move - but an important and essential part of my everyday life - use of a hot tub and the pool - remained as before.

I immediately resumed my daily afternoon routine of a half hour in the hot tub followed by a rigorous 100 laps in the pool, which was not bad for a man of my then age, even considering that I count each lap as "10". To complete the daily ritual, I dried off as best I could with my rather small standard Hermosa Beach townhouse pool towel, Then, I put on my flip-flops and exited the pool area via the large tiled anteroom and through a door into the slick marble-floored main lobby. Here, I called for the elevator which took me to the fifth floor marbled foyer leading into a carpeted corridor toward our unit's entry.

After a couple of weeks of firmly establishing this wonderful routine, I was accosted by the building's chief super, Luis, who politely told me, "You are <u>dripping</u>" and, "This is dangerous since someone can slip and fall". Since Luis, at that time, was working with his swab and bucket on the anteroom floor and since this was almost my first contact with the building's supervisory hierarchy, I chose to ignore his admonition, thinking that his remarks might be spurred on by sour grapes in objecting to mop up after me. Moreover, I could not detect any substantial drippings outside of the immediate pool area.

I was also expecting a different treatment since, in Hermosa Beach where I had served long and valiantly as an (unpaid) officer of the Homeowner's Association, it was the custom that a Board Member - him or herself in person - would apply an admonition in a warm friendly manner, until the unruly perp ultimately acceded under threats of a fine.

Thus I was doubly shocked when, a few weeks later on October 18th, my landlord sent me a copy of a letter sent to him by the soon-to-be-dreaded Management Company to whom the building's Board had ceded their rights to govern. In the main, the letter stated,

"It has been brought to the attention of the Board of Directors that when your tenants use the spa or pool, they drip water from the pool area throughout the lobby into the elevator and in the 5th floor lobby. This creates a liability if someone were to slip and fall in the water. Please remind your tenants to dry off after using the pool and spa in the future."

Since I liked our landlord and was embarrassed, I wished with all my heart that the message would have been delivered to me via a personal meeting or phone call from a member of the Board or at least the Management Company official to whom Luis and his assistant, David, reported. In the true American way, it would have been nice to know my accuser, but I assumed it was one of the supers just doing their job. I later learned that the evil Management Company had earlier convinced the Board that tenants were basically turds and should have no standing or recognition as individuals. Nevertheless, seeing as how they apparently were serious about this heinous offense, I promptly asked Luis how one avoids "dripping" since there were no changing facilities other than in the relatively remote small bathrooms off the pool area anteroom. He advised me to wrap my towel around my waist after I had used it to dry off. This I did after that conversation - thus to my mind solving the problem.

However, a precursor of impending doom occurred on Friday night, Dec. 8, when we heard a knock on the door. It was the lady-next-door. She announced herself as the Chairman of the Board - and did I know that, "despite the warning letter, I continued to drip!" She then launched into a diatribe about how, just last week, a visiting cleaning lady had slipped on a Foyer floor and was suing the Association for damages. 'Oh", I said, "Was I responsible for this accident?" "Oh No!" she said, "But you could have been!!" I then assured her that I would continue to be careful, and asked if she had any suggestions as to how I might reduce the dripping? She advised employing a really big towel - which made so much sense that I immediately purchased one such and thereafter used it assiduously. Later, I decided to go to the pool area in a beach kimono, and used it as a shield as I removed my bathing suit when I was ready to go upstairs. The wet suit was then placed in the towel, where the sucker could not possibly drip.

Well, you could have knocked me over with a straw when the next day's mail brought a copy of a dunning letter sent to my landlord - a letter the lady-next-door must have known about since it was dated Dec. 6, the day after the monthly Board meeting: *"It has* *been brought to the attention of the Board of Directors once again that your tenants are continuing to drip water into the lobby causing a trip and fall hazard. A warning letter was sent on Oct. 18, 1995. At this time, the Board has unanimously decided to assess a $50.00 fine against your unit. Please remit $50 by check made out to the 531 Esplanade HOA, c/o ------------- Management, Inc. no later than December 16, 1995. Further occurrences will result in a $50 line for each occurrence."*

I immediately contacted the billee - my landlord - and assured him that I would pay the fine- but under protest. I sent my $50 cheek to the newly named, "Ruthlessly Efficient Management Company" on December 12, noting on the check that it was for an "Illegal and Contested fine". My letter, slipped under the door or the kindly lady-next-door, with copies to my landlord and the R.E.M. Co., stated: "In *response to the Dec.6 dunning letter from our ruthlessly efficient management company, I have enclosed a check for $50, which I trust will be returned to me unsullied after you have considered my plea for mercy in view* of *the circumstances in this case outlined below*":

Then, in exquisite detail, I documented the events leading up to the unexpected delivery of the fatal notice. I added the sage suggestion, *"If the Board is really concerned, I suggest the addition of two or more changing rooms in the anteroom area. I notice that now some people inconveniently disrobe under the cover of towels or robes on the patio with much sheepishness and discomfiture, but with true Stalag 17 obedience"*

I then made three specific comments in lengthy paragraphs: <u>One</u>, I suggested the issuing of advisory warnings, followed by a summons to appear in person before the Board before fines were levied; <u>Two</u>, I suggested that they keep in mind the notion of 'presumption of innocence' and, if they didn't like suggestion One, that they use the ruthlessly efficient management company to make suggestions to the offender as to how to regain a state of nirvana with the Board; <u>Three</u>, I pointed out that I did not believed they acted legally within their own Rules and Regulations. I ended by saying, *'In the future, I would appreciate dealing directly with* me *rather than my Landlord. Hoping for a reply or a meeting as well as a pristine uncollected check.---------'*

When nothing happened for over a month, I thought that they had heeded my advice. However, on Feb 5, 1996 I received my bank statement and discovered that they had cashed the fine-payment check on January 17. Early in February, I tried to attend the annual Board meeting, but had no proxy since my landlord was out of town when I sought to act in his stead. My real purpose in attending the meeting was to point out some of the structural and amenity shortfalls of the Building - and perhaps, if the occasion arose, to suggest that that tenants should be recognized as part of the human race. I was rudely booted out of the meeting by the lady-next-door, who said that tenants were "never allowed" at Board Meetings. In Hermosa, we welcomed the advice and bitches of tenants since they were often plausible and helpful.

This unseemly attitude galvanized my letter of Feb. 4, 1996, which documented some of the points I had intended to make at the meeting, along with a veiled threat of contemplated legal action should the check in question be cashed. Additionally, I officially noted for the first time that the building had some fundamental structural problems. I told them that I had previously demonstrated our patio/balcony's inherently dangerous flexible guard rail problem to both Luis and my landlord, but neither seemed to be singularly impressed by the incipient possibility of an unwarned guest doing a Brody from our fifth floor balcony down to the pool area below.

My Feb. 4 letter which pointed out these shortcomings read:

"In view of the fact that I was unceremoniously denied observers rights in attending the recent Annual Meeting , I will volunteer the advice and admonishments that I might have discussed at the meeting had the opportunity existed: There is a dangerous safety situation on every patio. The guard rails are not fastened along the tops of the railings. (i.e., the three risers which attach to the railing tops are cantilevered (!) from the patio floor, and the two top railing ends do not attach to the building! When the rail is leaned on, the risers bend markedly). The problem evidences itself in the cracking of the concrete floor and the tiles. Please take corrective action immediately before anyone gets killed!"

I further provided four additional greatly helpful suggestions dealing with slippery conditions poolside; guest parking spaces (there were none); storage compartments in the garage; cover for the hot tub to conserve gas, followed by the final fatherly advice:

1) Don't levy fines based on indefensible rules and procedures, lest your court costs exceed your fine revenues manifold!
2) Finally, a personal gripe. You have not seen fit to answer my letter of December 12, which is not courteous and is, in effect, holding my check of $50 in abeyance. Moreover, your ruthlessly efficient management company has not acceded to my request far a copy of an earlier warning letter, thus delaying any further action that I may wish to take. Please let me hear from you in all good time so that we may adjudicate our mutual grievances. At the least acknowledge that you received my earlier letter, as well as this one!
But, please take care of the rail situation immediately - at least in my unit!! (I have already temporarily tied down one end.)"

Their cashing of my check made it clear to me that a decisive blow must be struck to cause fear in their callow hearts! On February 23, I opened an action in the City of Torrance small claims court with the charge, *"Defendant owes me the sum of $150, including court costs, because of cashing my $50 check, # 2468 of 12/12/95, for an illegally and maliciously levied fine. I have asked the defendants not to cash the check, but they did on 1/17/96. I have asked the defendants to pay back this money, but they have not done so."*

The same day *as* the filing, I sent the Board a letter informing them of my action. I usually sent copies of my letters to them by slipping the goods under the door of the lady-next-door - a practice that seemed to infuriate the recipients. On the petition, I had asked for $15O; $50 to replace the check, $40 for court costs, and $60 for normally unallowable 'pain and suffering" cloaked under the guise of wear and tear on my trusty Macintosh. Although I may have worded the official court charge poorly, I acquitted myself nicely in the informing letter to the Board by quoting the now-famous "rush to judgment" words of Johnny Cochrane - the OJ trial still being fresh in everyone's mind. For the first time, too, I made the subtle suggestion that the management company might not be running on all four cylinders. The letter read;

"On this date, I have initiated a small claims court action against the Board (and its ruthlessly efficient management agent) seeking a return of my "illegal and malicious" $50 fine, my court costs of $40, and a sought-for penalty. The notice is being is being served to the above noted ruthlessly efficient agent. Earlier, I had informed my landlord of my intent to start this action in case he cared to seek counsel with you.
I remain dumbfounded by your apparent lack of sophistication in dealings with your owners and tenants; your senseless "rush to judgment" against a perceived, but totally innocence scofflaw without the obviously called-for (and requested) conference; your unwillingness to open discussions in a neighborly manner; and now your seeming gross negligence in failing to take timely action vis-a-vis the unsafe *railing situation which I recently wrote you about.*
On my part, I will *be willing to immediately settle my grievance out of court for the $90 I have already invested, thus allowing you to possibly avoid additional expenses which are the court's to grant. I take it that you understand that* my *grievance is not about money, but about trying to make you into responsible thinking citizens who do not need to hide behind the skirts of your ruthlessly efficient (but basically stupid?) management company."*

The above letter, coupled with an earlier pontification that the Board was probably being fleeced by the R.E.M.'s fees, caused a quick, outraged response to my landlord on February 29. This letter, reproduced faithfully below, should forever set the textbook standard as a model of tenant- management relations statemansbip:

"It has been brought to the attention of the Board of Directors that your tenant (Dr. RF Brodsky) has been sending letters to Board Members harassing them over a fine which was assessed against you, but which your tenant actually paid. Apparently you informed him of his continued problem and made him pay the fine. In fact, the on-site manager had also informed him of this problem.

The problem revolves around the fact that when he leaves the pool area he drips water into the lobby and in the elevator creating a trip and fall hazard, In fact he admitted paying little attention to verbal requests (Ed. note, actually only one such request was ever made by Luis) to dry oft by the on-site manager. It appears that from his letters he is being more inconvenienced by having to follow association rules, and then compounds the problem by writing long dissertations with his opinions and slanderous comments on every thing else that bothers him.

Dr. Brodsky should understand the basis for the Board's authority and get his facts straight before he continues his unwarranted written abuse and personal harassment. He has absolutely no justification for his sarcastic and unfounded remarks. The rules are very clear about the problem he is creating. He needs to follow the rules, plain and simple! For you (sic) information no one is picking on him. In fact there are other owners and tenants who have in the past been sent warning letters and subsequent fines for CCR's (sic – I think they meant CR&Rs – Covenants, Rules and Regulations) and rules infractions. What the Board did was merely notify you of the continued violation and consequences set forth in the rules.

To set the record straight, the Board has always and will continue to follow and enforce the CCR's, as well as the Association rules with the best interests of all owners and tenants in mind.

His latest letter, which was attached to the Board President's door (Friday, February 23. 1996) now asserts his intention for legal action in small claims court. Because he wishes to play the "role of tough guy", the Board will be contacting the Associations (sic) attorney and proceed to file a lawsuit against him, for harassment, slander, and libel. (Ed. note, what chutzpah!)

It is strongly advised that you sit him down and advise him of his responsibility to follow the rules, as well as to cease and desist from sending his 'opinion letters'. (Ed. note; this is a mild reprimand, since from the Sicilianish family name of the R.E.M., it might be suspected that he may have been 'connected'. Now, THAT' S SLANDER!).

As for the letter you recently sent to our office concerning your tenant's claim of the loose handrail, the on-site manger investigated this on Friday, February 23 and found nothing to be loose. (Ed. note, apparently he was not impressed by the over three inch outward movement of the cantilevered railing when it was leaned against!). It is true that there is a gap between the railing end and the wall, but the patio rails were designed and installed according to code. As far as the posts are concerned, they are installed into the patio flooring but are not loose. As you know the tile is the owners (sic) responsibility.

114

Finally, the Board requests that any future correspondence in regards to the unit or its occupants be sent from you, as the owner of the unit. (Ed. note, I always showed a copy to my landlord in my angry letters).

The Board of Directors appreciates your attention to resolve this problem. Naturally, if you have any questions, please contact this office"

The above finally unmasked the megalomaniacal nature of the ruthlessly efficient manager, indeed justified his well-earned sobriquet! Even my landlord, to date a passive figure in this passing melodrama, felt that the threat of a law suit was a little beyond the pale. However, despite the harsh tone of the R.E.M.'s letter, my previous remark about "gross negligence" vis-a-vis the railing situation provoked the hiring of a consulting firm, Palos Verdes Engineering, "to inspect the fragile rail situation and consequent concrete floor cracking damage" in all nearby units in view from our balcony. This was done on March 21 - only four days before the court ease convened. The expert structural engineer's report - suppressed by the Management Company for at least 6 weeks-completely vindicated my concerns. The repair work that their report recommended ultimately led to a massive assessment, over $2000 per unit, for all 90 units, three years later, but only after pieces of concrete started falling off the building. But, wonder of wonders, in the rework they still did not secure the railing ends, except for my unit. They simply did not understand the power of a lever, and will undoubtedly face another major assessment in 10 or so years.

Let us now return to the courtroom drama. Having related the back ground of my petition to the already impatient Judge, I now mounted the attack to destroy the opposition by dint of the pure logic of my case and exhibits. To my great surprise, my opponents had not only appeared to fight the case, but had appeared in force! There was the R.E.M. himself, along with Luis, and a third gentleman who was later introduced to me as a member of the Board. It appeared that he come only to show the flag, since he never said a word. I finally met the evil incarnate R.E.M. face-to-face at the earlier court-required evidence exchange meeting. He, by a combination of mean visage and "chip-on the shoulder attitude, turned out to be one of those people that you instantly dislike. My sight-unseen sobriquet fit him like a glove!

I had appeared at court armed with the sure conviction of my righteousness, and my conclusive and damning evidentiary exhibits: the original "small' beach towel and its much larger successor, and the copy of the already inadmissable "Who's Who In America" write-up, which I had hoped would help convince the court that I was not a flake despite my opponent's written allegations. I also had a copy of the 531 Esplanade Home Owners

Association Rules and Regulations (CR&Rs) - its only pertinent article being #25: *"Cover ups and footwear are required to be worn in the common areas of the building when returning from the pool or beach area. Water and sand must be removed before entering the common area and elevators"*

Also noteworthy are the concluding remarks concerning breaches of the CR&Rs:

"1. First offense: Written notification from the management company, with the exception of violations of the use of emergency exists (sic-exits?) and the move-in and move-out rules.

2. Second offense: The amount of the fine to be levied by the Board of Directors. This will depend on the severity or frequency of the offense"

My opponent's legal armament consisted of a copy of the self same CR&Rs and the prior-signed affidavit that I had indeed read, understood, and nurtured them; as well as a sense of self righteousness and indignation that clearly equaled my own.

Picking up the thread of my argument, I showed the Judge the evolutionary change of pool-side bath towels that I had employed by ceremoniously unfurling them. I next demonstrated that the CR&Rs were not specific either about the definition of "dripping" or about the frequency, size, and distribution of drops, let alone proof of drop ownership (I was, after all, born in Philadelphia), Moreover, I added that the CR&Rs did not address a statute of limitations; "Was one warning letter to cover time immemorial?" Nor did it give a menu of felonies viz fines. 'Isn't $50 rather stiff? Let the punishment fit the crime!" Lastly, I reasoned that the fine was probably dunned as a knee jerk reaction to the threatened suit of a cleaning lady who had been working in the building and had slipped and fallen on a supposedly wet floor. Having vented my spleen, I finally sat down, to the Judge's great relief.

Now, it was the R.E.M.s turn at bat, and he sanctimoniously referred to the CR&Rs and my lack of responsibility in first signing that I understood them and then not obeying them. He further cited the absolute right of the Board of Directors to rule their realm and fine their fines as cited in the sacred Covenants of the Association. The Judge then asked Luis if I had been "dripping lately" and received a negative. He then tried to see if there really was a possible tie-in with the maid accident incident and the fine assessment. The R.E.M. guessed that the incident was far removed in time from the fine action but, when queried by the Judge, Luis acknowledged that it did occur less than a week before the levying of the fine. At closing, the Judge asked me, "How old are you, sir?" I proudly acknowledged to being 71 (pushing it a wee bit, since my birthday is in May). Where upon he smiled and said that he would make his judgment known tomorrow.

Sure enough, as the Gods had ordained it, a favorable judgment for $90 arrived in the next day's mail! The ploy to get a penalty imposed obviously didn't work, but I must say I was tremendously pleased. Even my dear wife, who had never been a party to the drama, fearing we would both alienate our landlord and the building's supers, altered her opinion on which part of a horse's anatomy I best resembled. The ruling did say that the Board had 30 days in which to make an appeal. Knowing their demonstrated perversity, I sat back and relaxed, expecting the check to arrive on or about the 30th elapsed day.

One would have thought that the song was over and that the final victory would be sealed on or before April 25. On that date, knowing that he had attended the last Board meeting, I called my landlord to see if further action on my part was required. He told me that the minutes of the Board meeting showed that the small claims loss had been acknowledged, BUT he had been dunned $90 by Board action - due immediately! (and presumably before they paid me the $90). I advised him to go back to court if he could not convince them of how ridiculous their action was. I also decided to send the Board the following letter, with copies to my landlord and the R.E.M.:

"Dear Friendly Board

It has now been over 30 days since the Small Claims Court found in my favor in the matter of our great dispute It awarded me $90 and gave you 30 days in which to make an appeal, which you have apparently (and, wisely, since such would have caused an exposition of all the correspondence involved) decided not to pursue.

I now seek the $90 payment, and following your deadline approach when you levied the fine, wish to have it by May 10. Should it not appear by then, I will take the necessary steps - which, of course, will only cost you more money (I had found out that I would need to engage and prepay the services of the Sheriff to collect).

Incidentally, upon leaving our court appearance, your ruthlessly efficient manager said that I would be hearing (presumably via my landlord) about action being taken to correct the dangerous situation on my balcony railing (to say nothing of the equally dangerous conditions prevailing in nearby balconies which I, who after all have a PhD in Structural Engineering and who has acted as an expert witness in two legal cases, feels borders on criminal negligence). I have had no such input to date and hearing none- will ask my landlord to petition you for action

Very truly yours - oar friendly neighbor who us only seeking your love and approval"

The letter did stretch a point for effect- since my doctorate actually was in the engineering physics field, It is true, however, that I have twice served as an "expert witness" in airplane crash cases involving structural failure. I was so incensed by their lack of action following the damning report, especially on my balcony railing, that I felt they had this coming. The "criminal negligence" allegation must have taken its toll, for shortly thereafter, following the next Board Meeting, Luis was instructed to tie down the remaining loose end of my balcony railing.

On May 2, I felt impelled to write a few suggestions to my landlord who was scheduled to appear at the May 7 Board meeting. He invited me to attend, but it was the night of giving my final Final Exam at USC, marking my passage from academician to author. My letter was in response to his concern that they might put a lien against his property if he didn't cough up the $90. It suggested several avenues of counter-attack, if the basic approach of reasonableness did not win the day:

(1) Ask them if they were aware of the body of law called Tenant's Rights"? (I wasn't, but a lawyer friend said it probably covered unjust tenant harassment); (2) Argue that they are trying to collect the $90 twice; and in any case they should only hold you liable for $50; (3) Threaten to pay them and then take them to small claims court for attempting to circumvent the court's prior ruling. I told him that if he wanted to do the latter, I would send him a check for the $90, and then go after them myself. I ended the letter by asking him to insist on their securing the remaining loose end of my balcony railing ASAP, under threat of my inviting the Redondo Bench building inspectors to view, from our balcony, the cracked and spalling concrete chaos besetting the balconies of at least five nearby units at the foot of the railing uprights. As indicated before, this was done.

From my viewpoint, that meeting was a great success. Not only was *my* railing attended to (albeit I supplied the L-shaped aluminum bracket), but also my landlord, absolved of the $90 assessment, received the following letter on May 28:

"The Board of Directors would like to thank you for your recent attendance at the Board meeting on May 7. 1996. As you know the Board is currently reviewing the information contained in the P.V. Engineering report. As we discussed, the Board will have the engineers investigate further the concrete balcony slabs as well as any other areas which show any sign of distress or spalling. Once this comprehensive report is received and reviewed, the Board will solicit contractors to submit repair bids.
The Board will make even effort to expedite both the report and subsequent repairs. The Board of Directors appreciates your input, as well as that of your tenant (I gave my landlord a written suggestion of how they could repair the damage considerably under the $200,000 job cost being bandied about but, as usual they did not take my advice and spent

118

a bundle beyond the 200K figure), and thanks you in advance for your support in the continuing maintenance of the Association.'

On June 4, I received a $90 cheek in the mail from the management company: "In accordance with the terms set forth in Small Claims Court, please find enclosed a check for $90. This represents full and complete payment." I would have appreciated an apology, too, but Johnny Cochrane would have been no less proud of the outcome than me!

TACKLING A GIANT

My lay-off notice, when it finally came in a memo dated April 22, 1988, was not a complete surprise. I had been warned and I empathized with the company plan to relieve their payroll of the older high salary engineers in this critical post-cold-war time of aerospace industry belt-tightening. But, because it was the first and only lay-off notice that I had ever received in a 48 year career in Aerospace, it still came as a shock. In view of my seniority and international recognition, I really didn't think that they had either the chutzpah or the cojones to make such a move which, in today's spin-infested society, is labeled 'downsizing'.

My job in the last couple of years at TRW had been to act as a systems engineer in short term advanced studies or to help write proposals for new work. I had no permanent home or sponsor. A few weeks before the fatal notice, my Boss had suggested that I look for an essential spot in a funded project; fully knowing, I think, that such assignments were all being filled, post haste, by the younger less experienced system engineers that reported to him. I recognized, however, that he was giving me a 'heads up' to protect my ass and his. When he gave this advice, I looked at him like he was crazy. "Dick", I said, "You must be kidding! I thought I was unfire-able." He only smiled sadly and told me to pay attention.

The sign on the top of the e-2 building read 'TRW' in my day

At age 63, I was not quite mentally prepared for retirement, always having planned on getting closer to the traditional 65 before hanging them up. Moreover, in another year, I would have 10 years with the Company – and this milepost would increase my retirement pension considerably. Also, I did not really know if I could afford to give up wage-slaving. I responded to the new situation thrust upon me by taking four essential actions:

First, before receiving the formal notice, I wrote and distributed an internal memo sent to my friends in the Company advising them of my availability and desire to find a home where I could weather the storm, while also fruitlessly applying for advertised position openings within the Company.

Second, still before the notice, I took on a Financial Advisor – a former engineer at TRW with a Doctor's degree in Physics who had become fascinated by finance and who had been recommended to me by a trusted member of my 'Old Farts' sailing crew.

Next, but after the death-knell notice, I successfully bought more 'adjustment' time by getting an extension in my termination date due my impending stint on jury duty.

Finally, availing myself the recently passed Congressional bill which permitted people to see their own company files, I requested, poured over, and made critical copies of information I deemed might be pertinent should I decide to initiate a grievance.

A few fact-filled consultations with my new financial advisor immediately relieved the pressure. It became eminently obvious that I could retire comfortably without reducing my standard of living, and would not need to seek work. So I relaxed my internal brown-nosing job-seeking efforts and, cheered by some very flattering unsolicited letters of praise I had found in and copied from my personnel folder, began thinking of fighting back. My new attitude of insouciance and goal-expansion was further brightened by an offer from a friend and former colleague to join his burgeoning start-up company as a consultant, working as much as I desired.

It soon became obvious to me in my efforts to find a new home in the company that the "fix" was in! Management thwarted any effort by my friends in the Company to fill their appropriate openings. Those jobs were going to my compatriot younger, less well paid, engineers who they wished to stockpile during the downturn. Not that my fellow workers were not competent, but they were certainly less qualified. After all, I was also a professor at USC and had taught the niceties of spacecraft design to literally hundreds of graduate students.

I applied for two advertised high-level 'in–house' positions both of which carried bonus pay features. One of the job descriptions looked as if it had been written with me in mind! In both cases, I was refused by a curt "experience not applicable" notation, which I thought at least showed that the company management had a healthy sense of humor. I checked out quietly on July 1, 1988 to face an uncertain afterlife.

As I later thought about it, I came to believe that I had a prima facie "Age Discrimination" complaint, which I decided to exploit as a hobby following my termination. Money was not my object, though I did wish to make up for the future pension income I would lose from several sources by not working full time 'til age 65. Also, probably hurt in the ego more than I wanted to admit, I decided I wanted to show 'them' that they could not push around working stiffs of my caliber. I came up with a number of $500,000 in damages consisting of one - plus years of lost salary and consequent lost pension incomes for the next ten years. I visited with two law firms who specialized in age discrimination cases, and who took hopeful cases on contingency. Both assured me that I had a good case, but that I should expect to invest about $10,000 of my own money to pay for depositions, etc. But, they said, a large settlement would not be a surprising outcome.

Not feeling that frisky, since I was just groping my way into retirement, I turned to the State Of California *Department of Fair Employment and Housing*'s downtown LA office to seek assistance in my quest. The DFEH did not charge for their services if they accepted the case, but warned that their settlements were limited by law to considerably less than the half mill that I had hoped for. But, I would only risk my time, plus mailing and commute expenses, if I opted to have them take on my case. Their legal expert listened to my story and opined that I had a good claim and that they would be willing to work with me. He then suggested that I write up a bill of particulars to assist them proceed. I came up with the following long diatribe:

"11/28/88

MY CASE FOR AGE DISCRIMINATION

DR RF BRODSKY

BACK GROUND

At age 63 and earning ~$80,000 per year from the Space and Technology Group at a time when I was at the peak of my technical prowess, I was unceremoniously "laid off ", less than two years short of achieving full (10 year) pension vesting, I was told that all possible positions had been surveyed for openings and/or "bumping" possibilities, but that "no weak sisters were found, and it would be difficult to 'bump' lay off persons doing even an average or slightly below average job". Moreover, "jobs are now controlled by the Program Offices. All top jobs are now taken (see later comments about "squirreling away" favorites) and they just want to retain low paid technical people". I was "looked on as a future tools developer and no loose research funds were available".

At the time of my lay off, my credentials were impeccable. I was an internationally known engineer and educator (then, Adjunct Professor of Aerospace Engineering at the

122

*University of Southern California) with over 40 years experience in the aerospace indus-
try. I am listed in "Who's Who in America" and several lesser national and international
Who's Whos. I am a world wide lecturer on space and educational subjects, and likewise
am well published in US and foreign technical journals. At the time of my layoff, I was one
of four active engineers (of the others, two are Vice-Presidents and one is the company
CEO) who have been awarded "Fellow" status in the technical society (the AIAA) that
serves the aerospace industry. Additionally, I am a Fellow in the LA-based "Institute for
the Advancement of Engineering", an honor I received in 1971. Two company VP's just
recently were so-named, making a total of three, to my best knowledge. I am a Professional Engineer in the states of California and Iowa, a university academic program accredi-
tor, and an Advisor at various times to NASA, the Air Force, and the National Academy of
Engineering*

MY LEGAL CASE
*I believe I can establish a prima facie case of age discrimination as the basis for my layoff,
for the following reasons:*

- *I was discriminated against in the lay-off selection process (approximately 5-6
people in my immediate organization of ~50 people) because I was within two
years of full retirement eligibility; my advanced age (despite a near perfect health
record); my substantial outside commitments which brought favorable publicity,
but no revenue to the Company; my generally known position of being able to "afford" unemployment because of past pensions earned; and my work situation of being normally employed in overhead activities, such as proposals, research, consulting; thus not damaging an on-going program by my dismissal.*

- *It is my further belief that they established a pattern of age/salary discrimination by
the selection of others that they laid off in the period surrounding my notice. I have
made a list of others that I know were laid off; and all appear to be in their 50's
and 60's, and relatively high paid. The State of California DFEH agency (my assigned consultant is Stan E., phone no. ---) is attempting to get details on the others
laid off during this crucial period. Note that none of us victims were given the opportunity to take jobs at lower pay, or to attempt to "bump" as was permissible in
the published "lay off" instructions to management(I have a copy).*

- *During this same period (a sharp business decline was easy to forecast) my management took the opportunity to 'squirrel away' many younger presumably lower
paid favorite-son engineers (I believe professional jealousy may have played a part
against me) into safe haven jobs in Program Offices that had adequate long term
funding, or into research work of a longer term nature. I was informed that I
needed at least 4 months of full time support to escape from the lay off list. My ability is such that I could have performed well at any of these jobs. I have made a list
of the people that I think were so 'squirreled away' and the DFEH is attempting to
obtain such an official list from the Company. It is significant to note that I am the*

holder of a special clearance which cost the Company many thousands of dollars to obtain. Yet, despite the shortage of personnel with such clearances, no attempt made to find me a job in that arena!

- *The most damaging action (fully documented!) taken by the company was the incomprehensible refusal to consider me for a job for which I was superbly qualified (and for which I applied shortly after receiving my notice) and which would have enabled me to again be placed on bonus (more about this later) status. The turndown cited "minimum requirements not met" and "inappropriate experience/skills". Nothing could be further from the obvious truth! I thus finally realized that the "fix" was in for my case This refusal followed two other not quite so blatant turndowns (also fully documented) in 1987-88 for bonus-eligible jobs for which I was very well (but not superbly) qualified. Here, the turndowns had a ring of reason, if not truth- but were made by the same VP who let me go.*

- *The timing of my lay-off coincided with my withdrawal, at management's strong suggestion, from the various outside activities with my technical society which had placed the company name in the forefront on the local technical scene, and for which I had a separate overhead budget. Indeed, they would not let me spend funds for preprints of a technical paper I had written, thus causing delay in its publication. Specifically, I turned over membership on a key AIAA technical committee to my boss; completed my term as Chairman of the AIAA LA Section Advisory Council; and turned over guidance of its company Chapter to a protege. It should be noted that I was penalized for this outside work (my involvement commenced when it was a key part of a previous job) by being dropped from the bonus rolls at the start of 1988.*

In fact, my treatment vis-a-vis the bonus situation has always been a bone of contention, and indeed the subject of an earlier formal grievance in which I was only successful on one of the two counts of disagreement. I have documents to show that I was lured away from the campus and a tenured-for-life position with the promise of much gold via the bonus process. I was not informed that the bonus process could be turned on and off like a faucet: I was dropped from the bonus rolls as soon as it was decently feasible! I re-achieved bonus status due to a later promotion. I was relieved of this job when the position was abolished after I told management that their expectations were not, in my opinion, realizable.

Finally, note that during the 8+years I was employed at TRW, I always received an annual raise in addition to the substantial bonuses I received several years. In fact, I have available several recent voluntary letters of commendation about my work.

Without counting penalties due to impugning my considerable reputation, I can easily show financial losses of at least $500,000 due to my "forced" (I assure you that there are

no $80,000 jobs around for 63 year-old engineers no matter how capable-I have tried. I
shall detail these losses separately)."

On December 7 (a day that will live in infamy!), 1988, the DFEH informed me that they had started a file on my case and that I must give them a timely notice of my intent, should I choose to do so at any future time, to initiate a private lawsuit. Thus began a series of meetings and information exchanges in which I named names and provided various witness letters and letters of commendation from my company files. They, in turn, sought information through the offices of the Company's internal lawyers, who – from remarks made by my project officer – stonewalled as best they could, while gladly providing statements from my former colleagues as to my shabby performance; quite contradictory to the nice letters of commendation that I had received (and had copied from my file) from several of the very same people! In some cases, the slander was downright nasty, but I recognized that my old friends were under the gun, and that all of this was merely 'show biz'.

Finally, on July 6, 1989 – a year after my lay off – by the command of the Director of the DFEH – a formal 'accusation' notice was served on the senior counsel of the Company. This included a notice of hearing, the accusation, a copy of my complaint, a notice of defense, statement to respondent, right to interpreter, administrative procedure act and 'new regulation' – i.e., all the boiler plate documentation needed to legally support the righteousness of their suit. The DFEH further established tentative dates for a hearing for September 18-19, and provided company counsel with papers to request such a hearing.

No such hearing proved necessary. Apparently the Company, at the advice of their counsel, decided to fold and sought a settlement. I signed the agreement on July 28, 1989, accepting recompense, in two bundles, for back pay as well as for 'emotional distress'. In total, the agreement yielded a bit less than half a year's salary – but the 'win' was very satisfying. As part of the agreement, I had to agree to not sue the company in any other related action, and not to disclose the settlement financial terms. The Company, for its part, had to agree to take steps to that this unfair practice was eliminated and subject themselves to a future review to determine that they had complied. The same day, I sent out a letter to the friends who had supported me:

"Dear Friends:
*   You will be pleased to learn that on this date I signed an agreement negotiated be-*
tween the black hats (TRW management) and the white hats (the State of Calif. Department
of Fair Employment and Housing) which will bring me modest recompense for the shabby
way I was treated (and thus further ease my so far successful retirement!. Alas, I will have

to pay income tax on half of the settlement; the other half being for my "pain and suffering".

I could have chosen to take them to court and might have ended up with a real bundle of moolah, but I was advised that this would probably take another year; mean an $8 - 10,000 investment in deposition and other costs with no guarantee of recovery; and a 40-60% split with the lawyers
(my 60%). So, since we'll be leaving for Israel in late September, I decided to take the money and run.

In letting them off the hook, the company was admonished to a) post notices advising employees of their rights and how to redress grievances, b) use non-discriminatory practices when selecting employees for lay-off, c) review their policy on ranking of employees (which is purely subjective and " what have you done for me lately" now), in addition to my pay off.

So, I guess I'm vindicated and reasonably happy. I will forever of course wonder if I shouldn't have gone for the big banana - but maybe Ed McMahon will call me on August 3.

Anyway- the point of this note is to thank each and every one of you (and, my wife, dog, and heirs join in) for both your moral and verbal/written support for this great cause against the sinister military-industrial complex that has nurtured us all. For you, my everlasting gratitude and a sailboat ride whenever you're in the neighborhood. We will return from Israel in mid-February. Have a great summer, and for real fun - sue somebody!"

For all my ventures into the mysterious world of the LAW, this of course has been the only one with a big money pay–off. Still, as I later thought about it, look how smart, albeit somewhat unethical, the Company really was! At very little expense, they simultaneously got rid of a high salaried engineer past his peak; saved two years of paying his high salary; saved on payments of his pension, which would have been greater at reaching of 10 years of service. They actually came out of it smelling like a rose, with only a slap on the wrist – for by the time the DFEH stomped down on their evil practices - they had achieved the 'mean and lean' watered down complement of engineers that was right for the time. Although word of my victory got around and I received several inquiries as how to proceed, I am not aware of anyone else 'winning' a jackpot. I think my case was somewhat unique.

Even if I had had the guts to go for the big money and had won, as was probable, they still wouldn't have been hurt too badly. That's why they are a great company. My hat remains off to them. I bear them no ill-will. In fact, I remain today an active member of their Retiree's Association, and support their docent and travel programs.

But, the beat goes on! On Sunday, July 1, 2001, many newspapers in the U.S. carried a story by Adam Geller, Associated Press Business Writer. Its headline was, "FORCED OUT AT 50? Older Workers Allege Age Discrimination in Job Cuts". An accompanying graph inset was titled, "Age discrimination complaints increased 15.4% last year".

A 'FINE' ROMANCE
(WITH NO KISSES)

Opportunity comes in many shapes and sizes. In this case, opportunity meant an opening to again return triumphantly to the Small Claims Court arena, after a 4 year run of favorably settling equally minor grievances by mere vitriolic letter exchange cum cajolery. While these out-of-court victories were satisfying, there's nothing better for a rush than a good Small Claims battle against a corporate bully, especially when you know you're destined to win!

While we were on our round-the-world trip in the spring of '99, our middle son David stayed at our condo and used our car. Unbeknownst to him, or so he said later when it came to light, he was awarded a $50 parking citation. It occurred in San Pedro where he was visiting a friend and had inadvertently parked on a street-sweeping side of the street on the wrong day. Some months later, the fine showed up when we got our annual car registration renewal notice with an unanticipated 'late payment' $75 illegal parking dun added on. Some difficult research revealed what had happened, but only after we were able to get a copy of the citation. We ruefully paid the fine in order to re-register the car with the State Department of Motor Vehicles in February, 2000. This turned out to be a prelude to a kiss.

Sometime later, in the summer, our former landlord of 3 years ago, now living in the condo we had rented from him, forwarded a City of Los Angeles Parking Violations Bureau notice that had been incorrectly addressed. It said we owed them $86 dollars for a parking violation which we had ignored. Without reading the small print, I naturally assumed that they were still trying to collect on the already-paid fine and had added more 'late' charges; figuring that the left hand (the LAPVB) never knows what the right hand (the DMV) is doing.

With some pain, I dug up the DMV bill and the cancelled check which paid it, made copies of both, and sent them back with their notification letter. I wrote on the latter that I had already paid this fine to the DMV and had enclosed the evidence. I also noted my correct address. Thus began a cycle of 2 or three exactly similar exchanges, although I do recall that the third one was finally mailed to our correct address. No notice was taken of my complaint. I retain the reply of November 21, 2000 from the City of Los Angeles Parking Violation Bureau, sent to my correct address, which noted that I had 15 days to act, and further said:

"UPON REVIEW OF YOUR LICENCE PLATE, OUR RECORDS INDICATE THAT THE PARKING CITATION<u>S</u> (!) LISTED BELOW ARE VALID AND REMAIN UNPAID. PLEASE SEE BELOW FOR THE TOTAL AMOUNT DUE.

PLEASE SEND A CHECK OR MONEY ORDER MADE PAYABLE TO THE CITY OF LOS ANGELES TO THE ADDRESS ABOVE. WRITE THE CITATION NUMBER(S) ON THE CHECK OPR MONEY ORDER. DO NOT SEND CASH. NOTE THAT FAILURE TO PROMPTLY PAY THIS AMOUNT COULD RESULT IN ADDITIONAL CHARGES, WITHHOLDING OF YOUR VEHICLE REGISTRATION AND MAY SUBJECT YOUR VEHICLE TO IMMOBILIZATION OR IMPOUNDMENT"

At the bottom of this curt missive was a citation number dated 7/27/00 along with the $86 bill. At this point in the saga, I apparently did not read this fine print which, of course indicated that the alleged misdeed had occurred only a few months earlier. I marked up their letter by circling "citations" and writing, *"What citation<u>s</u>? I never got "them"! Can you send me a copy of the 'citations'? I never got any notice, if 'these' are different from the DMV citation."* I also added the following letter to the package:

November 26, 2000
PARKING VIOLATIONS BUREAU
Sirs:
I am almost 76 years old and you are driving me to an early grave. Once more, I will try to convince you that the fine you are trying to get from me was paid long ago: I have enclosed:
My last vehicle registration renewal notice from the DMV, clearly showing a charge for a parking violation. copies of my check (front and backsides) showing I paid DMV the FULL AMOUNT, including the charge for the violation.
A copy of the letter (Feb 3, 1999) that I sent both to you and DMV noting that the fine should be reduced by $25
What more can I do? I do not want to pay the same fine twice, and I am certainly not aware of a more recent violation. Please advise me by phone (310 937 1811) or make it go away. I do not wish to spend the few days I have left in this vale of tears in a running battle with you.
Thank you for your consideration.

Not surprisingly, I received a semi-responsive reply a few days later (Dec. 20) which said that if I had already paid the fine, I should send the documentation; again with the usual fifteen day warning. But they did send a copy of the citation. For the first time, I saw that it was for a supposed $35 parking incident at the LA Airport, inflated to $86 because it was ignored or not contested in the allowed 21 period. It also said, in part, *"IF YOU WISH*

TO CONTEST THE CITATION, YOU MUST NOTIFY THE PARKING VIOLATIONS BUREAU IMMEDIATELY AT THE NUMBER ABOVE". When I did, I was told that the magic '21 days after the issue' limit had been exceeded, and I had no recourse but to pay the fine. I riposted furiously:

Dec. 22, 2000
Parking Violations Bureau
PO Box 30420
LA, CA 90030

Re: Citation 505018765

Dear Sirs:

On Dec 20, 2000, I received in the mail, and for the first time I and my family saw, the Citation which we never knew existed. It correctly listed our car's license plate number, incorrectly called the car 'gray' (it is a very obvious 'Silver' at 7:30 am PDT), correctly placed the car at the upper level at what would have been the right time for my wife to be letting off our Massachusetts son, Jeffrey (see his FAXed statement attached) who was on his way to Hawaii. My wife and son dispute everything else about the citation, and if this letter does not result in redressing our grievance, my wife would like to plead her case before a Traffic Judge or some other proper authority.

I would like to request a review of this citation, even though the protest date is way past due. I will cite the reasons for the delay in making a protest, which starts with the fact that my wife (the driver in this instance - I was not along) was never given a Citation at the supposed place of the crime, nor was she aware that she had done anything wrong. She routinely pulled up the car near the departure stand, possibly in the second lane if the curbside lane was not available, opened the rear compartment by remote, and waited in the car while he removed his baggage. She never left the car; she was never talked to or warned by an authority, and was certainly never given a 'ticket'!

The comedy of errors continued by your apparently sending the first delinquency notice to our old address on the Esplanade (an error you continued to do as little as 2-3 weeks ago. Eventually, I did get a notice and, until a few days ago thought the notices concerned an old citation (LA County 1078 47611, since we had received no other citation) which I had long ago paid via DMV re-registration. I started a long fruitless correspondence with you trying to prove that I had paid for that Citation. You must have a file on this whole series of letters and counter letters. I have enclosed a copy of a recent sample of our correspondence. You never took the trouble to point out that this is a different case, nor did you call me as I requested. The point is – had we been presented with a citation or been advised in a timely manner, we would have protested immediately. Thus, the fact that a $35 fine has now reached $86 is very unfair- to say the least – and would never be upheld in a hearing.

As soon as I discovered that this was a 'new' citation a few days day ago, I called your office and requested a copy of the original citation (since we had never seen it, nor did we know the date of the citation). When we received the copy on Dec. 19, my wife immediately said that she did not agree with its findings and confirmed that she was never presented with a ticket; nor – since she never left the car while our departing son 'unloaded' his baggage – was one such put under the wiper. She never left the car; she never blocked traffic; she never was in a 'third' lane. The fact that the Officer cited our car as gray makes me think that he was after another car, but got our license number instead.

I would appreciate a hasty conclusion to this affair, as I just received my vehicle registration renewal notice with $86 fine on it – and don't want to start another cycle of confusion.

Merry Christmas,

Dr RF Brodsky
110 the Village, #410
Redondo Beach, CA 90277

Agreed to in its entirety:
_____(_signature)_____

Mrs. RF (Patricia W) Brodsky

PS: On Dec 20, in accordance with instructions in your letter #209 (12/12/00), I called in to inform that we were contesting the fine. The lady said that we could not!!! This is truly violating our civil rights to having a hearing, since it was your error that started all this.

This letter was followed shortly thereafter by the following – which finally cut to the chase; Shape up or Else!:

Dec. 27, 2000
Parking Violations Bureau
PO Box 30420
LA, CA 90030

Re: Citation 505018765

Dear Sirs:
Your letter (#245) of 12/20/00 (which came before we could mail out the enclosed letter package dated Dec. 22 which <u>formally</u> asks for a review) convinces us (my wife and I) that we can not get justice via the mail. I therefore have decided to pay the fine under protest and seek redress in the courts. The enclosed check for $86 is dated January 25, 2001. If we have not been informed by some means ((310) 937 1811 or email address) about what avenues we have to seek redress by court action, I shall place a stop order on the check at that date.

The reason you <u>couldn't</u> give us a favorable review is because of the time factor. But, as you will see in the enclosed: 1) you never gave a ticket at the scene of the 'crime', and sometime later you must have sent the first dunning letter to the wrong address, and still later, after I protested because I thought I had already paid the fine, you did not inform me that I was on the wrong case. How- under these circumstances- could we have appealed within your time limit?

Please tell us the appropriate parking fine court (preferably in Torrance) were we can seek a trial or a hearing. Otherwise, we intend to take you to Small Claims Court in Torrance, if they will support such action. The result of this action – which we, as Senior Citizens, shall surely win –will be that you will not only have to repay us for the fine, but will also be charged with court and record subpoena costs, etc.

Please advise us ASAP. We'd like a conclusion before we die. Happy New Year!

Dr. RF and Mrs. Patricia W. Brodsky
110 the Village, #410
Redondo Beach, CA 90277

Encl: Letter Dec. 22, 2000; letter Nov 26, 2000, affidavit from son, Jeffrey of Massachusetts. (stating that no ticket was given, and no infraction occurred; on the check for $86 , I noted that the payment was under protest)

Their return letter of January 2, 2001, which only reiterated that the time limit for appeal had long passed, coupled with their crass cashing of my check before my Jan. 25 deadline drove me to seek the free help offered by a pro-bono Small Claims Court lawyer. She advised me that before I could file a small claims case, I must first file a "Claim for Damages" form with the city, and provided me a number to call to get the proper form. She said that they would inevitably deny my claim, finally allowing me access to the Small Claims Court. So, on behalf of my wife and me, I mailed the acquired form on January 15, claiming the $86, all court costs, and incidental mailing and copying costs plus depreciation on my trusty PC. I began to salivate at the prospect of once again attacking the windmills.

On January 19th, in separate letters from the Los Angeles City Clerk's office, we were each given a basic claim number (my wife's was –01, mine –02), followed by complete silence. But then, on February 5, a new and unexpected voice emerged. A letter arrived signed by Madeline R., ARM, Risk Manager I, of the *Los Angeles World Airports* acknowledging receipt of our claim. "It is being reviewed for appropriate determination and handling", it said, and gave the name of the person handling the case. I subsequently called him twice seeking a progress report. After the first call, at his request, I sent him copies of my complete file, since the LAPVB apparently saw fit not to share their file when they assigned the case to the people at the scene of the alleged crime. The second call resulted in a lukewarm, "I'm working on it" reply, necessitating – after a decent interval - the following note sent to Madeline's above designated minion, one Joseph N.:

Mr. Joseph N.   March 27, 2001
Los Angeles World Airports
1 World Way
PO Box 92216
LA, CA 90009-2216

                    Re: LAWA Claim No.: 2K00117
Dear Mr. N.
It has been almost a month since I talked to you about progress on findings concerning our (my wife, Patricia and me) parking fine case. You said that "You were working on it". We had hoped that our case would have been adjudicated by now, and are wondering if we are being "stonewalled"?
We are about (April 16) to embark on a short trip and will return by the end of April. If we have not heard favorably from you by then, we will take our case to Small Claims Court, and will add to our claim interest (at the rate of 18%/year) on the money we sent the Parking Violations people under protest. This will add to the court and service fees that you will inevitably be charged for.
Thank you for your consideration.

Dr. and Mrs. RF Brodsky

Upon our return on April 28, we found the following letter from the LA World Airports, signed by a new ARM, Risk Manager II named Roberta (I presume that Madeline had either been forced to resign in disgrace as a result of this nefarious affair, or had been busted to Grade O, or had committed hari kari, which in my mind would have been the correct thing to do):

"DEAR DR. BRODSKY
THIS OFFICE HAS INVESTIGATED THE INCIDENT REFERENCED ABOVE. THE CITY OF LOS ANGELES / LOS ANGELES WORLD AIRPORTS IS INTERESTD IN SETTLING THIS MATTER. WE HAVE ENCLOSED A 'GENERAL RELEASE OF ALL CLAIMS' IN THE AMOUNT OF $100. WE REQUEST YOU SIGN AND DATE THIS RELEASE, WHERE INDICATED ----- ETC., ETC.

PLEASE EXPECT TO RECEIVE YOUR SETTLEMENT APPROXIMATELY SIX WEEKS AFTER WE HAVE RECEIVED YOUR SIGNED RELEASE. -----".

Sure enough, around 6 weeks later, we received a check in the mail drawn against the CITY OF LOS ANGELES BAIL REFUND ACCOUNT – only it was for $86! This irresponsible action immediately and angrily engendered the following:

June 5, 2001

Dear Roberta:

In view of your letter of April 23, 2001 (copy enclosed) indicating that I would receive a check for $100 in ~6 weeks, I was flabbergasted when I received a check for only $86 (copy enclosed) today.

Please let me know when to expect the remaining $14, or advise me to go the Small Claims to collect.   Very truly yours,

On June 19, in a conciliatory letter, Roberta said, " ------------*As we agreed to settle your claim for $100.00, we have attached check no._____ for the remaining settlement balance of $14.00. ---------*". The check was covered by LAWA's insurance underwriter, again confirming the complete lack of cooperation between these vital government bodies.

Oh, sure, it was a reasonable and unforeseen denouement. I had full intentions of subpoenaing the Parking Violations Bureau to obtain the records of my case for our planned Small Claims appearance. But, dog-gone it, I have again been snatched from the jaws of victory and deprived of my day in court – a day that I know would have resulted in an unequivocal and probably uncontested victory. A day when my wife would be able to vent her spleen on others rather than me. A day when the big city folks would have gotten their comeuppance, and the downtrodden Seniors a new burst of hope.

Now, I can't wait for somebody to kick me in the shin or to be set upon by a rabid dog!

Chapter 5

ANNALS OF WRITER'S WORKSHOP FOLLIES

- **SHAKESPEARE A'RIOTING**
- **ZEALOTRY**
- **THE NEW 'WOBBLIES'**
- **THE XMAS POEMS**

When I started writing in earnest, my famous author friend advised me to join a writer's workshop group. He said that these groups, if properly operated, were intended to provide ready criticism for your work, to hone your own critical senses, and to be a fount of practical advice on getting published.

I soon found the "South Bay Writers Workshop" group meeting at an Anglican church about mile down the street, and settled in for what has now become a routine. We meet from 1-3 p.m. on Thursday afternoons, and conduct serious business for all but a week or two before Christmas, when we have a pot-luck meeting, exchange pleasantries, and listen to my always beautiful annual Xmas poem.

As we arrive, usually early for social reasons, we sign in if we wish to read — first come-first served. If you miss your turn this week, you'll be on first next week no matter when you arrive. Each reader is limited to ten pages double-spaced and is exhorted to speak up. The women, in particular, do not project. At this stage, my hearing is deficient and I will tend to nod oft if I can't hear clearly. At the completion of the reading, going clockwise, each person makes a helpful — if possible — criticism. The readers are not permitted to explain themselves. To allow for more reading time, the critics are urged to say "same as so & so" if they have nothing to add. It works well!

The group varies from 8 to 12 or 13; the basic core cadre these days being about six. The average age must be about 60, although we do get some young people occasionally. They come from all walks of life, and with various levels of talent. We have writers of novels, adventures, fugitivism from chain gangs, non-fiction, children's stories, scripts, poetry, travelogues, vampirism, and OpEd stuff. You'll hear more about the cadre of characters later in the chapter.

134

SHAKESPEARE A' RIOTING
(Or)
WHAT FOOLS THESE MORTAL TEMPESTS BE!

My home town* is a one-horse town,
But it's good enough or me.
Its writer population is scattered and small,
You won't find them on any literary map at all.
But, it means the world to me,
To be there with Jody and our author family.
My Writer's Workshop is a hinky-dinky,
Hunky-dory sort of a Group,
But it's good enough for me!

When I returned from a trip East, via back-logged messages on my e-mail, I found that all hell had broken loose in the life of the normally sedate and sane "South Bay Writer's Workshop", with whom I have been associated for Lo! these last 3-4 years. It's difficult for me to understand precisely why the great brou-ha-ha had developed. Clearly, it was precipitated by the addition of two new male swashbucklers to our group; the added numbers causing an irritating backlog in the reading program. And this, in spite of the ameliorating addition of a half hour to our session time. Fortunately, I saved the entire spate of e- mail messages that roiled the air waves from October 11 to October 16, 2002 and, interpreting them to the best of my keen analytic ability, I shall try to re-enact the whole sordid episode. Where necessary, I will employ wonderfully clever nom-de-plumes to protect both the innocents and the protagonists.

As you arrive for the weekly seance, you deposit a dollar for the church's benefit and put your name on a reader's list, if you desire to read – first come, first served. When your time comes, you read your piece and the attendees give you their comments. By tradition, critiquers always start by saying, "You're stuff was great, BUT --- ", then commencing to the meat of the criticism or suggestions, if any. When I fall asleep during a dull reading, I usually 'pass' when my turn comes, or say, "Yes, I agree with so-and-so's comments".

---

*Taken from the college song, "My Home Town". See my book, "Songs My Mother Never Sang to Me".

Otherwise, I don't hold back – being polite as possible if I feel strongly in the negative, but being as lavish in praise as jealousy allows me when one of our 'stars' read a good bit.. Alas, I have been known to say, "That was terrible!" on occasion, which wins me no friends, but opens the way for equal retribution without guilt when they tear into my superior work.

When I first found the Group, they consisted mostly of women, generally of a certain age, but all sincere about their writing of prose, fiction and non-fiction alike; some being addicted to poetry and some to play-writing. Gradually, more men of an even more certain age, like me, began to show up. The Group has a nominal leader, Jody, a gentle poet given to writing with such lovely 'imagery' that I sometimes choked on the treacle when I felt it was used in showboat fashion – art for art's sake. The rules she established frown on a reader fighting back or explaining on a criticism, although it is permitted to tersely answer a direct question. Following this format, the Group rolled on harmoniously, though when the participants reached 12-14 lately, one or two readers had to be placed first in line for next week. This frustration, I think, may have precipitated the explosion.

When a member needed publicity, we put out a bulletin

The Group is eclectic – a mixture of male-female, now almost even in numbers; black, white, yellow and brown rainbow colors; with topics and stories spanning from the ridiculous to the sublime in prose and poetry. It includes a 'Grand Dame', the author of several children's book and a fellow designee of 'Who's Who', who is the ultimate arbiter; a very able script and short story writer; an unusual documenter of man's cruelty to man in the southern chain gang genre; a self-published ex-femme fatale who knocks herself out pushing her book; some really top-notch insightful reviewers who are always helpful to me, and the rest of us – wannabees who get published now and then, but all of whom have 'day jobs'.

The two new male participants who star in this unfolding drama are "The Mad Doctor" and "The Satanist". The former writes in several modes, one being science fiction; He also has the tendency to fight back or go off on a tangent when criticized, and has to be mildly chastised for excessive verbosity on occasion. The latter is slowly walking us through a tale of satanic priests with all the accoutrements and gore that go along with these types of folks. Of course, the old nucleus of us had already been subjected to the ghoulish writing of Frances Tuck, now no longer with the Group, who featured well-meaning ghouls and their friends fecklessly roaming around in the Crescent City. So, we were immune to the Satanist's gore – but the Mad Doctor apparently couldn't stomach it. In two e-mails sent to the nucleus group, he first vented his spleen about the Satanist, and then proposed a radical new set of governance rules for the Group to consider:

His first outburst came as a reply to Jody's e-mail response to a complaint that I can only surmise. She wrote back to him, in part, " --------. *I'm sad that you feel most of the writer's are not qualified. They have been writing, critiquing, for a long while with the exception of a few. And the Satanist isn't writing a screen play about the cult. I believe it's a novel. ------*". In a lambasting and long note he first riposted strongly to the Satanist oeuvre: "---------. *I, for one, do not choose to listen any more to his vile garbage and hope you will ask him to read before I get there. I do not want him to critique my work. I have no idea of his education, professional qualifications, or resume. To me, he is a passive aggressive agent of Satan too sick for our mission. -------*", and, later, "--------. *If you want to hear more of his gore, ask him to read before 12:30 or after 3:00 p.m. Or be sure he brings us a chapter of socially redeeming value.------* ".

A couple of days later, undoubtedly trying to solve some our Group's problems and improve its efficiency, the Mad Doctor sent a massive message, well thought out, to all on the e-mailing list, asking for comments, and very nicely adding, *"Thanks for breathing life into my existence"*: Among his many proposals, was a call for a $25 yearly membership fee – presumably on top of the $1 donation to help defray the churches recreation room expenses; a call for a fee of $10 per reading which I immediately found obnoxious – Hell, my wife only charges me $5 to listen to my stuff! - ; a suggestion that each participant submitting a curriculum vitae for the purpose of evaluating how seriously the reader should regard the critiquers comments; limiting reading times to 10 minutes followed by critiquing by a reader- selected critic for 3 minutes; the bringing in of a paid expert to give a lecture on occasion with an additional admission fee; permission, plus an exhibitor's fee, to display or sell one's works; using the rule that someone else – a writer-designated reader - should read your work; the assignment of written critiques for the writer to take home; and other thought provoking ideas.

The reaction to the proposal was immediate and frothy – ranging from the analytical to the plaintive *"Do this and I'm gone!"* The most analytic reply deserves some further discussion since, like the initial proposal, it contained several gems, which I shall now disclose: *"First, you have eliminated poor struggling writers like me from being able to read ----.; Are you stating that someone with a resume as an editor is more qualified to judge what is well written?; A writer doesn't always have a chapter that extends 10 minutes and sometimes has chapters that go beyond 10 minutes -----.; If you really want to know the truth, there are only two things I would change about the Group. First I don't think ANYONE should read their own work, period, no ifs and buts. I believe it is it is the biggest detriment and disservice you can do to your own material. Second, groups should NEVER have more than 8 members. BREAK THE GROUP INTO TWO!"*

An obviously deflated and chastened Mad Doctor immediately wrote back to the Analyst, copying the mailing list: *"My suggestions were not intended to be mandated rules. - - - Let's debate among ourselves and yield to the majority. - - -".* In a long poignant e-mail response in color, entitled *"Writer's Group Guidelines, OR TEAPOT TEMPEST, Part Two"*, the Satanist, somehow released from the evil spirits that guide his pen and warp his otherwise keen mind, first presented a paean to the Group:

"In weighing in on our Thursday writers group, let me first say that the group has been wonderfully helpful and healthy. I've come to appreciate all of you and value your generous, diverse, yet compassionate feedback. This is by far the best writers group that I've ever had the joy and privilege to participate in. I thank Jody for her excellent soft touch in leading us and each of you for your many kind and gracious offerings of wisdom." [He then continued] *"-------- . If it ain't broke don't fix it! I see no reason to raise money and find any hint of additional charges to be elitist and insensitive to the economic realities of struggling writers, which most of us are. -----------. Personally, I see us having very few problems. Remarkably, almost each week, every person who desires to read I given that opportunity. When there is not sufficient time they are moved to the front of the pack the following week. ---------. Listing one's credentials is bovine excrement. They are irrelevant here. The world already has enough educated fools and opportunities for them to tout their*

useless academic degrees. -------. I love our group. I prefer not to leave it. I believe that the group will become better not worse for dealing with the issues the Mad Doctor raised-."

About the same time – still before my return to the battlefield – another voice was heard from,

"Since the recent furor about how Thursday Writers is run/handled has been generated by the Mad Doctor; since apparently no one wishes to implement the changes he mentioned; since all of this was generated by an issue between the Mad Doctor and the Satanist, I strongly suggest that these two gentlemen and scholars meet privately before the scheduled 12:30 starting time and settle their differences between themselves as they wish. I myself have no intention of listening to a rehash during critique time which would be better served by critiquing."

On October 16, 2002, the day after our return home, the Mad Doctor folded,

"I yield to the will of the majority. I think my proposal has received sufficient consideration and hold no grudge. I have already written to the Satanist to tell him I think he writes well and has much to offer my writing. He was gracious in his reply to me and has clearly explained the dynamics of the type of group we are. Look forward to critiques as usual tomorrow. I wish you all well."

When I showed up at 12:50 the next day, I found that absolutely nothing had changed except the Group had decided to return to a much appreciated 1 p.m. starting time. I like this better since I am addicted to the daily soap opera, "All My Children" which I still have to abandon 10 minutes early to make the one o'clock sign-in, which usually dooms me to a 'next-week' reading if the whole gang is there. Apparently there had been zero discussion about the crisis. Sanity had returned!

When, in spite of my wife's Archie Bunker-like caution to "stifle", I read this story to the group one week later, it was miraculously acclaimed for the gem it is! One suggested that I entitle it "It Happened on Broadway!" and immediately send it out to the media, omitting this last paragraph. The Mad Doctor said, "It somehow sounds as if it were almost real!" and said he was astounded by the patience and dignity of the Group. The Satanist snarled that "He would do a ritual on me tonight!" I went home and prepared a wooden stake.

ZEALOTRY

Zealousness comes in many flavors, as does irony. There is a gentleman in my Writer's Workshop group who is trying mightily to save sinners and correct the ills of the world. He is a conscience wracked, iron bound Christian and carries around with him not only his own guilt baggage, but the guilts of the unwashed multitudes counting back to those halcyon days in the Garden of Eden.

Right after I wrote this now-slightly-altered piece, I sent the original to its subject via e-mail, asking him if he had any objections if I read it at our next group session. Normally I get almost instantaneous replies, so when none such appeared I figured he was probably out of town for the Christmas holiday. But, two days later, I ran into him at a party given by our group leader, and asked him what he thought of it.

"Completely inappropriate", he said, "It looks like a personal attack on me". This reply startled me, and I told him the whole point of the bit was to show the many faces of zealotry and the irony thereof. I asked him if he was mad at me because I am a professed atheist. "No", he said, "I was one myself in the past". It turned that one word had also peeved him. I described him as 'pious', which he said was derogatory. I therefore have removed it from the text.

I then told him my plan: I certainly would <u>not</u> read it at one of our sessions. I would however, in its present form, include it in one of my books, "A Pilgrim Muddles Through". I told him the chances of my getting this book published legitimately were slim. So it shall be!

The fact is that he is a very good writer and can express all these feelings fluidly, albeit at times somewhat preachily. He has written a book on ghouls and exorcisms, and is now writing one on 'how he got to be the way he is'. The words flow – you can feel the indecisions, the pain of youthful excesses and mind wanderings, the problems of sexuality – all the demons that probably hound people who are of a strong religious bent.

He does good works by leading retreats: 'Using the STEP Method: <u>S</u>piritual <u>T</u>herapy for <u>E</u>motional <u>P</u>ain'. He thoughtfully counsels those who seek his help. To quote from his retreat flyer ad, he is 'a published author, was a Pastor, a spiritual psychotherapist and chaired the counseling department of a Bible College. With degrees in psychology and theology, some call him a *Christian Deepak Chopra*'. Nobody can deny that he is a good and sincere man – but clearly a zealot. But, as they said on Seinfeld, 'Not that there's anything wrong with that!'

But, to me, there is something wrong! I told him the other day after his Workshop reading that his life would be a much happier one if he gave up all this zealotry. Of course, I made that statement from the viewpoint of a 'closeted' semi-militant atheist and a person who spends a lot of his latter days busily and verbally, by lecturing, espousing the purist joys of worshipping and writing about New Orleans Jazz – a now obscure art form that only five or fifty other people in the world appreciate!

It reminds of the story about two psychiatrist friends who passed each other on the street. One said, "Have a good day!" The other mused to himself; "What the hell did he mean by that?"

THE NEW 'WOBBLIES'

Long before most of you were born, there arose the IWW –derisively called 'The Wobblies' – The Industrial Workers of the World. They were at the vanguard of the labor union movement, and - though few in numbers – made a disproportionate dent in the public reality. They were generally dismissed by a scurrilous press as obstructionists – and, even worse, Communists. But their raison d'etre was pure and simple: The workers of the world were being viciously exploited and needed to rise up and assert themselves. They were browbeaten by the police and defeated by scabs and company hoodlums hired to 'protect' plant property.

Last week, at the Writer's Workshop meeting, one of the Group read an impassioned theme calling for the globalization of Women's quest for equality. She spoke of the need for women to escape the rule of the male society that has kept them in chains – barefoot and pregnant –for all these eternal years. Her writing was clear and crisp and logical. It predicted that women were now beginning to stir – beginning to realize their chattelry – and were becoming aware of their second-class situation all over the globe. It was a fine and stirring piece but, alas, offered no prescription for action. It offered nothing more than a hope that this universal awareness might lead to reform, but had no call for action. For this, at least one of the Group (guess who?) chastised her, and did offer a program:

My solution, naturally, is for women to form the IWW – the *International Women of the World*. Its job would be to educate and instruct women how to take their rightful place

142

in the world as real people – not sexual objects or baby-making machines. It would instruct them that if they were really serious about attaining some status – really rocketing through the glass ceiling - they should (at least in the United States) in this Summer 2004 atmosphere:*

- Vote the straight Democratic ticket all the way down the line.
- Get behind vocally, financially, and action-wise the true female leaders such as Hilary, Barbara Boxer, Diane Feinstein, etc.
- At the same time, eschew and vilify anyone who supports the Eagle Forum, Phyllis Schlafly, Rush Limbaugh, and their ilks.
- Don't listen to any radio or TV station the is a part of the FOX dynasty
- Join and participate in NARAL ('right to choose' organization)
- Join and participate in the ACLU (Amer. Civil Liberties Union)
- Join and participate in NOW (Nat'l Organization for Women)
- Keep you and yours away from the 'family value' proponents, especially those who talk to you from pulpits in cathedrals, churches, synagogues, and mosques. Their job is to assure the continued subjugation and demeaning of women, while providing them with shelter and a living.
- Run for political office yourselves, or at least support the people who are on your side, being careful to avoid or counter those who merely want to get into your pants.
- Start your area branch of the IWW. Put out newsletters, have meetings, influence the vote, become activists.
- And, finally, emulate my dear (said sincerely) first cousin, Alyse O'Neill of Naples, Florida, the ultra right wing family troglodyte who rules the south Florida Eagle Forum with an iron hand and a golden fist. She holds a once-a year $10,000 per plate gala with either Rush or Phyllis as the featured speaker. She captures all those nice society rich folks who helped Dubya get elected. But, the point is – she cares and does something about it!

---

*It is spookie, but not entirely unexpected, that 4 years later in the throes of the '08 political year, a real life woman candidate for President arose from the masses and was enthusiastically backed by most Democratic white women, but lost out on the nomination by her vulnerability to be ignored by most Black women voters with an Obama to champion and by a woman republican vote. So went women's chances for many years to come.

Ladies, I know this program may be hard for some – probably most – of you to take. But, if you really want to become mensch's, this is what you've got to do. But, being women, I know you're not up to the task. Your husbands and boy friends and Daddies will get mad at you.

XMAS POEMS

Two weeks before Christmas, we usually devote most of our session to enjoying pot-luck food and drink and each-others company. The women usually bring the food, though the Mad Doctor might come up with an entrée. I usually bring wine – now 'Two Buck Chuck' – for those of you acquainted with California's great wine bounty available only at Trader Joe's – brazenly smuggled into the very boo-som of the church.

When we finally do get around to some light reading, the pieces are usually designed for the occasion. I must modestly say, however, that my meaningful, soulful Xmas poems usually bring tears to the eyes of the listeners. Part of the reason for this is because I am of the now long-gone school of poets who firmly believe that the stuff should rhyme. None of this haiku nonsense!

Here then, in all its glory, is my work for the year of our Lord, '04. You will recognize our glorious leader, now under nom-de-plume, our Grand Dame ex-English teacher, our swashbuckling playwright, our mad doctor and satanic clergyman, our traveler and raconteur, our ethnic star, and truly beautiful Maria, whose stories and poems (which don't rhyme) of growing up in Mexico are simply lovely.

XMAS, 2003

ANOTHER BEAUTIFUL CHRISTMAS POEM

It was a year of severe losses and nice recoups
    For the fabulous South Bay Writer's Workshop group
The Group expanded hugely and then got small
    Our glorious leader wondered about 'After the Fall'
We lost Charles, Jean, Irvin, Nina and more
    Some of them left willingly, some of them sore
But, a core of old-timers hung on, and I'll tell you their feats
    As well as mention some of the deserters, with stories replete:

Dear Edith caught a touch of the bad old Big C,
    And bravely and brownly took her radiation therapy

Mel, too, had medical problems, but branched out in his writing

    He now covers the world and comes out fighting!

Charles also fought illness, but managed to get two stories in print

    We will miss his insights and rantings and eyes with a glint

Bob, head down –ass up, continued to charge ahead

    His writing of interest to only the dying and dead

Dale joined the group with stories of World War II

    Intrigue over Japan, with much derring-do

Eric too dropped in – an erudite breath of fresh air and spiritual hype

    His stories have action of the inspirational type

Jody began to write clearly - in the Hemingway style - terse

    Eschewing her usual mystical, lofty, beautiful-picture verse

Ken was a big winner who will be published – isn't that peachy!

    But he continues to be chided when he gets too preachy

Nina published a second book, and wrote a paid story for 25 bucks

    And that, my friends, is artistry, not beginner's luck

Maria, my other dear one, continues to spin her magic

    Her stories are sweet, poignant, and often tragic

Gail, without fail, added her critical expertise; as did Laurie

    Those two really know how to enhance a story

Who knows what next year will bring?

    A resurgence, we hope, and hearts and pens that will sing.

Chapter 6

ANNALS OF AN OUTRAGED CITIZEN

- **THE POLK CITY POLKA** – an inappropriate speed trap is uncovered.

- **BIX'S BLUES** – a motel owner is chastised for gouging at the Bix-fest.

- **STACKING THE STACKS** – the ISU library is told how to operate.

- **MAMA DON'T 'LOW NO SST's HERE** – Des Moines International Airport and Hot Dog Stand is also told how to run its business.

- **MY WIFE WAS A ROTARY ANN(NIE)** – resigning with a bow to NOW.

- **FEED FOR CHATTEL** – rabble-rousing for portable pensions.

- **BILBO BAGGIN'S LAST STAND** – fighting for our miniature Schnauzer's territorial rights.

- **INTRIGUE AT THE SSA** – a new retiree tries to collect Social Security.

- **WHY I HATE GTE** – A 3-block move wreaks horrific havoc.

- **GULLS WITH GALL** – our schwimbad is under siege.

- **"YOU LOST A GOLD MINE WHEN YOU LOST ME"** – MCI feels the sting of my revenge for their French antics.

- **"WHAT A DUMP!"** – the gull-ravaged swimming pool loses temperature and the Home Owner's Assoc. hears about it.

- **MORE HOA FUN (and SEQUELS)** – more noise, elevator and pool temperature complaints.

- **ONE SWEET LETTER FROM YOU** – The world's energy crisis is solved, but nobody cares

---

In these ANNALS, I draw from the original letters, newspaper articles, and notes of some of my more interesting fun-loving tilts at the windmills of pomposity and bureaucracy. In most cases, I retain the originals or copies thereof for those who demand verification.

This Chapter chiefly consists of letters that I have written in protest of outrageous fortune. As you will see, in most cases my 'outrage' is more cerebral than visceral. You might also detect some partial tongue-in- cheek attitude, and the guarded use of excessive hyperbole.

POLK CITY POLKA

When we rolled into Ames, Iowa in June, 1971 to start our new life there, we were trailing our newly acquired sailboat. "Poulet de la Mer, II". It had been purchased in Kansas City, our last road stop before relocating in Iowa. Poulet II replaced the original "Chicken of the Sea", a Venture 24 sloop, sold at a loss just before we left California. After an exploratory trip to Iowa, I had deemed Poulet I too large for the local lakes; the newly developed "Big Creek" and the even smaller "Little Wall" lake. I daresay it was maybe the hundredth sailboat in Iowa, the majority of sailing activity then being concentrated at Lake McBride near Iowa City at the eastern end of the state.

But, by the mid-70's, Iowa had become a sailor's delight. Not only was Big Creek developed to accommodate the rapidly expanding sport, but the Des Moines River was dammed, forming Saylorville Lake. This became a body of water about a half mile wide and almost 10 miles long, replete with marinas and beaches. The Big D river (in Iowa, I decided that Des Moines would be 'Big D', and Davenport, 'Little D') was also dammed further downstream yielding large lakes in the middle and southeast end of the state.

The main entry to both Saylorville and Big Creek for all aficionados north of Des Moines was via perky little Polk City, which was finding new prosperity as a way stop on the way to high seas adventures. One day, as I was trailing my way through the township's narrow road approach to the lake district, I was stopped and cited for speeding – a wholly unreasonable and unjust citation. On June 22, 1977, I reacted after my court hearing by writing the letter below to my friend Victor Preisser, Director, Iowa Department of Transportation:

"Dear Victor

They're running a tyrannical and probably illegal (in the sense that one claims the Vietnamese War was morally illegal) speed trap in Polk City. The trap is just like in the funny papers, i.e., replete with hidden police car and deviously placed speed advisory signs. On the other hand, without the aid of the DOT and the Conservation Commission, they really will have a traffic and speeding problem, which will only become worse as, with Saylorville finally filled, Polk City becomes the boating center of Central Iowa.

The way to solve the problem is <u>not</u> to continue alienating those boat people who are and will continue to bring prosperity to Polk City by perpetuating the speed trap, but to solve the problem. For example, it used to be possible to get to Big Creek without going through Polk City! Now, by collusion with those who control routing, Polk City thinks it can have it both ways – getting the traffic <u>and</u> collecting fines. Clearly, the routing prob-

lems have to be better thought out; better advisory signs need to be placed; and better access roads provided.

I would hope that you would make the proper people in your organization aware of the problem so that a sensible solution is found before the Polk County court docket is swamped. -----------".

I note that I sent a copy of this letter to both the Mayor/City Council of Polk City and to the notorious hanging judge before whom I appeared. I apparently lost my court case, since I recently found a receipt for $32.50 issued to me by the Clerk of the Iowa District Court, Polk County, also on June 22, 1977. I also found a copy of the note I appended to the Judge's copy of my letter to 'Dear Victor':

"Dear Judge Anania:

While I'm muckraking, let me express my disappointment that you did not have the courtesy to reduce my fine since I was both harassed by the State in the matter of my driver's license and also took the unnecessary trouble to drive 40 miles with my obviously wasted message when I could have just as easily mailed in a check."

Unfortunately, there is no moral to this story. My suspicion is that there is still a speed trap and that Polk City continues to prosper from the take of its traffic fines alone. When I left Iowa in 1980, I'll bet the sailboat count was already over 2000 and I'm sure the number continues to rise exponentially. I imagine that the modern day Iowa state budgets are based heavily on the loot emanating from Polk City speeding fines.

BIX's BLUES

We looked forward to the last weekend in July, when the annual paean to the legendary "Young Man with a Horn", the Bix Beiderbecke Memorial Jazz Festival, took place in Little D. Each year, the protocol was the same. About 15 Dixieland jazz bands, from all over the country, came to Davenport, the city of Bix's nativity, to participate in a three-plus day open-air jazzfest during separate, morning, afternoon, and evening sessions. Except for the more impromptu Thursday night session which took place at differing covered venues in the city, the foot-stomping music, lightly amplified, emanated from a band shell at the dead end of Le Claire Park, right on the levee of the mighty Mississippi.

Bix Beiderbecke Memorial Jazz Festival

(From Wikipedia, the free encyclopedia)

The **Bix Beiderbecke Memorial Jazz Festival** is a jazz festival dedicated to the music of Bix Beiderbecke. It is a four day festival held simultaneously in four different venues in Davenport, Iowa. The main venue is Le Claire Park on the Mississippi River. It is held on Thursday through Sunday, usually in a week in late July or early August.

The festival got its start in 1971 when Bill Donahue's Bix Beiderbecke Memorial Band of New Jersey traveled to Davenport, Iowa to play music at Bix's grave at the 40th anniversary of his death. People in the nearby neighborhood heard the music and a crowd slowly began to form. The people of Davenport saw an opportunity to turn this gathering into an annual event. The first "official" festival was held the following year.

Those who didn't want to pay admission anchored their boats and drank their beers within 50 feet of the bandstand. The admission price was modest and typical attendance per session was 800 –1000, with some dancing space maintained up front. Chairs were available, but blankets and backrests were also popular. Along the street side of the park, were line-ups of vendor's tents; selling refreshments, mementos, beer, fast food, and records.

The scene at Le Claire Park. The band shell ahead provides excellent acoustics. There is a dance area in front of it. The river is to the right; close enough so that boats can anchor and hear the music. Vendors are to the left. The author is front and center – in his mid-forties

We usually drove in from Ames in caravan with friends on Thursday afternoon or Friday morning. Before rushing to the music, we first checked into our favorite motel which was in easy walking distance to the festivities. We usually made our reservations for next year as we checked out. If you didn't, you might find yourself commuting from Bettendorf or Rock Island/Moline across the river. Sometimes we tried the Thursday night session to whet our appetites for what was to come. Came Friday, we were off to the sessions, and the 3-a-day routine which I usually religiously followed. We packed it up after the Sunday morning session, satiated with that satisfying old time music- always the same evergreen tunes, always played differently.

All was happiness and light until the fateful 1979 bash. The nefarious action then resulted in the following tasteful letter of July 30th to Mr. Chen, Manager of the Quality Inn / Midtown motel at 6th and Main in greater downtown Davenport:

"We have been coming to the Bix Beiderbecke weekend since its inception in 1972, and for the last 6 years we have been staying at the Quality Inn. We like its service and convenient location - within walking distance to Le Claire Park. Moreover, we have consistently brought friends with us who require three or more additional rooms (e.g., this year, the Newbrough's - who made our reservations – Mr. Case, and the Speer's). However, my wife and I and our friends will no more book at the Quality – because WE WERE GROSSLY OVERCHARGED!

The room (523) which my wife and I occupied Friday and Saturday nights was posted at $32.50 (a reasonable price, albeit higher than 1978's price) – but you charged us $45.00(!) (less tax). We were not told (a) that a special price had been established to gouge festival go-ers, or (b) that twin beds cost more than the large double bed we preferred and requested. To repeat, such information was not given when Mrs. Newbrough made the reservation, or when we (all) checked out on July 27.

The idea of upping your price for 'Special Events' is the surest way to kill off people's enthusiasm for such events, and to give the City of Davenport a bad name. It is certainly antithetical to the aims of the Bix Beiderbecke Memorial Society.
You should carefully review your counter-productive pricing policy. The last weekend was so expensive that I'll think twice about coming in the future."

Of course, I sent copies to the President of Quality Inn International in Silver Springs, MD; the President of the Davenport Chamber of Commerce; and to Don O'Dette, the Director of the BBMS Festival. We did not return to the Quality the next year – instead July, 1980 found us on our way back to California and work in Industry (TRW, in this case).

Despite our absence, the annual tribute to Leon Bismark Beiderbecke, has continued unabated. Indeed, twenty years later, we revisited the festival, along with the Newbrough's and the Speer's. As we rolled past it, we thumbed our noses at the site of the Quality. This time, we stayed at the 'swank' Blackhawk Hotel, two plus blocks away in the heart of the downtown district. I think we paid $80 a night.

152

Iowa Engineer, October 1977

Another Young Man With A Horn

STACKING THE STACKS

In addition to meeting townspeople, I met many distinguished faculty members with whom I would not normally interact, at the Monday noon Rotary Club meetings. One such was Dr. Warren B. Kuhn, the Dean of Library Services, who proudly presided over a library which had recently passed its one millionth acquisition. On February 1, 1980, I felt moved to send him the following Interoffice Communication:

"Message from an Outraged Citizen:

*As you might gather from the above, please expect my annual crank letter to unfold below. Since I was not here last year (*ed. note; I was on Sabbatical at Hughes Aircraft*), the invective will be more bitter than usual.*

On this very day I sent a young innocent over to your shop to borrow the December 1979 version of the monthly magazine, ACTA Astronautica TL787; As891 *published by Pergamon Press. Would you believe it - - I was told that I was allowed to have this in my possession for two hours only (it is a smart 250 page issue). It appears that these are the rules for all periodicals until they get "old", i.e. dated before 1970.*

It is my conservative estimate that there will be exactly three calls for this particular issue within the next decade – and consequently, it would not have hurt to have let me borrow the issue over the weekend (or for the next year, for that matter).

I demand that you immediately drop everything else and carefully investigate whether such rules are truly in the best interest of peace, brotherhood, and the pursuit of higher learning, especially where ACTA Aeronautica is (are ?) concerned."

On February 12th, I received Warren's IOC reply, which gave a reasonable, but abjectly unsatisfactory account of their reasoning, which read, in part:

"Thanks for the "citizen's message". We need these to keep us on our toes, although in this instance your comment, as far as I know, is an isolated one. The non-circulating policy for journals – bound and unbound – is one we've had for a decade now with little or no negative reaction and plenty of positive support. The reasoning was simply that journals are like reference volumes, answering a need for generally short-term perusal of a few articles. However, like reference works, the policy has been to circulate them for special needs for two hours, or if there is longer need for research, our public staff makes a longer exception. ----- The two-hour period, incidentally, was selected to accommodate researcher's desire to photocopy materials for their own use."

Needless to say, for reasons you will gather by noticing the near-moving-out-time-from-Iowa dates of this exchange, I never availed myself of the ISU library services again!

MAMA DON'T 'LOW NO SST's HERE !

The airport that serves central Iowa is one of the few capitol city airports that does not call itself "International". When we first arrived in Iowa, the main building was merely an overgrown shack. But like the great improvement in the waterways, the airport continued to grow and to this day is still in a state of upgrading. As a swashbuckling Department Head, I had many occasions to use the facility on the way to and from various academic and professional soirees. The angry 'Letter to the Editor", also dated February 1, 1980, (I wonder what else I did that day other than write poison pen letters?), directed to the Des Moines Register and Tribune (in truth, you must believe me, it was a truly top rank newspaper in anybody's league) is self explanatory, and was published shortly after its receipt. It was written on ISU stationary and carried my full pompous title; Dr., Professor, and Head were all included:

"Dear Sirs:

Some weeks ago during a raging storm, I embarked on a business trip which necessitated departure from the Des Moines 'International' Airport. Since I am aged and decrepit, poor, and unable to afford the dollar tip for a porter to carry my bag from the curb to the airline, and I am physically unable to carry my bag from a parking space in left field, I left my car at the curb, spent about three minutes checking my bag and returned to permanently park my car, only to find a $5 ticket on my windshield.

I complained to the local "speed trap" gendarme and was told that leaving cars at the curb was not permitted, unless there was an occupant in the car. I subsequently wrote an impassioned letter to Councilman Nahas pointing out the bush league nature of this ordinance and noting that this was not standard practice at some of the other airports in this country which have even more serious pick-up and delivery problems than the Des Moines airport (if that can be believed). I cite Washington National and Los Angeles, for example. In a subsequent conversation with the Councilman, I was informed that the situation was being thoroughly investigated.

Last week I again had occasion to leave from the Big D airport, again in weather that would freeze an Eskimo. This time, noting the ever –present public servant writing tickets, I quickly (as fast as my ancient legs could carry me) took my bag into the lobby and left it there unprotected while I rushed back (ditto) to snatch my car, in the nick of time, for permanent parking.

Kidding aside, if we in Iowa ever hope to achieve a certain degree of sophistication, we ought to take steps to take the straw out of our teeth."

I did try to have the ticket 'fixed', as you will see in the excerpts below from the letter I sent to Councilman Nahas on November 29, 1979, another day of infamy that will forever be stamped on my heart:

" ---------. *It became obvious that a police officer was just waiting to 'pounce' (I have done a similar routine hundreds of times with impunity). In fact, the officer may be in cahoots with the porter (whose services I unwisely refused - to save a dollar).*

I find this completely unreasonable - - it is as morally wrong as a 'speed trap'. I do not intend to pay the fine - - nor will I drive in from Ames to make a traffic court appearance. I would hope that you attempt to (a) quash the enclosed ticket, (b) investigate my allegations and change the "rules" (e.g. "Parking for Luggage drop-off Permitted" signs). In any case – stop the harassment of innocent citizens, and not force them to employ a porter if such is not necessary. Note that if the car had not been 'unattended', no citation would have been given. Does this make sense?   ------

Incidentally, the incident caused my blood pressure to rise to a dangerous degree. If I had had an attack, you can bet I would have sued the city!

Thank you for the consideration of my plea,"

I have no recollection of ever paying the fine. I must have, for they never came for me in the middle of the night, nor did I lose tenure.

MY WIFE WAS A ROTARY-ANN(NIE) !

I'm not a natural 'joiner'. Except for my life-long affiliation with the Democratic Party (I've always voted the party, not the candidate), and on-again off-again dances with the ACLU, I tend to avoid organizations, secular and religious. But when I arrived in Ames, Iowa, I immediately perceived a major problem that comes with living in a town whose sole raison d'etre was to house and feed a large University and all its accoutrements. I saw that unless aggressive steps were taken, you and your family would only associate with the 'Gown' part of the 'Town and Gown' hierarchy (except for your local grocer, doctor and pusher).

My solution – and it turned out to be a good and happy one – was to join the local Rotary International club. I chose Rotary over the Lions and Kiwanis at the suggestion of my Department Head predecessor and our mutual Dean, both Rotarians. The Ames Branch appeared to encompass most of the higher officials of the University, including its beloved president, as well as many bankers, lawyers, mayors and ex-mayors, and men of affairs. Here, I met the makers and shakers of the community every Monday for lunch. We schmoozed prior to taking our seats, suffered a sweet mostly non-denominational invocation, sang nice songs and heard, sometimes, interesting commentary (like, for instance, when I told the assembly about the wonders of the space program and the Space Shuttle).

My participation accomplished what I had wanted to accomplish. Despite my liberalism, I did not really miss the company of female faculty and business executives. In Rotary, at that time, all females were relegated forever to the sole role of being helpful Rotary-Ann's who, at our occasional family events, were assigned the tasks of serving food and refreshments. You can bet that my wife loved being a "Rotary Annie"!

When I knew (but the news of my impending departure was not yet generally known) that I was again going to follow Horace Greeley's immortal advice to, again, 'Go West', I bravely seized the opportunity to make a bold statement for emancipation. Realizing that I would probably never again be a Rotarian, I made a great liberating statement, dated June 30, 1980:

"It is with regret that I tender my resignation from ROTARY International as of this date. As you know, I have been at odds with the organization for refusing to admit women. Since, at the latest conclave, this stance was not changed, I take this step in protest and hope that you will have it noted for the record.

Aside from that, Mrs. Lincoln, it has been a great pleasure to have served in ROTARY and I will miss seeing the many friends I have made in this organization on a regular basis"

I frankly doubt if this bold declaration was the one that swung the tide. Several years later, an affiliate in the Los Angeles County area (Monrovia, I believe) announced to Rotary National that it was declaring its independence from the National and admitting qualified women. This started a series of international 'hugging and chalking' sessions which ultimately resulted in glass ceiling limited women now being knowledgeable of the secret handshake, upgrading the quality of the singing in the higher octaves, and themselves being served by Rotary Annies at the picnics. I'm proud to have done my part!

FEED FOR CHATTEL

As befits a liberal Democrat – a rarity in engineering circles – I always felt that it made sense for engineers to have the opportunity to be unionized. In the 50's and 60's, sporadic efforts towards unionization were made in some of the major Southern California aerospace industry giants. I tried to get my technical societies to at least discus the matter, but they, dependent on Corporate funding sponsorship, were never keen to enter the arena. Management, everywhere, was vociferously against such organizations for engineers, whom they have always considered necessary but expensive chattel. However, one company, Lockheed/ Burbank, did permit the formation of a so-called "Company Union". This organization was a voluntary one and had no dues, but did have the right to elect a spokesman to intercede with management. It turned out to be a paper tiger, and did nothing to solve a problem that has always plagued the industry: The problem of Pension Portability.

At that time, most aerospace companies contributed to, or at least managed, employee's retirement pension funds from the first day of employment. However, in the 50's and 60's, at least, the employee was not 'vested' (i.e. given the right to receive such accrued funds upon retirement) until 10 years of service had been attained. If an employee left the company before vestment, he or she was given the money that had been deducted from their salary, but none of the company's contribution. In those days, due to the great competition with consequent salary bonuses for switching companies, and the ability for Californians to commute to many plants without having to move their residences, 10 years with the same company was the exception, not the rule.

In the case of skilled hourly workers at these companies, most of whom were unionized, the individual's pension fund, managed by the Union, went with the worker as he or she changed jobs in the industry. Why shouldn't the same be true for engineers? Again, through my technical societies (which eventually merged to become the AIAA), I agitated for portable pensions and was not alone in this quest. The harsh reality of how my fellow engineers and I were being screwed really dawned on me when I went from Industry to Academia in 1971. In a letter to the Editor of the March, 1972, issue of the AIAA monthly magazine, *ASTRONAUTICS & AERONAUTICS*, I wrote:

Letters

A PENSION EXPERIENCE

I must believe that the problem of "portable pensions" is being delayed by a series of apparently "immovable obstacles," which to me merely indicates the aerospace industry's unwillingness to face up to the inevitable.

My own pension experience illustrates vividly the current inequities. Until July of 1971, I spent 22 years in the industry at three companies. For this service, I will be rewarded for only 12 years of vested retirement benefits. The pension, assuming reasonable economic growth, will be about $500 to $600 per month.

Upon reentering the academic world, I found that the TIAA-CREF (Teachers Insurance and Annuity Association-College Retirement Equities Fund) system provided me immediate vestment in a program considerably more generous than in industry, and one that IS portable to most U.S. universities. If I retire at age 65, 18 years from now, my pension will be from $1200 to $1400 per month, based on a present salary slightly less than my industry rate. If this problem can be handled so readily by the academic world, I cannot help but feel that it can also be solved by the aerospace industry and/or its allied technical societies. I feel that this problem is presently being attacked in a negative manner – only the barriers are considered

Let us adopt a positive attitude, define what we want and- hopefully with the willing aid of industry - provide a program which at least achieves what workers in the electrical, automotive, transportation, and construction industries have had for many years.

R. F. Brodsky
Head, Aerospace Engineering Dept.
Iowa State University

As with much of my windmill tilting, nothing ever came of the concept of portable pension for engineers. Fortunately for me, as it turned out, the pension payments both from industry and teaching are higher than quoted earlier. True, several companies have reduced the vesting period to a fewer number of years. But, in my opinion, engineers – the lifeblood of the aerospace industry – are still treated like chattel. The funny thing is that most engineers know it, and apparently like the status. They have always said, "I want to deal with management head-to-head. No one can represent me better than me. Little do they know!

BILBO BAGGINS' LAST STAND

During our last winter in Iowa, we acquired one Bilbo Baggins Brodsky, a roly-poly lovable fuzz ball of a miniature Schnauzer puppy, who soon became "Baggins". This valued addition to our family was made possible by our youngest son, Jeffrey, having grown out of the asthma problem that had beset his pre-teen years. We moved to Hermosa Beach, 2 blocks from the water. Both my wife and I loved dogs, so we happily shared the 3-a-day dog-walking duties. After I retired from TRW in July, 1988, I took on most of these chores. I did so because I greatly enjoyed the company of the many friendly fellow (and girl) dog-walkers who usually followed the same time-of-day routine.

Moreover, we had available a prime dog walking area - the renovated, vegetated strip, only a half block from our house, on which the once proud Pacific Electric red cars used to wend their way, bringing the 'Big City' dwellers to their sea shore bungalows for the weekend. We shared the former right-of-way with power strollers and jocks, but there was room for all, and the camaraderie was superb. Dog walkers are truly the salt of the earth – surely a higher class of human being - as any dog owner will attest. I knew them all well! We were family!

The right honorable Bilbo Baggins Brodsky - a lovable ball of fluff
who was a family member for over 14 years and brought us much joy

One day, our idyllic aura was threatened by the ill-conceived notion of a good friend of ours; indeed the wife of one of my staunchest crewmen, and a figure of power and stature in our town. Via a "Letter to the Editor", she complained bitterly of the prolific supply of 'doggie-do' on the tarmac walkway and demanded that all hunds be heretofore barred not only from running free, but perhaps also being completely banned from the walkway. This attack prompted the following letter, which was also dutifully published in the fabulous weekly *EASY READER*, September 21, 1989 issue, under the banner of

'INDIGNA*NT*':

"Dear ER:

Would you please consider publishing the note below in refutation of Pat Gazin's heartless and misinformed letter in a recent issue:

GONE TO THE DOGS

As much as I respect the normally calm logic of our former Mayor, Pat Gazin, I now find her completely misinformed about the burning issue of dogs running free on our city's wonderful combination dog and jogging strip between Valley and Ardmore. Moreover, our hund, the right honorable Bilbo Baggins Brodsky, who daily enjoys three romps on the turf also find gaping holes in her argument:

Most dogs I know who join us in our daily routine and who are allowed to run free are very well behaved vis-a-vis the passing jocks (Indeed if they weren't, their owners, not wishing a liability suit, would not take a chance on their running free). I am only aware of one incident where a dog threatened a runner, and I have not seen any accounts of such attacks in any of the local papers.

I admit that the turf is generally brown in color – but surely this is because that is the basic color of the tree shavings that line the pathway. Most dogs have the courtesy of doing their thing in the ice plants where no person in their right mind dares to tread. The new City ordnance which requires pooper - scooping seems to be working well for those noble animals who eschew the ice plants.

So, the thousands upon thousands of Hermosa Beach dog lovers beg the indulgence of the jocks and request non-users of this expensive turf to butt out. I would accept a compromise: in return for free run on the strip, no dog walking on the Strand.

Respectfully:
R.F. "Mad Dog" Brodsky
Hermosa Beach

I'm happy to report that the day was won, and the status quo remains so to this day. I'm sad to report that in 1993, after 14 grand years of promenading, Baggins met his maker and is now in that special doggie heaven reserved for all high ranking family members.

INTRIGUE AT THE SSA

My 1988 transition from Working Stiff to Retiree went pretty smoothly. I had chosen to start receiving my dole from the <u>S</u>ocial <u>S</u>ecurity <u>A</u>dministration at age 63, despite the fact that my monthly check would have been more had I waited until I was 65. Unless you are planning to live to be a very great age, a quick calculation will show that the early bird in the hand is always better than the delayed one in the bush. I very quickly got used to receiving the reliable pay check on the 3rd of each month, and counted on it to supplement my other pension checks.

Until the strange rules were changed, a retiree on Social Security was allowed to make something like $10,000 per year before deductions to the normal SS monthly pay check were made. The rule made it self-defeating to make more than this amount in any year, so I limited my income accordingly. The strange rule, just nullified in 2000, lasted through one's 70th or 71st birthday; thereupon you could make as much as you could and still receive the full SS allotment. One of the administrative peculiarities was the requirement that you guess and report on how much income you expected to earn in the next year. I think it must have been this factor that led to the following December 19, 1991 letter exchange with the local SSA, with copy to my Congressman:

"Dear Mary:

Thank you for your letter of Dec. 18, giving your interpretation of what happened to my October SS check. You spoke of a mysterious "computer notice" – which, of course, I never received. I would not be questioning you if I had received it and I believed its findings. I neither did receive it nor do I believe in your explanation. The SSA already gave me no check for Jan 1991, <u>based on the same $11,500 income estimate that I made last year and later, this year, confirmed.</u>

All I am asking for is an official explanation of why I didn't get my October check. The mysterious missing computer notice will do – however, it remains my belief that the SSA had goofed and they are struggling for a rational explanation. The before-the-fact withholding is not consistent with their past practices.

<u>Please, all I ask is a written explanation emanating from the source of check action. I think that's very little since you have ruined my life forever by your capricious actions.</u>"

The requested explanation never came! Instead, after a while the missing check arrived by mail with no explanation. I then learned never to estimate an income overage for the next year, and to be sure to stay below the limit. I was happy when I reached the serendipitous age of 70 or 71, and could mutter with impunity, "a pox on your house!"

WHY I HATE GTE

When they broke up AT&T, I rejoiced. I finally saw that it might be possible to get out from under the most heinous telephone system operator since the Big Bang. My resentment against the slovenly service and quirky pricing offered by their successor, the General Telephone and Electronics Company, merely smoldered for several years, until we suffered the indignity which I will now relate:

In mid-April of 1997, we opened escrow on our new home, a one-level condo about three blocks North (SeaScape 2, still in Redondo Beach, of course) from the Esplanade building that my wife characterized as the "Hotel'. I called the GTE business office and asked them to transfer our phone number as of the late May closing date. Here is where trouble, of an unbelievable nature, began!

The first thing they told me was that we could not transfer our now well-established two year old phone number. Why? Well, naturally "because your new home is on the other side of a major artery, Torrance Avenue" and, by the way, you will incur a $46.00 'service connection' charge. "Oh, sure, that's easy to understand! And what will our new number be?" We were assigned 792 9677, and we promptly ordered new bank checks with this number and our new address on them. We next printed up and mailed out 150 notices to our family and friends announcing our new address as of May 29, 1997 along with the newly assigned telephone number. In spite of the exorbitant installation charge, I felt the world was in its proper orbit and that we were ready for the move. What fools we retirees be!

Ten days before our move we received an advisory bill from GTE noting what our basic monthly rate would be, and indicating that they would account for the $46.00 service charge over the next three monthly bills. Coincidentally, we got the package of new bank checks in the same mail delivery. But, what's this? In the upper left hand corner of the GTE advisory, I noted "billing number 937-1811". What the hell was that? With much trepidation and a sinking feeling in my stomach, I immediately called for an explanation. "Oh, shucks and fiddle-de-de, on the very same day, we assigned the identical number to a John Aarons, and when we discovered the mistake, we reassigned you your 'real' number. Sorry we didn't let you know."

The Masked Avenger, his blood pressure at a new high, whipped into action. I found out John Aarons' work number, and begged him to cede his new home number to me.

"Oh', he said "That's why I've been getting these strange calls" and, angrily, "No, I won't change numbers - go screw yourself!" I then turned my wrath on to the phone company.

My approach was to prepare a one page annotated pastiche consisting of a sample from the 150 address change mailing at the top; a copy of the GTE advisory in the middle; and, at the bottom, a copy of our worthless new checks with the wrong phone number imprinted. The annotations on the margins were as follows:

"1) How could you do this to me?

2) At least, don't charge me $46.00!

3) Let me retain my present number (316 2323) at no extra cost.

(p.s. I've moved 4 blocks! Why should I have to change numbers anyway!)

4) Think of how you've also screwed John Aarons – who will be getting all my calls!

5) My costs for your mistakes, so far:

Printing checks (2 sets) 2x$10= $20

stamps (150x $.32) x 2 = $96

copies ,addr. change. 300x$.03= $ 9

for a total of $125. Please send cash or cancel the $46 switching charge."

By phone pre-arrangement, I sent this to Gary Sommer in the Legal Office of the GTE Executive Office at #1 GTE Place in Thousand Oaks with my usual threat to take them to Small Claims Court. Very quickly the $46 charge was dropped.

But, even now when my old nemesis has been swallowed up by a new outfit called "Verizon", I remain wary and have another company carry my long distance trade, and keep hoping that competition for the local calling business will somehow appear. Have you ever tried to run a rate comparison of competitive communications companies? It is a maze that even Einstein could not get through.

GULLS WITH GALL

In addition to the broad vista that can be seen from our balcony, stretching from the Palos Verdes hills to the left and over the ocean to the Malibu shore on the right, our condo's swimming pool/spa area is in full sight immediately below. Like a magnet, the pool has become a watering hole for the local sea gull* population, who must fly only a hundred yards from the harbor breakwater in order to 'take the freshwater baths'. They bathe periodically in groups of two or three.

At their August '98 monthly meeting, which I attended as an observer, the Home Owner's Association Board took note of this daily invasion and in vain sought a solution to preclude the unwanted visitations. It rejected the suggestion of an eager observer to apply a BB gun as probably unlawful and inhumane. But, all agreed that the birds were obdurate and not at all intimidated by swimmers splashing water on them to drive away. It is true that they are not an ill-mannered bunch. I have seldom seen a 'dropping' in the pool per se. However, the walkways around the pool do get soiled and one must carefully watch where one steps.

Being a daily swimmer, I decided to helpfully enter the fray. I had recently noticed that the *LA Times* was about to inaugurate a new column every other Sunday, entitled "Living with Wildlife", proprietress Andrea Kitay. I promptly e-mailed her a description of our predicament, which read:

"We live in a condo complex very close to the ocean. Despite a wind-actuated 'singing string' and a plastic owl, the sea gulls are becoming more and more brazen and fearless as they come for a bath in the pool several times a day. They make a mess both in and out of the pool. Short of enclosing the whole area, do you have any suggestions?"

In her Sept.13, 1998 column, in which she repeated the QUESTION, from R.B., Redondo Beach, she gave her ANSWER:

"Keeping sea gulls out of pool area is one of the easier tasks in the business of controlling pesky wildlife.

---

*For a person of my ethnic persuasion, this bird is pronounced "Segal", as if they were members of one of the twelve lost tribes, which some obscure oriental sects purport them to be.

Many restaurants around the country, including one on Cannery Row in Monterey and another at Disney World in Florida, have successfully repelled gulls by suspending a simple network of mono-filament line or non-rusting wire over the area needing protection.

This tactic can also be applied to your pool area to prevent the gulls from landing. ----------- .

To create a barrier, string several strands --- over the pool area. Attach the lines to whatever's available or install posts if necessary. Run the lines eight feet apart at whatever height seems appropriate and safe. Make sure that people can easily walk beneath the lines and that they don't interfere with stairs.

If the birds still penetrate the line, fill in the existing spaces so that the lines are only 4 feet apart. And so on. -----------."

A member of the lost tribe who has found his/her way to our pristine schwimbad

Later that morning, I dispatched the following e-mail:

"Andrea:

I thank you, my wife thanks you, my sainted mother (from her view from the gull-less void) thanks you, and perhaps the SeaScape 2 Home Owner's Association Board of Directors may someday thank you after interminable debates which should consume the rest of the year, at least.

Your solution, applied here, would require some uprights but is feasible. However, I fear the installation might cost over $1000.00. So, the outcome will be determined by the tradeoff between money and the Board's desire to do away with the pests humanely.

Again, thanks for the column. I will let you know the outcome and results."

At 2:32 p.m. that afternoon, Andrea sent the following:

"Bob, glad you liked the column this morning. You should know I've received several letters from various homeowner associations regarding gulls and other birds in their pools ... you're not alone.

For what it's worth, $1000.00 split between 300 units (did you say 300 or so?) (actually, it is 178) is cheaper than a Happy Meal from McDonald's. You might tell the association that the other option is a professionally installed full net from a place like Bird Barrier (a very reputable shop, by the way) – my guess is it'll run you several thousand minimum. Of course, a full net from BB would last a long time ------ ."

I passed this information exchange along to the Board. As predicted, they are still mulling it over, and new generations of the lost tribe have found their way to the mineral baths.

"YOU LOST A GOLDMINE WHEN YOU LOST ME"

This time, the wicked perpetrator was my heretofore valiant, frequent-flyer-miles-giver long distance telephone company, MCI World Com - the dirty bastards! The bad news, $68.29 of it, arrived via the phone company's bill "statement ending Nov. 1, 2000".

During our late September - mid-October jaunt in France and Germany, I had occasion to make local calls as well as France-Germany calls. Being ever aware of the vicious surcharges that hotels add to phone calls and, having been advised by MCI on several occasions to "always use your phone card when abroad", I naturally availed myself of their service with confidence. After all, I did pay them $8.95 per month to secure low rates to France, Germany and Israel.

In fact, I had to make two 'emergency' local calls from Neuilly, our old Parisian neighborhood, to hotels a few miles away. Not having a French phone card to insert in the booth's coin–slot-less phone, I was nevertheless triumphantly able to make the calls using the MCI card. However, the November 1 statement showed that I had paid a high price for this triumph, as well as for the calls made from hotels; none of the calls being over two minutes in length. The bill showed charges of $10.16 each for six less-than-two-minute calls and $7.33 for a call less than 1 minute! This insult brought on the following retort:

"*Nov. 11, 2000*

MCI WORLD COM
Customer Research
PO Box 460
Iowa City, IA 52244-4600

Sirs:
You have scammed me royally on charges for MCI card calls I made while in France and Germany in late Sept and early October. For six calls billed at 2 minutes each, you charged $10.16 each (two of these calls were to a friend's hotel 2 blocks away!); and one 1 minute call was billed at $7.33!

As a result of your callousness, I intend to pay only $10.16, and you can send a bill collector after me for the rest. I have also dropped your service - which you can win back if you care to make a reasonable settlement (you will note that I have been a long time and good customer).

I pay $8.95/ month for what I thought were very low international rates to Germany and France. You have instructed me to use my calling card when I make such calls when I am on the road. How dare you then charge me outrageously for calls which would cost *only a few Francs or Deutsche Marks had I used the Hotel's notoriously high (but actually a pittance compared to yours) rates?!*

I would like a letter of explanation, an apology, and a reasonable settlement offer, preferably accepting my more than generous $10.16 offer. THEN, I will consider renewing my service with you.

Very Truly Yours,

Cc: VeriZon, Federal Communications Commission"

As soon as I could, I dropped the MCI service in favor of an outfit called Econophone, who said that their rates were uniformly low, and that I would soon get two tin cans and a long length of string in the mail. Despite the sharply toned letter above, I kept getting notes from MCI like the one in late December which began, "You made an excellent choice when you selected MCI WorldCom for your international calling needs. -----" I called them on the day after Christmas to see if they really understood the basics of commerce, only to be told that they had given me credit for around $60, and would I like to rejoin their happy outfit? I told them I'd await official confirmation of their settlement, but, in truth, I was happy with Econophone, to date. Some months later, Econophone went bankrupt without warning. After a few days of no long distance, I hooked up with another cut-rate outfit, ECG, and am holding my breath.

WHAT A DUMP!

It was déjà vu all over again! We had just returned from a short vacation in delightfully warm Palm Springs to the mysterious cold and clammy mists that surround the local seashore in May and June and were prepared to enjoy the Memorial Day holiday weekend – sun or no sun. The mail in our crammed box included a note from our condo's Home Owner's Association that our monthly maintenance bill would increase by a meteoric $30 due to the recent run-a-way electricity and natural gas price increases. This, just when we were recovering from the shock of paying over $2 a gallon for our drive back from the desert. An addition to the notice was that the staff had been instructed to lower the pool water temperature from 84 to 82 degrees, again in the interest of conservation. Thank heavens for small favors, the Jacuzzi temp would remain at 104.

On reading the notice, I immediately had a 'flash back'. Some years ago, when we were living under the tyranny of yet another Home Owner's Association in a townhouse in Hermosa Beach, a similar energy crisis led the HOA to declare a moratorium on pool heating for three winter months. I had just left the Association's service after a two year term and angrily told my former colleagues that I would take them to Small Claims Court if they did not relent. I explained that we had bought our home for the amenities it presented, and we would not settle for less. After much haggling, they turned the heater back on. Would I now face another gargantuan struggle with the powers-that-be, I mused?

I soon discovered that my worst fears had indeed materialized, which led to the following letter composed at the end of what should have been a life-renewing holiday frolic:

May 28, 2001

Board of Directors
Seascape II Home Owner's Association

Dear Board:
"What a dump!" I echo the opening lines of "Who's Afraid of Virginia Woolf" to express my disdain at an outfit who, on a rare 4 day holiday, runs an ice-cold swimming pool and an inoperable elevator in Building ll0, my alma mater. And THEN wants to collect $30 a month more in dues! Fat chance - sue me, if you can't fix it:

On May 19, I returned to my unit after a delightful 76th birthday celebration in Palm Springs. There, the pool was warm and the elevators worked. I read my mail and noted the dues increase and the supposed lowering of the pool temperature to an acceptable 82 degrees. I immediately restarted my daily (rain or shine I must do my ten laps to maintain my precarious health) routine of hot tub and swim. When I dove into the pool my heart immediately stopped from the cold shock. Three minutes later, by continually pounding on my chest, I fortunately (for you, for my dear wife would have most certainly sued) got it started again and complained to Penny. She measured 76 degrees (I, 75) and, she says, told the pool man to get it up to 82. It hasn't been there since and I now suspect chicanery by evil forces trying to save a dime at the expense of an old man's health. On the other hand, the elevator continually breaks down because it's no damn good!

If you're going to raise the dues, raise them enough to maintain services which I believed came with my unit when I bought it. At my age, it's a strain to walk up and down steps. Right now, you're running an upscale tenement!

By the way, I've analyzed the budget and think that in your panic to make up for unanticipated expenses, you've overshot how much is really needed. Finally, since I tried to raise hell over the phone on this lost weekend, I request that the next Bulletin list all of your home phone numbers (I could only find Jill's in the phone book, and she wasn't in) plus Penny's cell phone or page number. Trouble usually comes on a weekend! Recognize that harassment from your 'tenants' is part of the job you took on.

Seriously, if the pool situation is not straightened out and maintained at a reasonable temperature, I will pay only $15 additional per month and will take you to small claims court when you put a lien on me.

With love and affection: Herr Professor Doktor RF Brodsky

Seascape 2 – Redondo Beach. Crowne Plaza Hotel pool, garage/Gold's gym is in foreground. 110 the Village, our building, in background – a football field distance from the ocean. Our condo is on fourth floor, right, above swimming pool/gym/ locker rooms (pool can be seen mid-picture, 80-90% right).

The letter did some good. By Monday afternoon, the pool temp was reasonable and, when later in the week, it again mysteriously dropped down, I got a quick response which jacked it up. I now am hoping the crisis is over, but am remaining vigilant and measuring the temp whenever I feel the slightest chill. I attended the HOA meeting the following Tuesday. The Board Members, except one (who dubbed me, "Brave Heart"), said they enjoyed my letter but weren't quite sure if I was mad or not. They also decided to formulate a new set of emergency procedures for weekends and holidays and to replace the old fashioned pool temperature thermostat with a digital one. Of such stuff are heroes made!

MORE HOA FUN

As you may have gathered by now, I am on much better terms with the Seascape II Board of Directors than I had been with the "dripping incident" Board on the Esplanade, whose deliberations were closed to the renting tenants (as were we). The Seascape Board appreciated my interest in their transactions, welcomed my attendance, and felt shortchanged if I didn't have some bitch to liven up their meetings. They also appreciated my snide letters:

When we bought our unit in the newly renovated 110 building of the Seascape 2 complex, we noted that the single elevator had not been renovated, and was a bit slow and noisy, albeit seemingly reliable. As time went by, however, it became slower and slower, emitted more wheezes and, on occasion, stopped completely. The Board dutifully had it refurbished, but only its interior decor. I continued to have the feeling that when one pushed the button, the wheezing noise came from the mouth of the genie that sat on a bike in the elevator room and furiously pedaled to up the hydraulic pressure on demand. When the genie was out to lunch, we had to walk three flights of stairs to get to our car or to the pool. Many times when I got to the pool, the water temperature was below spec. All this frustration contributed to the following letter:

July 7, 2001
Seascape 2 HOA Board of Directors
Dear Board:

Another fun weekend at the SeaScape 2 tenement house and lodge! (And, although the pool thermometer reads 82, I think it is 'fixed'.)

1) Unlike organized Condos (531 Esplanade, for example), you continue to allow move-ins and move-outs on the weekend, which of course not only ties up the elevators (and in the case of the very sick 110 building elevator, probably kills it). This weekend also featured non-working indicator lights (ground floor, at least), making one wonder if it was truly inoperable), but opens up the building to marauders and pirates, since the unattended access doors are, of course, blocked open.

2) I wonder how many rental units do we have? I can only believe it is renters who have no regard for the other tenants. Case in point was a very loud party Saturday night well after 11 pm.

3) Possibly the building's fault: In two successive days, Channel 4 (only this channel) –broadcasting Wimbledon – failed and had to be called.

Let me suggest that Board consider some very simple solutions (before too many more "Safer SeaScape" seances are held). At the very least, post signs on the outside doors where loading takes place saying that these doors must be kept closed at all times and suggesting they borrow keys from their patrons. Next, rig a simple timer which rings a loud bell (tied into fire alarm?) if the door is open more than 30 seconds, say. Third, ask tenants to report time and place of infractions. Finally establish an automatic system of fines to the Owners for such security violations.

In the matter of after hours (11pm?) noise, establish an automatic fine system activated by a call to the police. (say $50 for the first call, another $50 for a second call, etc. Make these fine menus known to owners and renters alike. Add fines to monthly bill.

In the matter of the 110 building elevator, hire a local terrorist to blow it up, and use the insurance money to buy us a new one.

Respectfully yours RF Brodsky #410
   (My wife wants to state that wants no part of this rant)

This letter led to a lot of discussion, but essentially no action except to up the pool temperature. The elevator continues to be cantankerous, usually on weekends when the Manager is not on-site; and the genie is getting more and more ausgespieled; and I more outraged:

Feb. 19, 2002
Board of Directors
Seascape 2 H.O.A.

Dear Sirs and Mssss:

In traditional fashion for 3 day weekends and ordinary weekends, the elevator in the 110 building, the South Bay's most expensive tenement, broke down again this past weekend adding yet another chapter to its storied reputation. It is no wonder that no less a personality as Saddam Hussein calls it, "The Mother of all Elevators"? But, fret not – I HAVE A SOLUTION!

We obviously need a new elevator: Add to the dues of each 110 building owner a $10/ month surcharge until enough money is collected to buy one that operates consistently. BUT, in exchange, offer a $500 award to any person or persons trapped in the present elevator, and a $1000 award to the family of those who die in an elevator failure due to heart seizure or sheer fright. Since such cases would be expected to occur only 3 (trapped) times a year, and a failure-related death only once a year, we should have the means to purchase a replacement elevator in a mere ten years.

Although I personally do not expect to see the replacement in my lifetime, it will give me great satisfaction to know that my widow will no longer have to drag her osteoporosis-racked body up and down the stairs in her last days.

Your faithful servant
R. Foxroy Broadbeam, # 410

At the March meeting, the Board expressed their pleasure on reading my memo, and took the matter under advisement.

ONE SWEET LETTER FROM YOU

Occasionally I get moved to write a "Letter to the Editor", knowing full well that what I write is controversial and therefore will not pass the chicken-hearted editor's muster. I'm usually philosophic about the non-acceptance of my work. Sometimes, however, they do print "Letters" from others that do hit the nail on the head. But –blatantly – this was not the case in my latest windmill tilt.

The Page 1 headline in the June 28, 2008 issue of the rapidly declining *LA TIMES* was "What If Oil Hits $200?" Well. it was as if fate had sent me its blessing. I had been waiting for this one, and I knew the answer. Before the morning was over, I got the little beauty below off to the Editor:

Isn't it time?

Re: "What if oil hits $200?": page 1, Saturday, June 28

Isn't it time that we face up to a permanent solution to our energy problem? Isn't it time to recognize that the only fuel that is available in unlimited and replenishable supply, at a cost that can be very low and whose use is environmentally acceptable, is HYDROGEN; and that going onto the Hydrogen Economy is inevitable and can be initially accomplished with technology already on hand?

The 'cheap' Hydrogen comes from the ocean, separated by, at first, Fission nuclear plants, to be supplanted by cleaner more powerful Fusion plants when that technology becomes available (as it could sooner by a "Manhattan Project" approach). Storage and release-on-demand of Hydrogen is another problem which needs to be dealt with, though it is apparent that the light-weight, compact storage of Hydrogen in metal hydrides is a possible solution. But, the technology is here today to move towards the Hydrogen Economy NOW. Note also, a by-product of the nuclear plants is the possible production of unlimited quantities of drinking and irrigation water.

If the United States declares that this is what we are going to do, and backs it up with significant expenditures and obvious determination, what do you think will happen to the price of a barrel of oil? In my opinion, they will be giving it away on street corners.

In my book, "On the Cutting Edge", October 2006 (U. Nebraska Press or Amazon.com) (Chapter 7, p 186), I discussed my so far rebuffed attempts to organize a University-sponsored Conference to discuss all aspects; technical, economic, and political of the energy crisis. Isn't it time we did this – instead of romancing other solutions which can never solve the problem – individually or together?

Robert F. Brodsky, DSc
110 the Village, Unit 410
Redondo Beach, CA 90277
310 937 1811
rfoxbro@aol.com

I sent e-mail copies of the above letter to many of my friends, rightfully suspecting that it would not be published. I was amazed to see the firestorm it aroused. There appeared at least 20 'takes' on my letter ranging from one or two "Huzzahs!" to several "You don't know your ass ---"; with other intermediate comments ranging from tepid to outrageous. And, although the correspondence kept flowing for several days, that no one offered a more logical way to reduce our dependency on oil. A few spoke of going to completely electric cars - which makes good sense if we can make a significant "break-through" in batteries. In any case, I'll still stick with the Hydrogen Economy.

Well, finally, in the Saturday, July 5, 2008 issue, The Editors, under the '*Fuel for Pessimism*' banner dealt with the returns by printing three "Letters to the Editor", each of whom that were completely worthless:

DD of Leucadia started off the fun by bravely predicting that oil *will* 'hit $200'. Thus, he says triumphantly, the *TIMES* will introduce "What if Oil Hits $300?" This Letter of course did a lot to define the problem.

TJW of Huntington Beach chides the Editors: "And although the article presents a sprinkling of facts and economic opinions, almost nothing is concluded but that things will get worse --------" He offers no way to go but wants clearer exposition. His letter says nothing, but puts the words together convincingly.

Finally, PNK of La Costa completes the triumph of pertinent selections. His doozie refers us back to the movie "Three Days of the Condor" which, as you may gather, is highly apropos to the energy crisis happening right before our eyes.

So, the Editors have cleverly avoided the issue by printing garbage in a place that deserved my 'bit' and, I bet, several other 'bits' that dealt with the problem at hand. I think I'll send future "Letters to the Editor" to the tabloids. There, they will stand a better chance of being printed because they *are* controversial.

Chapter 7

ANNALS OF SAILING

- **WHAT IT'S ALL ABOUT**
- **BOATS I HAVE KNOWN**
- **THE 'OLD FARTS' SAGA**

Dating back to the late '50s, sailing has become an integral part of my life, especially since my 'first' retirement in 1988. Since then, rain or shine, I have generally managed to sail twice a week. My wife, Pat, says that if I miss a sail day, I fear the ocean may suddenly dry up.

It all started in my first summer of attendance at the Racquette Lake Boys Camp in the Adirondacks in upstate New York. There, at age 12 or 13, I learned to operate a sail-canoe. This was a conventional canoe that was retrofitted with an outrigger float on one side to prevent capsize, a 'clamp-on' foot pedal controlled rudder, and a hole in a forward seat through which the mast, with its sail and rigging attached, was inserted. It was as simple as that, and I soon became qualified and, later, expert in its operation. So good in fact, that I was asked to manage the 12-boat fleet in subsequent summers, with a significant reduction in my camp tuition. Clearly, I was 'bit' by the 'sailing bug' that stayed with me the rest of my life.

Since I left the New Mexico desert in 1956, I have always had a sailboat at my disposal. In this Chapter, I will tell you about the boats I have known intimately. My love of the sea has been transmitted to my children. Our middle son lived on a sailboat for a while, owned and operated a 65 foot McGregor tourist-carrying sloop out of Pier 39 in San Francisco bay, and is a professional ship Master.

In 1989-90, at age 64, while I was teaching in Israel, I crewed for an ancient Scottish Jew on his 22 foot boat. He had a wonderful authentic burr and single handedly did all the hard foredeck work, like spinnaker handling, during races, while I held the tiller. When one day he told me that he was 70, I marveled at his agility and said to myself, "Boy, I hope that I will still be sailing when I'm 70!" As I write this in May, 2005, a few days before my 80th birthday, I'm still at it, looking forward to my next venture on the high seas tomorrow.

WHAT IT'S ALL ABOUT

You don't know what you've missed until you try sailing on the Pacific on a nice day! People kid me that the route our twice weekly outings take is always the same. They say that the boat needs no helmsman – it knows exactly where to go: We exit Redondo Marina and, with the normal west wind, head South towards the shore marking the end of Torrance Beach; tack to starboard before we run aground and head towards the oil tankers that are moored off El Segundo by the airport, about a mile off shore from Santa Monica and the entrance to Marina Del Rey; then tack to port and head back to the 'barn'. Depending on the boat and the wind, this outing starts at 1 p.m. and ends at 4 p.m. – every time!

Sure, there are variances. In the winter, December to March, when the California Gray whales are running South to their winter birthing haven, Scammons Bay in Baja, and the wind is from the northwest, we head out towards Palos Verdes point where, until recent years, it was almost certain that you could spot the behemoths. Every year I offer a $5 prize for the first authenticated, by another crew member, whale sighting of the season. Two years ago, I won. So, this year only, to unruffle the crew, I upped the prize to $10, but there have been no sightings so far. And, sometimes, when we want to make a spinnaker run, or have ashes of our dearly departed to dispose of, we head out to sea towards the West and China. But most of the time, the course is the same overlapping excursion, and nobody on my 'Old Farts' crew of weather beaten experienced sailors complains. Like me, they are hooked on sailing, rain or shine.

But, that's boring, you say. No, Dammit, it isn't! It's the way it was meant it to be! What non-competitive sailing is about is peace and serenity in a company of old friends who are willing to say what's on their minds while taking turns at playing Captain of a wild machine that they have tamed. It's about the company of a compatible group, almost always ancient males who can freely talk about their operations, their impotency, heart disturbances, incontinence, and prostate difficulties while also solving the problems of the world.

It's about sometimes getting a knockout chick to join us, even though this means being on our better behavior, and avoiding medical ailments. Their presence raises our blood pressures just enough to avoid damage. I get big points when I can induce a young beauty like Jeannie or Chip to come along, but it's even pleasant to have one of our wives, or the widow of a lost shipmate come along. They usually bring some special goodies along to feed our faces.

It's about groping our way back home through a suddenly engulfing fog by hugging the shore and enduring the amplified yells of life guards telling us to move away from the beach – our only visible landmark. Sure, we have a GPS aboard, which displays the breakwater at the Harbor entrance vis-a-vis our present position. But, I don't trust these new-fangled navigation aids, even thought they can determine your position within 10 – 20 feet. I turn tail and run when the fog sets in // and generally beat it to our slip. Otherwise, my blood pressure rises dangerously. Is it no wonder that I named several of my boats, "Poulet de la Mer", -Deux", and -Trois"?

On our Columbia 36, Sea Toy, in October, 2007, at King Harbor

It's about Pat and me organizing 'Limburger Sails' with my sometimes boat patron, Rim, and his wife, Lily. They, from the beginning, and me only lately, love the stinky cheese that we do not dare use in our homes due to the overpowering residual smell. But, on the high seas, the odor dissipates readily in the breeze and the other crew can sit up-wind. Rim, who from the time I leased his Catalina '38 and later his Ranger '33, was then known as "the owner of Bob's boat". He and Lily bring the cheese and the authentic rye bread that they get at the Alpine Village, and we bring the onion slices and the wine. We usually bring some Brie for the others. These are soul satisfying excursions. Wine and beer are swilled.

It's also about where you sail. In the 60's, when we regularly trailed our Venture '24 from our home in Claremont to Alamitos Bay in the L.A. harbor. We not only made the trip to Avalon or Twin Harbors on Catalina Island, about 33 and 25 miles from the Redondo Marina, but we also trailed it to Santa Barbara, where daughter Bette was going to UCSB; and on forays to San Diego and to the Salton Sea.

In the '70s, we trailed our 16 foot Demon behind our Volkswagon Campmobile to all the main lakes in Iowa; Lake Perry near Kansas University; to the Lake of the Ozarks; and twice to California to camp at Newport Dunes. On the first such sojourn, wanting to show the kids a true phenomenon, we visited White Sands on the way. As we pulled up to the gate, I jokingly asked the girl attendant "Which way to the beach and lake?" She was aghast.

In the '80s, with bigger boats now available, Rim and I started our 'home and home' tradition of playing hooky from our jobs at TRW at 3p.m. on Wednesday afternoons; alternating between his Catalina '38 and my Mariner '31 ketch. We took many trips to Long Beach harbor, and in Catalina moored in coves all around the Island. Once we traveled from Avalon to San Diego, via a rest stop in Oceanside. We made the big leg at night – my first experience at night sailing. It was glorious! I learned that instead of gluing your eyes to the compass to maintain course, you could fix on a star and its angular relation to the main mast. For an hour at a time, keeping the angle the same, you could steer in a relaxed manner and enjoy the night air and quiet. Then, you had to make a new 'fix', since the earth was turning relative to the star you were observing. In the morning, at daybreak, we saw a row of cavorting Dolphins, at least 50 of them, moving across our bow in a straight line. What a sight!

And, of course, during our travels, in Israel, Mexico, Hawaii, France, Venice, Brighton Beach – in fact whenever we were by the sea – we never missed an opportunity for a rental outing. No doubt, for me, sailing is chicken soup for the soul! The money I've invested in sheer sailing pleasure probably might otherwise have gone to a shrink.

184

Sketch courtesy of Bob Cleland – Sedona, AZ

Finally, it's about mastering the filling and dowsing of the huge magnificent colorful spinnaker sails on the '38 and the '33. I first learned about spinnakers in Iowa. My neighbor taught me the basics on his boat, and I fitted out my 16 foot Demon to carry one. Spinnakers were not allowed in the local races, since they gave an advantage to those who could fly them. So, I never learned to erect them under racing pressure, and now only work one step at a time. Being amateurs at spinnaker work, and non-racers, my latter day crews have to be painfully taught the ropes. Sometimes, these days, it is a comedy of errors, done in slow motion. Sometimes due to repacking or rigging errors, the big sail has a disastrous 'Figure 8' in it. Once, during dowsing, we momentarily lost control and a crewman had to let go of a $100 line which unsnapped itself from the sail and sank. But, when all goes smoothly; when you can run before the wind, make a spinnaker reach, and gybe the spinnaker, and then douse it without getting it wet; you get a rush of pride and know what a beautiful picture you are making to other boats and folks ashore. You feel like the king of the world!

The Salty Sea Dog And Morris, the youngest of the "Old Farts" crew

BOATS I HAVE KNOWN

As I compiled the list of sailboats I have known in preparation to writing this story, a wave of nostalgia overcame me. Ah, these noble vessels – where are they now? Are they still sharing the glory that only the briny has to offer? They all have a story to tell and each a personality of their own – and I mean to share their glory days with you.

The first opportunity to resume sailing after my teen-age summer camp experience came several years later, in 1942, during my first year at Cornell. At Freshman Camp – a one week pre-semester séance where you got to meet your fellow frosh and various faculty and BMOCs – I met and befriended a townsgirl whose family owned Ithaca's biggest department store. We were compatible and dated throughout our freshman year. Before the winter cold set in, she checked me out on her well equipped *Lightning* sailboat, the "Nancy". Lightnings are roomy 18 foot sloops that carry a spinnaker. They are ideal for day sailing with a crew of two or three, but are a bit too bargy for serious racing. She taught me the ropes and by the time spring sailing was possible on Lake Cayuga, I had become competent. We enjoyed weekend outings on the lake, and as summer came about, we ventured up the lake and camped out in coves Saturday nights. Although our serious dating lasted a little over a year, we continued to be friends. Her parents took a liking to me, and had no problem with me asking them for permission to take out the boat, with or without their daughter, during the remainder of my stay far above Cayuga's rippling waters. The Lightning was a fine boat on which to learn the niceties, but because we did not race, left me lacking some of the finer points. These deficiencies later became apparent during later regattas in Iowa.

My service days during WWII were not without sailing adventures. While fearlessly fighting the war at Navy Pier in Chicago in 1944, I would appear in uniform at one of the several yacht clubs on the north shore and – heartily welcomed - hitch a ride on some magnificent sloops and ketches that were berthed there, as soon as Spring sailing started. The owners loved to accommodate servicemen who were risking their lives in their defense by venturing, unarmed and unafraid, into the fleshpots of the Loop. Sailing on Lake Michigan was a whoop! It could get very rough and reducing the size of the main sail by reefing was quite normal.

But my best sailing times during the Great War occurred in 1945 on Buzzards Bay, near Falmouth on Cape Cod, on a wonderful 22 foot 'Star' boat of which I was a third owner. I was working mostly on the flight line at NAS Otis Field. I was the plane captain for Lt. Comdr. Tommy Blackburn's F4U fighter, which had 5 Rising Sun meatball emblems on it – yes, he was an Ace and an Admiral's son, to boot. The job's working hours were from 4 a.m. to 11a.m., at which time Tommy and his two wingmen returned from their training or sub-spotting missions. My afternoons were generally free. Two flight line buddies and I bought the Star for $500 in the early Spring, and we sailed it most every day, getting to its mooring by bus from the base. It was a great boat, requiring a crew of two and some skill since, being an Olympic-class racing machine, it carried relatively large sails and was very tender. There were ankle straps in the bottom of the small cockpit, and you spent most of the time hiked out with your fanny on the outer edge of the spacious gunwales and your abs groaning. But the sailing was glorious. We crewed for each other, or my WAC lady friend sometimes joined me when she could arrange for off-duty. The beauty of it was that just before we shipped out, we sold her for $700. It was named "Speedy" – and it was!

When Patti and I, freshly married in 1959, moved into a rental house in Claremont, California, we did two crucial things: We bought a huge second hand Ford station wagon with a rack on its top and a used green no-named Lehman 12 cat-rigged sailboat, which the two of us could manhandle on to the car's roof. Nearby was the 'fabulous'' 3-5 acre Puddingstone Dam lake on the west edge of Pomona, which was hospitable to small boats and had a nice beach for the kids. The Lehman was like a big bathtub, but accommodated both parents and two kids in its ample belly. Its mast mounted well forward in the bow, and you had to duck as the boom went by on a tack. It was not very comfortable and had to be sailed straight up. But, it was a good ship to teach the older kids and a good way to spend a weekend day in the summer. In a few years they could take it out themselves when we took it down to Newport Beach for a day at the beach.

In the late 60's, we took a big step. We bought a Venture 24, the first "Poulet de la Mer", for about $2500. It was trailerable, with a retractable centerboard, and came with all the amenities: a head, a galley; and bunks for 5. Its mast was easily stepped using a pulley device. It trailed nicely behind our station wagon. It even sailed reasonably well – certainly good enough for the normal day sailing outings, although we did get it to Catalina on two occasions. Normally, we took it down to Alamitos Bay in Long Beach Harbor where there was a large launch ramp facility. We had to go under the bridge over Pacific Coast Highway before we could step the mast. The launch and recovery operations usually took and hour, and were always an adventure.

The Lehman 12 a beach on the shores of Puddingstone circa 1960.
David, Bette, and Patti are ready to challenge the high seas

Once the outboard motor crapped out at a crucial recovery phase and I had to jump into the water to direct the bow onto the half submerged trailer. On another occasion, we noted fuel dripping from // the car's gas tank as we pulled out of the water.

We immediately took the rig into the filling station next to the ramp, unhooked the boat, and had the tank sealed. I was sure I had re-hooked correctly, but as we pulled out of the station Pat yelled, "Where's the boat!" Sure enough, it was sitting back at the station, only a slight roll from where I though I had re-hooked it. Once, after we had reentered the bay from the outer harbor, son David inexplicably fell overboard. We had a hell of a time getting him back aboard as we had no ship's ladder. Again, we ran aground on a sandy reef in Upper Newport Bay, and would still be there if I hadn't remembered that all I needed to do was to lift the centerboard in order to free us. But, we had many great sails on the Venture, from Santa Barbara to San Diego. We regretfully sold it when I wrongly, it turns out, adjudged that it was too large for the lakes in Iowa, which would be our next home.

A faded picture of a Venture 24 launch adventure. Our big Ford station wagon was a dark blue color. Not sure of the launch site – maybe Santa Barbara

On our way to Ames, Iowa to take my new job at Iowa State University in 1971, we stopped to visit friends in Kansas City and saw an Ad in the newspaper for a sailboat-with-trailer that looked might it might fill the bill on Iowa's then small lakes. On inspection, it turned out to be a '*Demon*' – a 16 foot, 2-4 person boat. It had been fabricated inside a nearby well-lit limestone cave 'city' in Independence. The cave's temperature stayed the same throughout the year and the humidity was just right for fiberglass lay-ups. The same outfit made the more popular smaller '*Flying Junior*' and the beamier '*Sweet 16*' – both widely used in the mid-West, along with the more ubiquitous *M-Scows*.

The Demon was immediately dubbed "Poulet de la Mer, II", in honor of the late-lamented Venture. We soon found out that it was designed as racing boat; one that lifted up 'on a plane' after reaching about 3 knots, whereupon – its wetted surface being greatly reduced thereby reducing drag – it took off like a bat out of hell. It came equipped with two jibs and a spinnaker*, a "Cunningham" lash up that adjusted the shape of the main sail, and means of controlling the fore and aft stay tension which bent the mast to allow more speed

*The large, beautiful multicolored balloon-like sail that is used in races when running with the wind at your back

if you knew what you were doing. The center board could be partially retracted and the rudder could be drastically shortened. Both of the latter features were to reduce friction area when running before the wind. Like the Star boat, it had ankle straps and, we soon found out, required lots of hiking out. I later found out that the competition spent the winter at the gym strengthening their abdominal muscles.

The Demon with its faithful campmobile 'tug' as seen in 1972 visiting the Petrified Forest in Arizona on the way back from a summer visit in California

We couldn't wait to try it out. We were going to show these mid-western farmers what real sophisticated ocean sailors could do. The closest lake with a launch ramp was the small "Little Wall" lake, and we had a nice windy day for our first try. Armed with a six pack, we decided we would go to the far side of the lake, have a picnic and return. We got started on a reach and the acceleration figuratively jerked our heads back. The boat immediately rose up on its plane, a phenomenon that neither of us had ever experienced before, and we barreled into the far shore, having barely managed to lift the centerboard and bend the rudder up before we grounded. We felt we had escaped death by either drowning or impact with the far shore.

After a few more less exciting outings, we learned the rudiments of lake sailing. Finally, we thought we were ready to compete in the weekend races on the newly developed 'Big Creek' lake. On our first race, we watched in amazement as the other boats, driven by sailors whom we perceived to be cow herders or corn detasselers, steamed by us even though we had made a good start. The inland sailors were always making adjustments which were beyond our ken. They pulled on Cunninghams, bent their masts, lifted their centerboards, knew the quirks of wind shift due to local topography, and performed other bewildering feats to get more out of their boats. It took months to learn how the sail our boat competitively.

Our next-door neighbor had a 22 foot *Thistle* and was one of the great mid-West sailors. He taught me how to operate during races. When I skippered the Demon with my wife as crew, we usually came in second because it was an intrinsically fast ship. But when he ran our boat and I crewed for him, nobody – any size at all – could beat us. He knew exactly which lines to loosen or tighten and how to prepare for a wind shift which he knew would be caused by shore-side valleys and hills, and how to take the wind away from the competition by proper boat positioning. Who says it's the boat, not the skipper?

Races were wet. You usually could depend on at least one capsize per race due to sudden wind shifts or gusts. We got very adept at quickly righting the boat and getting back under weigh, even though the cockpit was filled with water. Once gaining headway, we then opened little bottom 'Venturi-effect' vents and the boat soon drained itself. It was exciting and fun sailing – and I've never lost my admiration for the inland sailors! They are indeed master sailors and have much to show ocean sailors.

On our relocation drive back to Hermosa Beach, California in 1980, we towed the Demon to Missouri and into the cave whence it was born. We sadly sold it under consignment to the manufacturer, to start a new sailing life on bigger and dryer boats. Thus, in the Fall of 1980, began the saga of ocean sailing that continues to this day and marked the eventual emergence of "The Old Farts Wednesday Afternoon Sailing Club and Discussion Society". The difference between lake sailing and ocean sailing immediately became apparent. On the Pacific, the wind always blows in the same direction and wind shifts are rare. The wind is not affected by topography and the weather is almost always good the year round. But, some of the hectic excitement is missing and everything happens in slow motion compared to the frantic mid-West race scene. Most important, the big sloops never capsize!

The first ship of the new Western fleet was a *Catalina '27* – then the most popular boat on the West Coast. As soon as I became half partner, for $3000 as I recall, it was renamed "Poulet de la Mer, III" by agreement with my new partner. He allowed the otherwise, by long tradition, 'no-no' name change since, wanting to get out of the boat business, he planned to sell his half to a new partner. So, after a while, Bob D. – a complete stranger - became my new partner and we lived in relative peace for 4 years. He hated the name, even though he never was quite sure of what it meant. Poulet III served us well and carried 5 passengers comfortably in its cockpit, and slept up to six – though not comfortably for the 2-5 day jaunts to Catalina. It had a crazy Swedish two-cylinder Albin 10 horsepower engine which burned either diesel or gas, having a moderately high compression ratio and spark plugs. Unfortunately, it wasn't equipped for a spinnaker, a sail I am very fond of because it takes some knowledge to deploy and looks so good both from the boat and from shore. It was a fine day-sailer and I began to organize crews who learned the ropes and took turns at the helm. We also established a route for our 3 hour sails that remains immutable to this day – making my wife observe that it is not necessary to steer, the boat knows where to go. It was on the '27 that we learned the joy of spotting the California Gray Whales as they headed South during the winter, then coming close to land at the end point of the Palos Verdes peninsula. In those days, they often cavorted near your boat – much to our delight. Now-a-days, they seem to avoid the sightseers by swimming on the far side of Catalina Island on their way South for the winter. We also spotted playful Dolphins many times. Most importantly, our crews learned to know each other better via our discussions on matters which were important to us. We generally decided political, environmental, scientific, and 'going to war' questions and drank beer (now, alas, a no-no for me due to weight and diabetes concerns).

In 1984, both partners and their wives fell in love with a *Mariner '31* ketch that one day came up for sale near our slip. We sold the Catalina '27 and bought the ketch, with my partner's proviso that it not become the 'IV'. His last name starting with the letters DUN, we settled on the "BRODUN" and with great pride began a refurbishment program. It was a handsome ship – it looked like what a real sailboat should look like. Although the hull was fiberglass, the lay-up was such that it looked planked. It came with a walk-on bowsprit, a two level cabin, round, openable port holes, and lots of teak deck work. Its masts were wooden and its lines old-time traditional. It was a boat you could be proud of and one you knew could be used to retrace its steps from Taiwan, where it was built.

It needed work, and I, Patti, and crewman Myron turned to. We sanded, teak oiled, painted, and even replaced a rotted-out portion of the starboard foredeck; plywood, fiberglass and all. The final touch, financed by me since my partner was not interested, was to buy a used spinnaker sail, and outfit the ship with the spinnaker halyard and top-of-the-mast swivel block, blocks and runners for the spinnaker pole downhaul and topping lift, and, triumph of triumphs, an authentic wooden spinnaker pole which Myron and I constructed from scratch, once having found a suitable pole at a second hand shop in San Pedro.

The Ketch "Brodun" – a 'Mariner 31' – sporting a classy wooden spinnaker pole and much TLC

We enjoyed several years of great sailing on the BRODUN, including trips to foreign ports such as Long Beach, Alamitos Bay, and Avalon, Twin Harbors, and all around Catalina Island. We used the ketch every other Wednesday on our 'hooky' sails, and Rim's Catalina '38 on the alternate Wednesdays. On windy days, the ketch sailed nicely on just the jib and mizzen sail. But you got the warm feeling of sturdiness in any kind of weather – kind of like the difference between a Chevy and a Caddy. It came with a huge 50 horsepower Cummings diesel engine, also a reassuring factor if fast maneuvers were called for. It was a great boat, and my wife and I still wonder why we sold out to our partner and kick ourselves for doing so.

Partner Bob D, who lived in Pasadena, wanted to move the boat to Cabrillo Beach in Long Beach harbor – a site more convenient for him. He said we should buy him out or vice-versa, and offered a very fair price for our share. Knowing that I could make a favorable lease deal with Rim for use of his Catalina '38, which he was using less and less, we decided to cede the ketch. In retrospect, this proved to be a less than wise decision in view of subsequent events, which twice made me a proverbial 'Wandering Jew' in search of a leasable boat.

But, the 3-4 years association with the first 'boat that Rim bought for me' proved to very happy sailing ones. The '38, designed as a combination long range racing boat and a day sailer, was rugged and fast. It always exceeded 5 knots in any direction and any wind. It was equipped with a huge spinnaker, and we had many 'Keystone Kop' adventures when we flew it – but the reward to our pride of seamanship when it flew gracefully was magnificent! Its large cockpit held up to 7-8 passengers in relative comfort. It was well equipped and made trips to Catalina or Long Beach for the weekend very pleasurable.

Rim's Catalina 38 'Lilyte' which I 'rented'

One day Rim said that he and Lily had decided to sell the 'Lilyte', if they could get a reasonable price for it. They recognized that they, themselves, were hardly using it all and were not attending their yacht club affairs anymore. They opted out of both. They found a buyer for the '38, and it was shipped off to Australia for refurbishment and resale at a large profit. But, it left me without a boat, at an age when I wanted to own as little as possible. I had a few friends in mind that had boats but didn't seem to use them very much of late. After a few weeks of sailing deprivation, I cajoled two partners, Budd C. and John S. – retired friends from TRW – to take me on as a lessee.

Their boat was a *Catalina '30*; a considerable upgrade from the no longer being built '27, which it had now replaced in popularity. But, for the first time, we were faced with a boat equipped with a dreaded 'Dodger'. This is a windowed windshield which has a canvas over-cover to delay the sun's devastating long term effect of discoloring and making brittle the translucent windows. The windows themselves always needed cleaning of water spots with much the same soapy spray as is used to clean house windows. The damned dodger caused us to spend an extra five minutes at both ends of a cruise. On the other hand, on cold winter days, it was nice to sit in its lee. Otherwise it was a pain in the ass. Moreover, one of the owners was extremely fussy about boat protocol and maintenance, and bullied us to keep everything spotless. The Old Farts never felt 'at home' in the year-plus that it provided us with our twice weekly jaunts. The '30 sailed well and had a comfortable cockpit. It had no spinnaker and not a lot of character. When the partners decided they no longer wanted to sail and sold it, none of us shed a tear.

Before the sale was consummated, I saw an ad posted at the entry gate to our slip seeking a quarter partner in a *Columbia '36*, an elderly boat that appeared to be in good shape. Despite ownership by 3 partners, it hardly ever appeared to go out. I approached the lead partner and proposed a lease deal similar to the $250 per month one I had on the '30, but spicing up my monthly rent figure with a good-will cash payment of $1000, to be returned if after 6 months either party wanted out. He kind of balked, telling me that one of the partners lived in Sacramento and was assigned the boat 10 days at a time every month I told him I thought I could work something out with him, and we agreed to meet for breakfast in Hermosa next week when he would be down. As I walked up to the table, I saw that the Sacramento partner was an old buddy from TRW. The deal went through and I hardly missed a sailing beat.

With my money infusion, the Columbia was repainted, adorned with new canvas, and thoroughly overhauled. Despite having no spinnaker and having a dreaded dodger, the boat was a joy to operate and the atmosphere with the partners much more relaxed. It was a rugged, dependable ship with a very large cockpit and an autopilot and other amenities. The year and a half that we operated it was a pleasant span, and would have remained so, had not Rim and Lily seen the error of their previous ways.

My friend from La Jolla, Howard, and his wife had a beautiful 38 foot *Cheoy Lee* ketch, the 'Harmony', which even had a wood burning fireplace. They were having trouble finding crew and finally decided that they, too, would go out of the business and priced it for $56,000. Several of the crew joined us in going South for a trial ride on the Harmony, and all fell in love with it. We decided to form a cabal of four, including Rim and Lily, and, at my advice, made Howard a low-ball offer which I thought he might accept. He didn't and sold to another party at his asking price, thereby making everyone sore at me for being such a tightwad. The truth was twofold: I really thought Howard would sell short, since money was not his problem, and I really wasn't anxious to become a boat owner again. But, out of the carnage, came some good:

The 'Sea Toy' – a Columbia '36 that could handle up to 7 crew comfortably

Rim and Lil realized that they missed the pride of ownership of a sailing vessel. So, they decided to 'buy me' another boat, as long as I assured them that I would drop out of my Columbia '36 cartel. Rim and I searched around and soon the *Ranger '33* "Argo" was purchased, with the new owners knowing full well that it was a 'fixer-upper' that would require as much money for fixing up as they paid for it. But Rim, a master builder, looked forward to the challenge entailed in the needed woodwork, electrical work, and painting and I looked forward to sailing it and once more running crazy spinnaker drills.

The Argo had obviously been used as a racing machine. Consequently, it had no drag producing and time consuming dodger. Its halyards and reefing, boom vang, spinnaker pole topping lift and downhaul, and Cunningham lines were all controlled from the cockpit, as was back-stay tension for use during spinnaker runs. But everything needed refurbishment and none of the instruments, including the ship-to-shore radio, worked. The cushions, both cabin and cockpit, had to be replaced. The engine needed overhaul and the gas tank needed purging. It was a mess – but as soon as we could get it sailing, it proved to be a gem! It needed only topside painting to achieve complete respectability and safety.

And the sailing was great! We have had major adventures. We were sailing on a 'quirky' wind day. We had to motor out quite a way to pick up a steady, but not big, wind on a relatively flat sea. Before you knew it, we were suddenly hit by a once-in-a-lifetime line squall which came out of nowhere. We were almost knocked over, and everybody was peeing in their pants, while trying not to show the panic. The rail was in the water and the mainsheet block was hard against a protruding bolt head precluding letting out the main sail to dump some of the wind. I adjudged that the crew aboard was not capable of reefing the main sail in the dangerous situation we were in. I could not send anyone up on the foredeck to facilitate the reef without concern for their safely. We did manage to furl up the jib, which gave enough relief to allow us to skim back into port safely. You can bet that in the next two sails, we conducted man-overboard drills, reefing drills and fixed the main sheet jam problem.

I was glad we did this because we later found ourselves in another quandary – my fault for not knowing that two red flags, which I had never seen before, on the Harbor Master's pole meant not just 'small boat warning' (one red flag never fazed us before) but 'gale warning'. I had known it was windy, so reefed the main sail and did not unfurl the jib before we left the protection of the harbor breakwater. What I didn't know was the size of the sea! As soon as we left the harbor entrance, we encountered 10 to 12 foot waves coming in at high frequency. I headed into them for a wild pitching ride trying to figure out how to turn tail safely without being caught sideways in a trough and knocked over. Finally, I found a period of lower wave activity, and jibed around quickly and headed back to safety.

We started making spinnaker runs as soon as all the necessary gear was in place. It was hairy at first. Two runs, including the last one, were successful. Crew error, mostly mine, were responsible for the two bad drills; one disastrous though not life threatening. The first boo-boo was almost unbelievable! I mistook one of the 'clews' or bottom corners of the triangular-shaped spinnaker for the 'head' or top of the sail when I attached the lines. Thus, instead of deploying right side up, there it was – in all its glory – sideways. I hoped nobody on land or sea noticed.

The later 'disaster' drill resulted in the whole spinnaker ending up in the water with the halyard that was attached to the 'head' of the sail having been pulled out through its pulley on the top of the mast as the sail, inflated with wind, flew away to its watery fate. The goof started by my noticing that I had forgotten to release one of the clew lines that I had tied to the boat's forward rail. As the sail was being hauled up, I yelled to the hauler to 'stop! and 'untie the knot'. Apparently, he loosely wrapped the spinnaker halyard that he was pulling on around a cleat. The sudden inflation of the sail must have unwound his loose wrap and away went the sail followed by the halyard, whose bitter end I had forgotten to secure to the mast. We gingerly successfully recovered all the soaked gear intact. Back in our slip, we used the mainsail halyard to raise the wet spinnaker sail in order to dry it our before repacking it. Naturally, a gust of wind hit and blew it over our neighbor's boat, and broke his radio antenna. It had been a bad day!

This is the kind of action you should expect, even after a lifetime of sailing in boats of all kinds. You would think one would learn by experience – but that apparently is not the case. On the Saturday following the wild Wednesday 'gale warning' ride, the wind and the sea remained high. I called off the sail. None of the crew complained. But, as I wrote this on that Saturday, at home instead of being on the high seas, I wondered if I would still be sailing three years from now – when I'm 80?*

---

*And the answer is YES! But, I'm back in the Columbia '36, since Rim sold the Ranger and is now, in 2008, into a C&C 38. My crew has therefore made me 'Admiral' of the two boat fleet.

THE 'OLD FARTS' SAGA

We didn't start out as "Old Farts'. In the beginning, when I first acquired half partnership in the Catalina 27 shortly after our permanent move to Hermosa Beach in 1980, I had no crew. New friend, Myron, a retiree but still spry, became my first regular crew member. Gradually, other regulars were added to 'man' the Wednesday afternoon 'playing hooky' sails and the legit Saturday sails. The mid week daylight-savings–time sails were usually crewed by people from work who could safely leave TRW at around 3pm without fear of recrimination. Mostly these were people who, like me, periodically worked several 7 day, 10 hour-per-day weeks per year on proposals, at no extra compensation. We had a clear conscience, feeling the company owed this stolen time to us.

The Saturday sailors were composed of social or business guests, worker friends from other companies, along with one or two regulars who knew how to run the boat. But, by the time I retired from TRW in 1988 and could sail twice a week completely guilt-free, the regular crew had mysteriously aged and, by our own acclamation, became "Old Farts". In this saga, I mean to tell you a little about most of them – so you can better visualize what our seagoing conversations were about. In the broad outlook, our repetitive day sailing is really just about camaraderie, since we most always followed the same over water route.

The early crews, in addition to my wife, consisted of Myron; and Rim, the 'Owner of Bob's (later) Boat(s)' with whom I had an amicable loose leasing agreement for his earlier Catalina '38 and then for his Ranger '33; and Vic, who now lives downstairs from me, and Charlie, both of whom took up golf in their dotage and no longer sail; Ellen, who worked with me on my TRW Affirmative Action Committee, plus Morris. All but Myron were co-workers at T.R. Wonderful. As time went by, we added Len, a Russian émigré from our Hermosa Beach Town house complex and then Mike, an English bloke also a town house neighbor who 'paparazzied' and wrote for the tabloids.

Around retirement time, when twice-a-week sails became de-rigueur all year round, we added Bill, a good friend from TRW who had been too serious to play hooky during our working years, and our former super-boss, Bob W. Later, Bill brought his work friend, Ken, aboard and I added Bob S, another 'civilian' from our town house complex. Other minor players came and went. Best of these, emotionally, were the lovelies that we could lure aboard to raise our moribund pulse rates: Chip, the sassy DELTA flight attendant from our town house area, and Jeannie, the beautiful zaftig lady engineer who was my next-door neighbor in Redondo. When they were aboard, all talk of enlarged prostates and ailing hearts ceased, to be replaced by topics of more current interest.

As I write this in 2002, most of the old farts, including me, are really old and some are ailing, but still manage to drag their asses aboard. The regulars, now that Bill died a couple of years ago and Mike moved North to Sutters Mill, are Myron, Rim, Ken, Bob's S and W, and Jim, a callow youth engineer I met while on sabbatical at Hughes, who barely qualifies for old fartness, although he recently retired. Len and Morris show up when they are not otherwise occupied. Morris took up flying a few years ago and now is engrossed in this pursuit, unless the weather is unsuitable. Len, newly divorced, has his two girls every other weekend. Wives and widows occasionally join us too, for limburger sails or ash spreading ceremonies.

A late development a couple of years ago upset our bliss! The stark reality of living in a capitalistic society reared up! Rim's money manager wife, Lily, the true 'owner' of Bob's boat, the Ranger '33 "ARGO", has objected to us calling ourselves 'The Old Farts'. She wanted to add some class to the old vessel and insisted that we now call ourselves "The Old Argonauts" – not a bad name, although you must admit it lacks a certain 'je ne sais quoi'. But, behind her back, we still call ourselves old farts and I'm sure Lily knows it. We can live with it.

Of the regular crew, Myron is taciturn and senior, both in age – he is 5 months older than me – and in crew membership time. We met him shortly after we moved to Hermosa Beach. He and his deceased wife, Pat – a former mayor of Hermosa, a 'macher' in the HB Friends of the Library, and an author of two historical books about Hermosa, mentored us as new additions to the "HB Friends of the Arts", of which Myron was then President. We soon found out that they were former boat owners, still remained affiliated with local yacht club, and wonder-of–wonders had lived in France the same time we were there. In fact our sons were in the same senior class at the American School of Paris. Myron's family emigrated to France under the aegis of Hughes Aircraft. He was a satellite field engineer working liaison with a French communications company. After returning to the USA, he retired to watch over his several low cost housing ventures, which continue to net him an income far in excess of his past work-a-day salary. Before his knees went bad, making his mobility in the boat painful, he was the 'clean-up' man. He took the helm as we re-entered the harbor under motor and did the maneuvering necessary for the more agile to bring down the main sail and put on the sail cover and neaten up the ship. I re-commandeered the helm to bring the ship into our slip, though Myron occasionally did this task, too. Now, alas, Myron is barely mobile and has difficulty getting on and off the boat. But, he rarely missed a sailing day until, in 2006, his knees gave out and he could no longer climb aboard or off.

Bob W., the other crewman not ready for America Cup challenges, was a delight at sea. He was witty, smart and loquacious, with a biting, snide and sarcastic, humor which I enjoyed, but which turned some people off. When I came to TRW, he was a Vice President and headed up my Space and Technology Group. He went to Cal Tech as an undergrad and MIT for grad school. I was protected from his idiosyncrasies at work by my boss, also a VP, whom he ragged unmercifully. Bill and I met Bob W. at a technical gathering after we had all retired, and had such a pleasant conversation that we inveigled him to join the crew. I also convinced him to start teaching UCLA extension courses in astronautics and loaned him some of my USC class notes to get him started. During his first sails, he just sat and enjoyed the company. Once he finally took the wheel, he really got bitten by the sailing bug, and is now a competent and eager sailor. Both Myron and Bob are big men – I imagine they were around 6'3" or 6'4" in their prime. Bob got pretty well banged up, mostly as a result of his continued proclivity of weekly road motorcycle jaunts with one of his sons over steep and primitive mountain and desert trails. He could be counted on to have one serious accident a year, which slowed him down for a while. He walked painfully with a cane and needed leg braces. A veteran of three back operations, a heart by-pass, and several other less critical procedures, his admirable credo is, "What the hell, if it kills me, that's the way I want to go"! In the meantime, his wife despaired. All these ailments caught up to him in 2007, and we painfully dragged him aboard and off into his wheel-chair. He died in July, 2008, about two weeks after his last sail.

Rim is the 'owner of my boat', and is a remarkable and talented engineer and artisan/builder. His forte is design of airplanes and spacecraft. He has an intuitive feel for problem solving and lives in the three-dimensional world where only visionary designers dwell. He has designed, built and flown six airplanes and one glider. He is also a glider pilot. He makes beautiful bronze pieces and is a master worker in wood and metal. He recently finished making two harps and one Lithuanian-type lute, using lovely wood combinations. He has also made spinnaker pole holders, new cabin entry steps, equipment-holding boxes, and made wood repair pieces for the ARGO. He likes the idea of owning, working on, and fixing up a boat more than sailing; and he also likes and attends hot jazz - the music that I so love - seances. He and Lily also like to see that I have a good boat to sail, and let me lease theirs when I don't have a boat of my own. What's not to like?

I first met Rim when he was assigned to a spacecraft study program that I was managing. It was then that we noted our similar likes, and started the Wednesday Afternoon Sailing Club that had the name "Old Farts" appended to it. We would alternate weeks for boat usage; one week in his Catalina '38, next week in my Mariner '31 ketch. When my partner bought out my half of the ketch, I started on the lease deal with Rim. After he sold his boat several years later, I made similar leasing arrangements until he 'bought the Ranger for me'. Rim was and remains the best possible landlord a sailor could ever ask for.

Some of the 'Old Farts' at my 80ᵗʰ birthday bash: himself, Bob W. And wife, Anne, Bea and Budd C. and Myron. Also at party were Jim P., Bob S., Len O., Rim K., Ken H., Jeannie R. Missing were Bill's widow, Jean D. (sick) and 'Chip' T. (her husband Paul made it)

We all miss Bill. In the things he knew, and he covered a considerable swath in the fields of control systems and basic physics, he was the smartest guy we all knew. To this day, when one of us poses a technical question that no one else can answer, we all say, "Where the hell is Bill when we need him"! Bill had many interests. He played clarinet in symphony orchestra, played badminton in the club next to his house, and was a serious mountain trail hiker. All this in spite of having suffered a very serious heart attack when he was a mere 57. He got his PhD in Electrical Engineering from Cal Tech, and I got him teaching for UCLA extension, and urged him to successfully apply for a fellowship to teach as a Visiting Professor at the Technion in Haifa. He had great stories to tell of his experiences as a bush pilot and a world traveler. He made the train trip across the Soviet Union from Moscow to Vladivostok. He and his wife were taken ill in Malasia while visiting in-laws there. He had 4 kids, three of whom have their PhD's. And, he was a very good sailor. When, a year after his death from congestive heart failure, we took his ashes out to sea, I was in good voice, especially on "Flow Gently Sweet Afton", despite the tears in my eyes.

There was a period when it seemed we were performing the ash dispersion ceremony every other month.
Now, surprisingly, 'business' has fallen off lately. Rim, a relative youngster, will take out mine.
(Sketch courtesy of Bob Cleland)

Ken, Jim, and Bob S. became the 'kids' of the crew, although Ken was nearing 70. I cannot take the boat out without at least one of them or Morris as crew. Ken had very little sailing experience when he joined us, but by now, having successfully weathered some bad storms and gusts without panicking while he was at the wheel, is an increasingly competent crewman. Like Bob W., he went to MIT and worked on a myriad of spacecraft programs at TRW. He is the first of us to get prostate cancer - though all of us have enlarged prostates and have to get up to pee 2-3 times per night. He studied the variety of possible treatments and selected the proton bombardment method, which – in its short documented track record – has produced complete cures with no follow-on treatment necessary. He had to undergo 40 radiation treatments – 5 a week – at Loma Linda, 70 miles away. He thus missed many Wednesday sails as well as the chance to win $10 for the first whale sighting of the season. In 2006, Ken moved to a retirement community North of San Diego.

I met Jim during my sabbatical year at Hughes Aircraft in the late 70's. We were drawn to each other by a mutual love of sailing – he had a Newport '27 then – and a similarity of political leanings. Jim is an excellent and fearless sailor, though the villain in the previously described spinnaker set-to caused by a mistake that I made in not untying a key spinnaker connection line from the front rail. Jim made up for the boo-boo by finding a co-worker at Hughes/Boeing, a former student of mine, who we hauled up to the top of the mast to restring the halyard, thereby saving $80 that the K.H. Marine Center boat yard would have charged. Jim has partially replaced Bill as a fount of knowledge. He has a very analytical mind and is a peerless system engineer. Unlike Bill, who had the facts neatly arranged in his head, Jim is expert on the web – and can find the damnedest information there to report back to us.

Bob S. is also a former boat owner and fearless sailor. He advocates going out in any weather, since he carries a GPS receiver which has Redondo Beach harbor breakwater maps on display along with 'present position'. Because the accuracy can purportedly be measured small numbers of feet, he does not fear the sudden onset of fog. Me, I don't trust these new-fangled machines, and turn tail and run for home as soon as we sight the mist curling around the Palos Verdes peninsula. Bob, like Jim, is adept on the PC and is the arbiter of many cyberspace questions. Of late, since his retirement from the FAA, he and his wife have taken to travel with gusto. He is a great photographer and brings his truly superior pictures on the cruises. He has slowed down a bit, what with prostate removal and heart problems, but still can do foredeck work.

It would not be fair to omit Ellen – the only female crew member, albeit from an almost forgotten bygone age of early '80's sailing. Another TRW colleague, she was a system analyst and a strong feminist. She didn't mind espousing her position to an all-male crew although often met with derision. She was a fair-to-middling sailor, but ultimately, because of her officiousness, she fell out of favor and, by popular request, I gradually stopped inviting her.

Not so for Len and Morris, two of the holdovers from mid-'80s to mid '90s sailing. Len is from Odessa and is a software engineer. He is our resident political iconoclast – an outspoken, but not far right-wing - Republican, in a boatload of Democrats or moderates. How he got that way is a mystery to me. I first met him in our hot tub in Hermosa and, I recall, took pity on him being a stranger in a new world. It turned out I had no need for this empathy. Len has learned to take full advantage of the American way and is a sage investor. He has managed to bring members of his family from Odessa and Baku to Southern California and has mightily assisted in making them independent. While we were in Israel the first time, he took over our ketch and helped with its expenses. We later used the boat to carry out his Mother's ashes. She had crewed with us, having been a sailor in the Russian Navy during WW II. He also has his own boat on a trailer, a dreaded stink pot that he uses for water skiing. But he doesn't want to use it in anything but fresh water.

Despite Myron's and my 'hazardous' duty during the Great War, Morris is really the only real Navy man among us. He served on a destroyer, doing real sea duty after the Korean fracas. He was a navigation officer, and early-on would bring a sextant aboard and demonstrate how he could find our position. He now eschews the old tools and brings his GPS aboard to do dueling matches with Bob S's. Morris is a great foredeck sailor, and has done such great things as unsnaggle a twisted spinnaker from a disheartening 'Figure 8' configuration into its full beauty. He now keeps us abreast of happenings in the light plane field; and has just bought his second plane; obtained his instrument rating, and is ready for another cross country flight.

When Morris flew us to Sedona to visit the Freres Cleland,
Bob, the artist in the family, understood Morris' predicament

206

It was sad day when, in 2001, Mike and his wife pulled up stakes to try something very new in Northern California. For one thing, Mike, a true Irishman, but from Yorkshire, sang an unusually touching 'Danny Boy' at ash strewing ceremonies. But he was best beloved as our intermediary with the fabulous world of Hollywood and the stars. Most of the time, he worked as a stringer for the London Times tabloid, working on commission. For a time, he worked as a reporter for the US 'Globe' tabloid. He got invited to all big movie star affairs and premiers as a 'foreign' pressman, and brought back wonderful stories to regale to crew. We never should have let him go!

I'll end this paean to the Old Argonauts by telling a story of recent vintage. It began with the following somewhat sad e-mail from Mike, who reports in periodically:

"To My Friends and Family:

There are times when we all wish we could do some good for our fellow human beings.

As I have become older, mellower and more aware of the virtues associated with lending a helping hand, especially to the younger members of our chaotic society, I feel better about myself, and better connected to the younger generation, and the world around me. I would like you to share in that happiness of helping the new generation that will succeed us.

To this end I am asking for your support in my latest endeavor. I have applied to adopt a set of young twins that have been orphaned by the conflicts in Eastern Europe. The twins are very concerned about their future and their ability to survive in a dangerous and competitive world, where our initial contacts and support group can make the difference between survival and abandonment.

Your financial support to get these deserving twins to the US would be appreciated. I know it is in poor taste to ask for money from friends and family, but I feel this is one of those special occasions. I know the twins, and I can assure you they are simply adorable and worthy of my and your support and generosity. I am sure they will be thankful, as well.

Just send whatever you can. Thank you for your support.

Mike
P.S. Attached is a recent photo of the twins, who will win your hearts as they have already mine."

When I downloaded the "Twins" attachment, there they were in living color!: Two beautiful, buck naked, fair haired, well endowed young ladies, very possibly sisters, sitting side-by-side on the beach, their legs bent at the knees and their arms stretched back keeping them upright. A lovely sight to see!

Will you help support these twins?

I forwarded the e-mail to the crew, noting, "Like me, you may wish to donate $2.50 per twin (from the famous song "My brother's a poor missionary; He saves young girls from sin; he'll save you a blonde for two-fifty; My God how the money rolls in!").

Me? What do I bring to the party other than organizing the twice weekly cruises? I tell stories. You've just finished reading one.

Chapter 8

ANNALS OF RETIREMENT

I am greatly enjoying my retirement and intend to live well into the eighties. There I expect to find true peace, as noted below. The stories in this Chapter reflect life in my latter years:

LIFE BEGINS AT 80!
(Author unknown)

I have good news for you -- the first 80 years are the hardest; the second 80 is a series of birthday parties. Everybody wants to carry your luggage and help you up the steps. If you forget your name or anybody else's, you need only explain that you are 80!

If you put things away and then forget where you put them and have to search for hours to find them, or if you forget what you went to the store to buy, it's all right because you are 80.

If you repeat a story two or three times in one evening, everybody expects it, for you are 80.

At 65 or 70, they expect you to retire to a little house in California and become a discontented, grumbling has - been. But if you survive until you are 80, everyone is surprised that you are alive, surprised that you can walk, surprised that you can drive a car, surprised that there are even some clear moments.

At 70, people are mad at you for everything. At 80, they forgive you for anything. If you ask me, life begins at 80!

THE 60TH REUNION

(or)

Where Were You on September 11?

The proud 177th class of Central High School in Philadelphia graduated in late January 1942, a few weeks after Pearl Harbor. We were a class of all boys, about 160 strong, and most of us had inaugurated the new building site in our sophomore year. Many came from the original building in downtown Philly. I transferred in from coed Germantown High, because of Central's excellent academic reputation and relative closeness to home via two trolley cars. It was then, and remains today, despite turning coed by forced entry in the 90's, ranked among the top twenty high schools in the country. It is the second oldest public high school, after Boston Latin, in the country and continues to award an anachronistic Congress-approved Bachelor of Arts degree upon completing school.

After graduation, we went our several ways. Many, as I, went into the service and several were killed. I stayed actively in touch with Obe, a newspaper editor and publisher with whom I had attended school from 3rd grade up; Hugh, also an aerospace engineer; and Dr. Max, a fellow Californian near neighbor who unfortunately died in his late 50's; and with the school itself via its active alumni organization newsletter which periodically listed inputs from fellow 177ers.

There may have been a 25th reunion, but I don't recall it. My first reunion was the 40th, which took place across the street from my mother's apartment on City Line Avenue near the Schuylkill River in 1982. From this excellent encounter, which whetted my appetite for more, I was able to catch up on the lives of most of my boyhood friends and schoolmates. As a result, I wrote the heart wrenching story of Stan, "The Class Failure" who, at age 57, reported himself to be "Very well, Bob, but out of a job and with no prospects" after just selling, for 18 million, the first two McDonald's shops franchised in New York City, along with some other assets.

The 50th reunion, ten years later and again on City Line, was even more enjoyable as, by then, most of my classmates were retired and had had time to recall their best stories. Surprisingly, though most were in their late 60's, about 85 showed up. Many still lived in the Philadelphia area, but two other Californians joined me, and there were people from Florida, South America, Sweden, and Texas who gladly made the trek.

The 40th and 50th had been organized by Philadelphians Henry and Seymour, both lawyers. Henry died after shortly after the 50th, and Seymour, who retained all the necessary addresses, announced that he was not up to the effort of going for another. Over the phone, Obe, from Arlington, Virginia, and I despaired of ever having another reunion, and schemed of us trying to stage a 60th from afar, abetted by Hugh who was now living in Florida. But it was all talk. No one grabbed the reins. It didn't appear to be in the cards.

Then in Spring, 2001 – like a bolt from the blue - came an inquiry from three of our classmates who apparently lived in Boynton Beach, Florida, at least in the winter. They were game to organize the 60th, and asked for a token deposit as an expression of intention to attend. Of course, I jumped at the opportunity. Later they asked for more money and announced the date as Wednesday, September 12, 2001, at the same City Line hotel where the 50th took place. My wife and I decided that we would combine the trip with a pre-reunion visit to our son and his family in Shrewsbury, Mass, about 30 miles west of Boston. We couldn't get enough of our then two (now 3) little girl grandchildren and their two huge Akita hunds who rule the household. The travel plan was a bit complicated. While I AMTRAKed from Worcester to the reunion and to also visit with boyhood friends in Philadelphia, my wife would fly to Iowa to visit our friends in Ames; both of us arriving home about the same time.

As the time for the trip neared, I more and more looked forward to seeing old friends and relatives. But, at the end of August, a sad glitch occurred. We got word, via her daughter, that our old and dear friend, Gretel of Esslingen, Germany had developed a serious inoperable brain cancer. Her prognosis was poor. We altered our plans so that my wife cancelled out Iowa and I would train back to Massachusetts after the reunion so that we could get a flight out of Logan airport on Friday for a short 'goodbye' visit at the Stuttgart hospital where Gretel was undergoing radiation treatment. Even so, with great anticipation, I planned meetings in Philly with Obe and another friend of bygone days, with visits to my best teenage friend, now laid up with a stroke, and to peer cousin, Betty B. I made 34 copies of the story about Stan, which would be included in my book in the "Annals of Retirement" chapter. I intended to distribute them to the attendees and packed them in my suitcase. It would be a hoot!

On Tuesday, September 11, 2001, I got on the 8:33 a.m. train out of Worcester bound for Philadelphia via New York City. Just before we got to the Springfield, Mass. stop, a strange announcement came over the train's P.A. system at around 10:30. It went something like this: "There's been a major disturbance in New York City and it is likely that this train will go no further than New Haven. There will be a bus at the next station that will take anyone who wishes back to Worcester". No more, No less! I mulled it over and decided that I could get a Greyhound bus or rent a car in New Haven and drive to Philadelphia, so I stayed on the train. As time went by, the Conductress filled us in on what had happened, although she said she was getting the news in bits and pieces over the phone. All of a sudden the reality of what was happening set in, but I vowed to get to the reunion one way or another.

Sure enough, they dumped us off at New Haven. I rushed to the Bus office in the train station, only to find that all bus operations had been cancelled. I looked in the AVIS office, also in the station, and was told that earlier detrainees had grabbed up all the rental cars in the vicinity. Then, I watched the unfolding events over a jury-rigged TV in the station and grasped the full horror of what had happened. Resignedly, with no option other than hitch-hiking remaining, I called our son, and he and my wife made the two and half hour drive to pick me up. My dreams of attending the reunion had evaporated. Back at our son's place, we soon found that all flights out of Logan had been cancelled, scrubbing our mission to Germany and leaving us stranded in Massachusetts.

From there, I called Irv A., one of the three reunion sponsors at his Philadelphia number, to tell him that I couldn't make it. He said he had lost about a third of the attendees because of problems like mine, but that they were going ahead anyway. Even more vexing than my case was Ed S's. He had flown from his native Malmo, Sweden to Orlando to stay with a son. There he was grounded, presumably doomed to visit Disneyworld daily until he could finally escape. Fortunately, Obe and his wife had driven up from Washington and did attend as scheduled. So did Hugh, who had arrived in Philly earlier. But my wife and I were stuck in Shrewsbury: The Boston airport, from which two of the ill-fated planes emanated, might never reopen!

On Friday, we made a false start, getting up at 4 a.m. to get a limo to Logan, only to find that the Thursday night report that the airport would open for our flight back to L.A. was not true. We cancelled the limo and gave up on ever leaving from Boston. We sought other escape routes, including the train, to no avail. We finally flew home on Sunday, leaving from Hartford, Connecticut, and traveling via Dallas to the Long Beach airport. Every bit of our luggage was hand inspected. We were delighted to be home. I mailed my 34 story copies to Irv A. and asked him to distribute them to the attendees.

I called Obe for a report on the reunion. He said it was delightful and that 24 had shown up, most – like him – with their wives in tow. A week later we got the nerve up to make a 5 day dash to Germany. Alas, by this time our friend could no longer speak words, but could answer 'yes and no' type of questions. So, the terrorists struck yet another blow.

A few weeks later, Irv A. wrote and sent a partial refund check. He wrote, "We missed you at the reunion. Do you think there's something to the fact that we graduated the month after Pearl Harbor and 9-11-01 happened the day before our 60th reunion? We had 13 last minute cancellations -----.

I'm enclosing your badge, the check, and the class picture. I'm forwarding the story of Stan S. to all the others -------.

There are about half of us left, so we've opted for a 65th in the hope that we'll have a better turnout and provided the world is still here. Stay well!" I'm already anticipating the event!*

Central High School

177th Class
60th Reunion

September 12, 2001

Bob Brodsky

---

* There turned out to be two 65th reunions- one in Philly and the other in Boynton Beach. We attended the latter, along with about 12 classmates and their wives.

THE FEGELA'S REVENGE

"Not that there's anything wrong with that", so they mused on Seinfeld about the gay and lesbian scene. I, myself, share that conviction, though I've got to admit that I felt better about them when they stayed in the closet. Nowadays, wherever you turn, whatever you listen to, whatever you see, the Fegelas are sending their message. And that message is increasingly militant. No more it's "all right to be gay and/or lesbian", but that it is indeed a state to aspire too, in order to be really hip. Not that there's anything wrong with that!

As I write this in Spring, 2004, the gay and lesbian community has just about won their battle for recognition and equal rights. I salute them for this hard earned victory – a victory as impressive as the one finally being won by the black community after so many years of civil rights strife. And they have won the battle against the same hard core 'family values' folks who are fighting to the last ditch to retain the "Under God" clause in the pledge. Not that there's anything wrong with that!

Another late triumph came in the beginning of 2004. They established that old fashioned marriage can include them, and my bet is that there will be no constitutional amendment to contradict what man has already put together. They can now enjoy the same tax privileges that heteros enjoy, and can happily go about the business of becoming families with children and mortgages. Not that there's anything wrong with that!

We already know how they are pervading the television scene. It is now almost de rigueur to have to have at least one sitcom character a genuine, rollicking Fegala. And they've taken over many off-stage executive positions as well. Their books are prized and their observations on a variety of subjects seriously quoted. And, they are now Mayors, City Council persons, and Congressional persons. Not that there's anything wrong with that!

Recently came their greatest triumph. Although, for reasons of being politically correct, the Academy did not give the Oscar to "Brokeback Mountain", they still can claim a great leap forward. Joining expatriate football and basketball players, it is clear that, just as educated fleas, cowboys do it! Where will it end? Maybe a movie a movie about gay priests? No! Perish the thought! There may be something wrong about that.

Ah, yes, speaking of the clergy: despite some discouraging words in the Holy Book, gay clergy of both genders, while being tsked-tsked at, are allowed to ply their trade in relative peace. Yes, folks, they're all over. Here a Fegela; there a Fegala; Everywhere a Fegala, Fegala! Not that there's anything wrong with that!

It's just that I remember the old world. We knew Fegelas were around, but they didn't broadcast. The only ones who 'came out' were entertainers and they were funny about their particular bent. I liked the old days when they weren't being flung in your face wherever you look. But, I suppose there is something wrong about that. It's just not PC!

Fighting back from the apparently the same ennui that I am carping about, a friend sent me a pertinent e-mail. I have modified and shortened it, but have not destroyed its intent:

"OK, I have had it. I've taken all I can stand and I can't stand no more. Every time my TV is on, all that can be seen is effeminate men prancing about, redecorating houses and talking about foreign concepts like "style" and "feng shui." Heterosexual, homosexual, bisexual, trans-sexual, metro-sexual, non-sexual; blue-, green-, and purple-sexual bogus definitions have taken over the urban and suburban world! "

"Real men of the world, stand up, scratch your crotch, belch, and yell "ENOUGH!" I hereby announce the start of a new offensive in the Culture Wars; the RETROSEXUAL movement:

Its Code :   A RETROSEXUAL MAN -

- opens doors for a lady. Even for the ones that fit that term only because they are female.
- DEALS with IT, be it a flat tire, a break-in into your home, or a natural disaster, you DEAL WITH IT.
- not only eats red meat, he often kills it himself.
- doesn't worry about living to be 90. It's not how long you live, but how well. If you're 90 years old and still smoking cigars and drinking, I salute you.
- does not dress in clothes from Hot Topic when he's 30 years old.
- watches no TV show with "Queer" in the title.
- does not let neighbors screw up rooms in his house on national TV.
- should not give up excessive amounts of manliness for women. Some is inevitable, but major reinvention of yourself will lead to you be-coming a froo-froo little puss, and in the long run, she ain't worth it.
- is allowed to seek professional help for major mental stress such as drug/alcohol addiction, death of your entire family in a freak tree chipper accident, favorite sports team being moved to a different city, favorite bird dog expiring, etc. You are NOT allowed to see a shrink because Daddy didn't pay you enough attention to

you. Daddy was busy DEALING WITH IT. When you screwed up, he DEALT with you.

- will have at least one outfit in his wardrobe designed to conceal himself from prey.
- should have at least one good scar he can brag about getting.
- knows how to use a basic set of tools. If you can't hammer a nail, or drill a straight hole, practice in secret until you can – or be rightfully ridiculed for the wuss you be.
- can chop down a tree and make it land where he wants. Wherever it lands is where he damn well wanted it to land. "

There are some special additional RETROSEXUAL rules, not that there's anything wrong with them:

Crying

"There are very few reasons that a Retrosexual may cry, and none of them involve TV commercials, movies, or soap operas. Sports teams are sometimes a reason to cry, but the preferred method of release is swearing or throwing the remote control.

Some reasons a Retrosexual can cry include (but are not limited to) death of a loved one; death of a pet (fish do NOT count as pets in this case); loss of a major body part."

Courtesy

"When on a crowded bus and or a commuter train, and a pregnant woman, heck, any woman gets on, the Retrosexual stands up and offers his seat to that woman, then looks around at the other so-called men still in their seats with a disgusted "you punks" look on his face."

Hobbies

"He may have hobbies and habits his wife and mother do not understand, but that are essential to his manliness, in that they offset the acceptable manliness decline he suffers when married/engaged or in a serious healthy relationship - i.e., hunting, boxing, shot putting, shooting, cigars, car maintenance."

Ethics

"A Retrosexual man doesn't immediately look to sue someone when he does something stupid and hurts himself. We understand that sometimes in the process of doing things we get hurt and we just DEAL WITH IT! "

Now, I'm in sympathy with most of those rules myself, even though they do emanate from my Bible Belt friends. Not that there's anything wrong with that!

MOVIES

Gay film fest is a first at Notre Dame

BY RON GROSSMAN
Chicago Tribune

SOUTH BEND, Ind. — Last year, the Princeton Review's annual survey of American colleges ranked the University of Notre Dame the most unfriendly to homosexuals. This week, the school's library is the site of the first ND Queer Film Festival.

"You have to understand what a breakthrough this is," said Richard Friedman, a fifth-year student participating in the event. "The university's administration had even barred gay groups from advertising in the student newspaper

."On many campuses, eye brows wouldn't be raised by ------

THE FIGHTING IRISH FIGHT BACK

From an L.A. Times newspaper article, circa 2000

BLIMPERY

About 5 miles due-East down the street from us, in a large open field at the edge of the City of Carson, off of 190th street, lives the local Goodyear Blimp. When it is not gainfully employed taking TV pictures of major outdoor events, it prosaically takes five lucky rubber-neckers on a half hour ride. It earns its living by looking down on the Rose Bowl, the Colosseum, the Dodger's and Angels' stadiums, and at other spectacles when there is action. At night, it is often employed exhibiting dynamic advertising messages on night flights by illuminating myriads of colored lights. The passengers fortunate enough to have made the cut are people who have done something nice for Goodyear – like equip their fleets with tires or manage a dealership.

Usually the Blimp goes straight West and overflys the Hermosa and Redondo Beach sea shores and marina before heading back to the nest. On foggy days, it might go South and fly over Long Beach harbor, an equidistant flight which is likely to be not so fog-bound. On a nice summer day, the Blimp might make 6-7 voyages on one hour centers. Oh, how we ached to get a ride! What a thrill it would be! But, it has proven to be very difficult for civilians to become sightseers. Some special gimmick was required, and I never found out what it was, until ------:

The local blimp 'down the street' from us about about 5 miles.
Like a wind vane, it swivels around the mast seen left middle

In the early 90's, as I was assembling my pack-ratted papers as a prelude to starting my book writing, I ran across a TRW interoffice correspondence, dated 12 November, 1982, that I had originated whose subject was, "Visit of Goodyear Representatives". We had just initiated work on a NASA 'Request for Proposal' for the design and construction of a protected hangar to be added on to the in-planning manned Space Station. The hangar was to be a large enclosed work area where Station engineers and technicians could assemble and refurbish spacecraft, to be later re-launched from the Station. A 'shirtsleeve' environment was desired, precluding bulky space suits.

My past experience suggested that an inflatable structure might be the best solution to the problem. I convinced the proposal managers to let me arrange a briefing which would demonstrate how such structures could be designed and deployed. I then asked Goodyear people in Akron, the birthplace of the blimps, to come and help with the briefing. At the end of an edifying day, the lead Goodyear engineer said to me, "Bob, how would you like a ride on the Blimp". When I answered affirmatively with much fervor, he said he would arrange it and that someone would call me. I salivated freely at the thought of what would soon come.

Well, as it turned out, the call never came. But now, 12 or so years later, on finding the ancient document, I thought, "Could this be the 'hook' to get us a ride"? Memo in hand, I went to the Goodyear blimp base in Carson and argued my case. They said they would take it under advisement, even though the Goodyear Airship Operations were now a separate company from Goodyear Tire and Rubber. As before, they said, "Stand by for a call!" I didn't hold my breath.

But, wouldn't you know it, a few weeks later, on the morning of the day our two German house guest's, Gretel and Gisela, were going to fly back to Deutschland at 5 p.m., the call miraculously came in: "Can you make it at 3 p.m. today?" "Nope, we have two foreign guests who must make a 5 o-clock plane to Germany. Can we have a rain check?". "OK, can all four of you make it at noon today, then?" You bet we could!!! My wife said, "I love it!", and our friends excitedly chattered away in their native tongue at such a pace that I couldn't begin to interpret – but I knew they were delighted. What a wonderful going away present for our guests and for us! An experience of a lifetime!

We arrived at the Blimp Port at 11:30, our car packed to go immediately to the airport after the flight. The good ship "Eagle" was perched on her swiveling mooring pole in the middle of a grassy field. Its small, in comparison with its overall size, gondola dangled a few feet above the ground, pointed into the prevailing wind from the West. Many manhandling mooring lines hung down from the hull and a crew of about 12 appeared ready to assist in take–off and landing operations.

Note the swiveling wheel which prevents 'grounding' of the cab, and the steps being put in place to assist passenger loading

The sole pilot, Captain Tom Matus, greeted us and escorted us out to the gondola, whereupon a crew member assisted the ladies aboard. The cabin actually had seats for 6 passengers, but Tom explained that new safety laws had prevailed and limited the number to five. The cabin décor was much like that of a medium luxury car, with big viewing windows looking in all directions. We put on our seat belts, were warned not to fall out, were positioned nose-up by the crew in the proper take-off direction, and with a whoosh of its two 210 horsepower engines driving large propellers at full throttle, rose quickly towards the West at a steep angle.

Unfortunately, it was an overcast day and fog covered our home area at the beach. Tom, therefore, headed us down towards Long Beach, parallel to the Harbor Freeway. As we leisurely cruised towards the Harbor area, Tom told us that the Eagle was 192 feet long, 50 feet in diameter, and carried almost 3800 flashing light bulbs. The noise level in the gondola was moderate – you could talk at a comfortable level of volume. From our cruising altitude of about 700 feet, the view was magnificent – over the extensive petroleum refineries, coke-making beehive ovens, and the huge LA Harbor cargo storage and handling areas adjacent to the water. We saw the many navigable fingers that compose the Long Beach and San Pedro Harbor areas; the huge cruise ships waiting for passengers; the graceful Vincent Thomas suspension bridge; and the harbor sea walls, with big ships moored both inside the breakwater walls and on standby outside.

The heavy mist did not preclude getting a good look at the stately Queen Mary and the adjacent huge dome which then housed the famous "Spruce Goose" – Howard Hughes' gigantic wooden flying boat. Our German friends wanted to know what everything was, and we and Tom did our best to tell them. Alas, soon we were headed back up the freeway.

Coming in for the landing was also exciting. Rather than dumping precious Helium gas, Tom nosed the blimp down at a sharp angle and again pushed the throttles to the fire-wall. We swooped down and our dangling lines were grabbed by the crew and dragged over and then attached to the mooring pole. What an adventure! Pat and I were knocked out that we had finally achieved the impossible dream! It was too much-too fast to take in the whole panorama – we knew we wanted more, but sadly knew that was our last shot in this lifetime. But, wait -- :

Two weeks later, I received an unexpected call. A nice lady called and said that she represented the Goodyear Aircraft Headquarters operations. "I see that you and your wife have been on our waiting list for a flight on the Blimp – isn't that so?" Without missing a beat, I agreed and said we would be "most pleased to take a ride". We settled on a date about 10 days hence. I could hardly contain my excitement.

This time the weather conditions were perfect and the flight leisurely went over our neighborhood. We saw our Hermosa Beach townhouse, and our sailboat in its slip in the marina, plus a beautiful bonus: Our fellow passengers were an out-of-town couple. The husband had been a blimp pilot in WWII and, of course, I piped up that I, too, had had blimp time in 1945 as a U-Boat spotter flying out of NAS Brunswick, Maine at a time when the Nazi subs were wreaking havoc with shipping. Tom allowed both of us to pilot the Eagle, which for me, at least, was a kick. Of course there was nothing to it – you just turned the wheel in the direction you wanted to go and pulled or pushed on it if you wanted to rise or lose altitude. Tom had adjusted the air intakes so that the basic altitude was main-tained. But, it was a new experience. My wartime blimp pilot and friend, Ted K., had never let either of his spotter crewmen take over the helm during the monotonous days we spent sub hunting over the North Atlantic. I suspect he dreaded the even more stultifying work as a temporary substitute spotter.

After the flight, we were the envy of all our friends, whom we bored to death recanting the adventures. In an expansive mood, I decided that I would try to share the wealth, since I now knew the nice Headquarters Blimp lady. I succeeded in getting a concession from her on behalf of the local Section of my technical society to allow the nomination of two passengers every year for a flight. I sold this to her on the true basis that our Society did concern itself with Lighter-than-Air craft; also promising favorable publicity in the monthly magazine, *AEROSPACE AMERICA.* For the next three years, the Chairman of the Section and a guest enjoyed the wonderful jaunt.

The next year, I was away teaching in Israel and no one took advantage of the privilege. I didn't realize that there had been a lapse in activity for a few years. Two years ago, at the urging of the then Chairman, I tried to renew the pact and found that my nice Blimp lady had retired. To date, the ubiquitous new Blimp lady that I tracked down with much difficulty has shamelessly evaded me, despite an initial assurance that she would consider the request seriously. Every time I see the blimp fly serenely overhead, I wonder if I should renew the quest and tilt at more windmills?

A year after this excitement, our German friends took us to the wonderful Zeppelin Museum in the town of Zeppelinheim, East of the Frankfurt airport. Here are models of all the zeppelins ever made, as well as uniforms, furniture and other artifacts from the Von Hindenburg and the Graf Zeppelin. It is a great and unique exhibit, but we, the noted Blimpers, were somewhat blase.

In retirement, little things made me testy. My wife
bore the brunt of my outbursts..
Courtesy of Bob Cleland of Sedona, AZ.

THE ACCIDENT

A "Law and Order" episode on TV brought back memories of a mid-1990's auto accident in which I may have played the naive dupe. The show dealt with an unscrupulous cabal, organized by ambulance chasing shysters, who planned and abetted fake rear-ender car accidents for the purpose of collecting insurance pay-offs via the old "whiplash" ploy. In this episode, a death resulted from their chicanery, but sure and just punishment was meted out by the hour's end.

In my accident case, I didn't know what hit me until suspicion set in 5 to 6 years after the incident; and the perpetrators, if indeed they were such, are probably still in business scamming the system.

I was driving East on 4-lane Torrance Boulevard heading for the Harbor Freeway on the way to a San Pedro second-hand boat outfitting store. It was mid-morning on a sunny day as I approached the completely dark and unlit entrance into the tunnel that went under the Freeway. For access to the Freeway South, I had to make a left turn at a traffic light about thirty yards before the tunnel entrance. I was driving our venerable Buick Limited, one of the free world's truly huge cars. In fact, it was more like a tank than a car and consequently had incongruously been dubbed, "The Yom Kippur Clipper" by our son David.

The 'Yom Kippur Clipper' in all its glory. It was an ~1988 Buick Limited
chauffeur-driven for the president of North American Rockwell (now part of Boeing)

As I approached the light, it turned green. Seeing no traffic in the opposing lane, I started making my left turn. Seemingly out of nowhere, as I was halfway through the left turn, I was suddenly sideswiped on the right by a speeding car, which then raucously careened to a stop. The Clipper was hardly perturbed and I slowly, in a small state of shock, completed the turn and pulled it over to the side of the road and got out. I couldn't imagine where the other car had come from. It must have come from the darkness of the tunnel, but I certainly didn't see it as I started to turn. I had a terribly guilty feeling that my careless driving might have injured the other driver, who was getting out of his car as I remorsefully approached him. His battered auto, a light weight Japanese variety, had a pushed-in wounded side, and pieces of his right-door-mounted rear-view mirror and rear tail light assembly were scattered over the road. This debris was in stark contrast to the small scratch mark along the side of the Clipper.

I asked my supposed victim, a bespectacled business-suit-dressed young man in his late twenties or early 30's, if he was ok? "I think so", he said, "but I feel a headache coming on, and my neck hurts". "You'd better see a Doctor right away" I said with concern as I repeatedly apologized for my senseless driving. I assured him it was all my fault, "I simply didn't see you coming". We exchanged the necessary information and I called to the Auto Club's insurance office from a nearby phone booth, reporting the accident and acknowledging my culpability. He drove his car away without any problem and, still shaken, I proceeded on my mission. Later that day I went to the Auto Club, showed them my car, and completed their accident forms.

A few months later, I learned from the insurance office that a court action had been filed against me, and that the Club had subsequently settled with my victim's law firm for $6000, in addition to his car repair costs. I, of course, was later offered insurance renewal at an exorbitant rate for a 3-year penance period, which I partially avoided by taking my business elsewhere.

It was only after seeing the "Law and Order" episode that it finally dawned on me that I had been taken by an expert professional. I am now convinced that he was lurking in the tunnel waiting for the right opportunity to gun his car and, with great skill, make the slight, but noisy, contact. The "right opportunity" obviously consisted of no other traffic for witnesses, a hefty 'mark' car to assure no real damage, and a senior citizen driver.

I'm sure the Auto Club knew what they were facing, but had no proof – especially after I readily admitted my fault. They had to make a settlement. But, in retrospect, it was done so cleverly – so professionally! To this day, I still harbor some doubt that it might really have been a legitimate encounter. Senior Citizens - Beware! And keep your lips buttoned if you are in an accident.

"NO BUS TO AMMAN"

Isn't it strange that visitors to your home turf always seem to know more about local manners and customs than the natives? This truism was brought home personally during the planning for and commissioning of our Summer '99 westward trip around the world. A major stop on this trip was Haifa, Israel. Here, we would visit with our cousin Susan and her husband, Dick, attend the wedding of their number 2 daughter, present an invited lecture, and see our many friends made in past visits during the two previous times that I was a visiting professor at the TECHNION. By using Royal Jordanian Airlines from New Delhi to Frankfurt via Amman, we ostensibly saved $400 each over El Al prices for the same route via Ben Gurion airport in Israel - but as you will see, there is more to this than meets the eye.

Before we left on the journey, I made inquiries about travel between Jordan and Israel. The logistics of travel between Amman and Haifa demanded an early solution, especially since we were to leave the Amman airport early on Sunday morning, June 6. On any given Saturday, the Jewish Sabbath, Israel is essentially closed down. I went on the internet and found that there are two buses a day that do a Haifa / Amman and vice-versa traverse, but I could not find out where you got the bus in Amman. By e-mail, I asked Dick to find out more about the bus, giving him the name "Trust Transportation Co" as the carrier. He shortly e-mailed back the first of "There is no bus from Haifa to Amman" proclamations, but allowed that he did find a daily Tel Aviv-Amman bus, which obviously solved no problems.

We agreed that on arrival in Amman, I would call him at our mutual friend's house in Afula- near the Jordan border crossing at the King Hussein Bridge (over the Jordan River). On getting my call, he and Susan would leave for the crossing and pick us up there. It seemed like a good solution since we had passed through the border stations at that same crossing only two years earlier on our jaunt to Petra and other outstanding tourist sites in Jordan and were thus familiar with the routine.

We arrived in Amman at 9:30 am local time and readjusted our wrist watches for the crazy half hour time shift that mysteriously occurs because there are times zones between Singapore and Amman that operate on the half hour. Little did we know that Jordan was on standard time, while Israel was on daylight time, which proved to be another complicating factor in travel planning. With some difficulty, armed with Jordanian Dinars purchased in India, I made the call to Afula to inform our cousins of our arrival and intent to immediately get a taxi to the King Hussein Bridge crossing. We carefully told the taxi driver where we wanted to go and felt sure that he understood. On the way out of the airport, he showed us the only near-airport hotel, the Alia, and we discussed staying there the night before our early morning departure to Frankfurt at the end of our stay in Haifa, since the airport is a smart 25 miles from downtown Amman.

The Shiek and Mrs Araby at an earlier visit in (then) Queen Noor's gift shop in Amman. We resisted purchasing the garb.

The drive to the border crossing seemed longer that we remembered from two years ago, but the station and interminable procedures seemed the same. When, after an hour of customs hi-jinks on both sides, including showing them the Jordanian Visas for which we had paid $60 each, we arrived safely on the Israel side. We wondered why cousins Susan and Dick were not there to greet us. We waited and waited and were just about to call Afula when we were tapped on the shoulder and asked if we were "The Brodsky's"? It turned out that the wicked taxi driver had taken us to the Allenby Bridge crossing, the one people going to Jerusalem use. It was some 60 miles south of the King Hussein crossing where our cousins waited. A $100 taxi ride and two hours later, we were in Afula and reunited with our family and friends, but the savings over EL AL travel were already being seriously eroded.

Our one month stay in the Old Country now began. Early on, to get it out of the way, I decided to plan how we would get back to the Amman airport for our Sunday flight to Frankfurt. It seemed obvious that there was no way we could leave Haifa very early on Sunday with any hope of making a 9 am plane, especially since Jordanian time was an hour earlier than Israel time, and the border crossing did not open until 7 a.m. It was also worrisome about traveling to Jordan on Saturday, since there is little public transportation in Israel on the Sabbath and our cousins cannot drive on the Sabbath. I went to a travel agency to buy a ticket for the bus between Haifa and Amman and to make a reservation for Saturday night at the Alia Hotel at the Amman airport. After considerable rummaging around on the computer, I was told in no uncertain terms that, "There is no bus to Amman" (confirming Dick's earlier pronouncement) and "There is no Alia Hotel"!

It became immediately apparent that the tenuous peace between Jordan and Israel had not really taken hold. The "Peace Process" (in Israel, they pronounce it "Piss" Process, and I have never been sure whether it is an accent or a political commentary) had been in force for over two years, but the Travel Agents were apparently still at war. Not discouraged, I called a number in Nazareth which I had taken from the internet, and was assured that there were two buses daily from Haifa to Amman, and was told where to find the correct agency in the harbor area of Haifa to purchase a ticket.

During the period of socializing and taking in the beach around Haifa, we combined a ride downtown on the Carmelit, Israel's only Metro, with a quest for Amman bus tickets. We easily found the travel agency where I was told I could get the tickets, but they advised us to walk "200 meters down Ha'Atzma Ut (Avenue of Independence)" and look for the terminal near the ramp entry to the Port. We did so, but found no bus terminal. I went into a travel agency right across from the port entry and asked where I could buy a ticket for the bus to Amman. They immediately said, "There is no bus to Amman". We trudged (it was very hot) back to the Agency, who reaffirmed the presence of a bus terminal and said we hadn't looked hard enough. For the nonce, we put it on hold.

As for a hotel reservation at the Amman airport, there was better news. I had asked our landlady, Mrs. Schindler (no relation) if she could help and she directed me to her "wonderful" agent (Ordinarily, Dick's travel agent, who had done us proud on our Jordan trip two years ago probably would have been able to solve our problem but, alas, he had recently died in the course of duty in Albania and Dick had not yet found a new agent). A few days later, we got a call from the Agent, who proudly told us that while there was no hotel Alia, she did book us into a hotel "near the airport which had the airport shuttle service" that we had insisted on. I was temporarily placated and elated.

A week or so later, I decided to make another try to buy bus tickets to Amman. I got into the rental car, drove downtown, and parked near the ramp entry to the port at what appeared to be a station. I went up to the ticket booth and asked for two bus tickets to Amman. The lady said that this was the downtown railroad station, and volunteered that "There is no bus to Amman". I thanked her and asked where a bus station in the vicinity might be. She suggested going up to the port entry gate at the top of the steps leading up to the ramp. The guard at that gate told me that the bus station I wanted was about a half mile away and pointed to the multistoried municipal bus station, which I knew very well.

Resignedly, I trudged down the steps, deciding to check again across the street at the same travel agency that I had been to two weeks ago. However, at the bottom of the steps, I spied four men in the process of opening up a little office-like outdoor cage. I asked them where I could buy a ticket for the bus to Amman, and one of them pointed and said, "Right over there"! Sure enough, cuddled under the rising ramp, but in easy sight of the depraved lady in the RR station ticket booth, was a small terminal clearly marked as the bus stop for Nazareth/Amman. Bemusedly, I bought two tickets for $30 and was assured that the bus ran every day, including Saturday

On our last Thursday evening in Israel, after dinner in central Carmel, I stopped at the taxi dispatch stand to arrange for an early Saturday morning pickup to take us downtown to get the bus to Amman. When I told the dispatcher the plan, he naturally said, "There is no bus to Amman", and the other zinger, "No buses run on Saturday." I thanked him for the information and asked him to humor me.

The bus ride to Amman was pleasant and uneventful, albeit it took over an hour to go through the King Hussein Bridge border crossing, and we were inexplicably charged $15 each to leave Israel! We were let off in downtown Amman and immediately transferred to a cab to go to the Airport hotel that Mrs. Schindler's trusty agent had proudly reserved for us. About ten minutes later, the cabbie left us off at the downtown Amman hotel where we had stayed at two years prior on our way to Petra. I said that there must be some mistake because our travel agent had assured us of proximity to the airport. I went to the desk and asked if they had shuttle bus service to the airport. "Of course", said the pretty clerk, "the taxis run all the time." Really teed off, I asked the Clerk if she would release us from our reservation and call the Alia for us. This was done, and we got to the Alia an hour later with not enough Dinars to pay the cab driver. He drove me to the nearby airport and a local ATM. After a pleasant evening and a great meal at the Alia, we were off to Frankfurt the next morning, with three weeks still left on our journey around the world.

For all the world to know, we had convincingly established that there really is a bus to Amman and that the Alia hotel exists!

ELECTION, 2004

I've never considered myself a real poet like my cousin Susan in Haifa. Oh sure, I dabble in poetry on occasion – enough to give me a feeling of inferiority when I run across a real winner. This was the case in the denouement of the recent election. I've saved the POEM in question for the last, as a whet to your appetite.

This was again one of those pivotal elections that threatened to change our lives. Only once before, in the heat of the Mondale/Nixon campaign, had my wife and I considered moving out of the USA in the unlikely case of a tragic outcome. In Tricky Dick's case, it was to Israel – then a seemingly more comfortable place to live with our Liberal principles. That we didn't make the move, and apparently weathered the storm, is a tribute to our steadfastness and hearts filled with eternal hope. But this time, it may be different! But, where, oh where, in this crazy firmament can we go now?

At the outset, our hopes for a favorable November '04 vote outcome were extremely high. It seemed to us that no matter who the Party nominated, he or she would be a sure bet to beat the encumbered incumbent. The war in Iraq was a shambles, the deficit was sky-rocketing, jobs were being lost by the hundred of thousands, Social Security was in a crisis, the fundamentalist right wing bible belters surely could not be taken seriously, the Gay Marriage issue was trivialized, and our Foreign Policy had resulted in us being disliked the world over. Hell, even I, a Jewish atheist, could probably be victorious if the Party had the temerity to nominate me.

Early on, before anyone considered him seriously, I threw in my lot, plus a handsome $10 contribution along with a piece of sage advice, with Senator John Edwards. I liked his boyish charm. He appeared to have the charisma of a Jack Kennedy and the ability to get along politically. Deciding that he needed an edge to beat out the myriad of potential candidates, I favored him with a trump card: "Come out strong for getting America on the road to the Hydrogen Economy! Release us from the grip of the US and foreign oil interests". I importuned that if he followed this path, he would clearly differentiate himself from the pack and win the grateful support of American motorists. It is now obvious that by not following my directions, he could only come out second.

Still, when John Kerry was nominated, we did not fret, feeling that the ABB (Anybody but Bush) syndrome would prevail. And Kerry, although not as likeable as Edwards, still represented us well in his thinking on all matters of importance. We could accept him as a leader and still felt reasonably certain that he, and common sense, would prevail in the upcoming election. And we were encouraged by the outpouring of Democratic sentiment evinced by Michael Moore and the Hollywood and Rock stars, by WEB- rampant organizations such as NARAL, Move On, the ACLU, the Democratic National Committee and others. Surely, their goodness and mercy would have a highly favorable impact on a public which seemed to include an inexplicably large number of 'undecideds'.

Though deploring the flimsy offensive effort mounted by our Party – in the same circumstances the republicans (sic) would have had a president with Bush's record up for impeachment - we went about our pre-election civic duties with some avidness. Large amounts of money – over a $100 dollars, I'll bet – were sent to good Democratic and liberal causes. A Kerry/Edwards sign appeared in our window, defying condo rules of 'no politickin'. My wife was a poll worker and we both went to poll worker's training class. We wrote e-mails to our Senators and Congresspersons as suggested by WEB messages. We did everything but pray, and Yea, There's the Rub, perhaps.

In the holocaust that followed the election we still do not understand why and how an incoherent and bumbling President carried the day? We are still sorting out the evidence. Apparently we greatly under-estimated the religious fervor that appears to be building in this country. The Jesus-Belt people really are serious about abortion, gay marriage, keeping the illegal 'Under God' in our pledge of allegiance, blurring the separation line between church and state, and converting (or banishing) Jews and other so-called minorities (that's why we continue to send the same huge amounts of money to Israel so that we'll have a place to go to when they turn on us). It is also apparent that the people were cowed by the 'terrorist threat' and the morass that is the conflict in Iraq.

Why they thought that Bush can handle this better than Kerry is a complete mystery to me, whose answer is probably known only to Karl Rove. What the Democrats can do now is also a complete mystery to me. For once in my life, I have no suggestions of any ideas that I could happily live with. Well, maybe one – Think of an Edwards*/Clinton ticket in 2008 and start doing the right things to support it now!

In the wake of the disaster, one bright shining light appeared: the poem referred to at the beginning. It wisely calls for the reunification of the American people, urging them to walk with confidence with the incompetent incumbent. Oh, how I wish I had the talent and foresight to write it. I did, however, have the good sense to send it over the airwaves to all my friends, in the following e-mail:

---

* In hindsight, in August, 2008, oops!!!!

"Dear friends:

I thought you would all enjoy this uplifting, unifying poem sent to me by a republican* friend in the wake of the election. It is a sincere call to work together in these next excruciating four years.   Bob"

A Poem for the Election

The election is over, the results are now known.
The will of the people has clearly been shown.
We should show by our thoughts and our words and our deeds
That unity's just what our country now needs.
Let's all get together. Let bitterness pass.
I'll hug your elephant.
You kiss my ass.

Bipartisanship, Republican style

---

*Yes, believe it or not, I do have a few -very few - republican friends, and even - Heavens to Betsy! - a right wing first cousin.

DEMOCRACY - AIN'T IT GRAND?

A feeling of revulsion and sadness swept over me as I watched the relentless waves of Mardi Gras media hype domineer telecasts heralding New Orleans' remarkable ability to put on a show amid its suffering caused by Hurricane Katrina. The utter hypocrisy came through when, flashing away from the revelry for the moment, they would sometimes show the scene down the street – the complete devastation of neighbor after neighborhood still in a state of upheaval and unimproved 6 months after the storm. "What kind of a country do we live in?", I said to my wife while reading a series of related horror stories in the *LA Times* February 28, 2006 Mardi Gras day issue.

Growing up in the then-exemplary elementary school system of Philadelphia, I was taught that, while not perfect, Democracy was still better than any other type of government. The fallacies of parliamentary government, such as practiced in Great Britain; the multi-party chaos of French governing; the gross failures of Socialism and, worse yet, Communism because of excesses due to human greed perhaps more than their basic theory of governance; and finally the utter deprivations caused by Dictatorships, were dutifully and patriotically taught. They were taught by teachers who for the most part believed in what they were teaching, and - in those times – there was more than a modicum of truth in that belief. I was led to believe that Democracy was the best, fairest type of Governance, and I still do – but certainly not the way it is now being practiced in our dear United States of America. We have allowed politics and politicians to pervert our government and, even worse, to preclude anything serious being done to correct the system. What we have now is CAPITALISM, not Democracy.

What kind of a government is it that cannot respond quickly, reasonably and compassionately during and after a crisis such as that wrought by Hurricane Katrina? Can you visualize other civilized Governments not coming to the timely rescue providing immediate and continuing help to the of thousands of families made homeless and jobless by the catastrophe? And, why can't Democracy response? Because there's no money in it! We are too busy making money by holding Mardi Gras' and by selling oil and supporting the 'war effort'. These are the engines that fuel the economy. To make things 'right', we would have to resettle and rebuild for the beleaguered New Orleanians and Gulf Coasters. Apparently, there's no money for this and an increase in Taxes is simply not PC.

What kind of a country is it that has to rely on charitable organizations such as the Red Cross and Church groups to shoulder the main burden of relief and rescue? Isn't that crazy, particularly in a country where church and state are supposed to be separated? Should we really build charities into a National Disaster plan? And, if so, shouldn't the Government support these charities with more than just a tax break? In the Mardi Gras day issue alone, I easily found a stark indictment of our Government process – one so strong that I wonder if the democracy that we are trying to sell to the outlanders really works, even though its theory – like Communism and especially Socialism – looks awfully good on paper.

To illustrate my points, let us examine selected articles from the February 28, 2006 morning paper:

HEADLINE : "Red Cross Had Been Warned of Inefficiencies".
"Years before Katrina, the charity was told its huge hierarchy could impair relief efforts."
   Washington – "The American Red Cross – castigated in a recent House report for its disorganization in the aftermath of Hurricane Katrina --------"

Now, is that calling the Kettle Black? And FEMA is a *government*, not a charitable, agency. It begs the question of what exactly is the role of the American Red Cross. Is it a quasi-governmental organization, and, if so, should it not be under FEMA. If not, which is the true case I think, why the hell are we depending on it to support all types of crises and then feel we have the right to 'castigate' it. I wonder.

BUSINESS: **"Investing Abroad"**
"The rush by U.S. investors into foreign markets reached a new level in January ----."

Given proper Government support and guarantees, I suspect investors would rush into the task of rebuilding the Gulf Coast, thus creating new opportunities and jobs for American and 'guest' workers. The only upturn in jobs there that I now know of, comes via my mariner son who is on the scene shipboard as a Mate, is in support of the oil platforms that were damaged. He says they can't hire enough qualified people and that no one is truly aware of the extent of the devastation from Biloxi to Port Arthur and even westward. Does the Government think that 'free enterprise' will figure out a way to make a profit out of the rebuild? And how long do they think it will take? Or, are the votes too few to care about? I wonder.

All through the paper that day I found articles that showed how capitalism had over taken democracy. Look at the following and decide for yourself:

HEADLINE: **"Stocks Get a Lift on Oil, Profit News"**

"A drop in crude prices and strong earnings from retailer Lowe's revive investor's optimism. Treasury bond yields advance."

HEADLINE: **"KBR to Get Back Most of Disputed Iraq Costs"**

Washington – *"The Army has decided to reimburse a Halliburton subsidiary all but $9 million of nearly $222 million in costs ----- for oil industry work in Iraq ----".*

HEADLINE: **"States Offer Grim Look at Curbing Corruption"**

"Many have rules that Congress is considering. But scandals underscore the difficulty of policing ethics, even with independent oversight"

Washington – *"As lawmakers wrestle this week with overhauling ethics and lobbying guidelines for Congress, they need only to look to the states for sobering examples of how hard it is to curb political malfeasance."*

HEADLINE: **"Port Deal Was Questioned"**

"Before the Dubai firm's takeover was approved, the Coast guard warned of intelligence gaps"

LETTER TO THE EDITOR: **"The high court and the gerrymandering puzzle"**

Re: *"Don't mess with Texas Districts," Opinion, Feb. 24*

HEADLINE: **"Shaken by Deaths, CHP Reviews Safety Policies"**

"After the sixth officer fatality in five months, officials will revisit procedures, including traffic stops and where they take place"

LETTER TO THE EDITOR: **"South Dakota's law against right to choose"**

Re: *"S.D. House Approves Abortion Bill" Feb. 25*

There is a grim sameness in these articles. All illustrate the failure of government and governance. They have fallen into the hands of the industrialists, zealots, and billionaires who have bought the best government money can buy. And, alas, we are unable to turn the tide. Like the Roman Empire of yore, I fear we are on our way downhill.

THE LAST HURRAH

(or)

TRAVELING AIN'T FUN LIKE IT USED TO WAS

The jaunt to Reno in January, 2005 was strictly an ego trip – and an expensive one, at that. About a year earlier, since its venue was in nearby Long Beach, I had submitted a technical paper to the annual conference, "SPACE 2003". It dealt with the design of a unique emergency rescue vehicle which I had 'invented' in 1962 to bring back crew members from a failing space station. I had spent considerable effort, starting in the late 80's, trying to convince NASA that such a device was needed for the International Space Station – to no avail. Surprisingly, the paper was not accepted. Now, further discouraged by the new US policy which had all but abandoned future development of the ISS, I reluctantly decided to give up the fight to legitimize my invention and submitted the paper to present at a Historical Session at my technical society's annual Aerosciences meeting. So, this, my presumably final paper* was to be the last hurrah for the Space Lifeboat. Moreover, I suspected that I would be the oldest person to ever present at this conference – perhaps a LANDMARK event!

Our flight to Reno was to leave LAX at 10 a.m. on Monday. Our Santa Fe daughter and her Santa Barbara son and his lady friend had been visiting us prior to winging it to Hawaii on an earlier 9 a.m. flight. On Sunday evening, I arranged with the usually reliable Yellow Cab company for a 5 passenger van to pick us all up at 6:45 a.m. next morning. The dispatcher said the driver would call us as he approached our pick-up point. Previous experience was that they usually arrived about 15 minutes early, so that when no one appeared by 6:50, I called in, slightly panicky. It was a mind-blowing revelation to find that she had never heard of me, but that she bet she could "have a cab there in 10 to 15 minutes". Thinking quickly, I asked, "Do you have any cabs at the Crowne Plaza Hotel", which is directly across a small street that runs between our buildings. She allowed that there indeed were two vehicles now stationed in front of the hotel. "Fine", I said, "please call one and tell him to come by immediately!" "OK, they'll be there in ten to fifteen minutes". Being no longer able to deal with incompetence, I told her to "forget it". I plodded

---

*For reasons I really don't understand at age 83, I expect to present two more 'final' papers: one in Sept. 2008 and the other in Jan. 2009.

across the street in the rain and commandeered a waiting cab at the hotel front entrance. The first crisis was over, but I was wet and out of breath, and short of temper!

At the airport, fortunately with plenty of pre-flight time, we ran into the vicissitudes of modern technology. You will see that this eventually led to an attack of apoplexy on my part, with an accompanying first notice divorce warning from my Dear Wife. Eskimo Airlines, our carrier of choice, has instituted a mechanized way to get their customers started on the long process of checking in baggage and getting boarding passes. Innocently enough, it started with a supposedly user-friendly computer screen and keyboard. My wife carries the tickets, so she took on the machine. The first thing it asks, once you get it energized, is "Confirmation Number, please". Alas, there wasn't a confirmation number on our Electronically-derived ticket. And try as we both might, by calling for "Help" on the screen and other futile stabs, we could not get past the first barrier. Thus stymied, we were not able to move on to the open Agent stations ready to immediately service those who were able to deal with the machine.

I then moved our baggage and my heightened blood pressured- body into the long line of those who also had not been able to use the machine and were waiting to be processed by a real person. In the meantime, my Dear Wife had found a minion lurking around the intransigent machine who told her that if you didn't have a confirmation number, you merely had to type in your name. She beckoned me to abandon my position in line and join her at an open machine. Giving up our place in the queue, I joined her while we tried the new formula. And, try as we might, we could not bring up an icon which asked for our name. Not being noted for patience, the evil twin within me began to mumble under his breath – speaking unkind words about our airline-of-choice.

But, before an explosion occurred, we spotted another floating minion whose job appeared to be of an advisory nature, since he appeared to be 'helping' another hapless soul at the adjacent machine. I signaled audibly for help and he replied, "Wait a sec, it's easy". With that, I roared, "Easy!! Fer Chrissakes, I've been here 15 minutes, and even with my PhD in Engineering I can't figure this dumb sumbitch out!" With that, he disdainfully declined to help me, noting that rudeness doesn't count and that he "wasn't being paid to take this kind of treatment!" So, I got back at the new end of the line, suggesting to my wife that she politely try him out. But he was too slick for her and told her that he knew "she was with the madman". Eventually, we got to the front of the line and checked in; noting to the Agent that we would could be contacted at the Reno Hilton. Blood pressures back down to their normal highs, we arrived in Reno, determined to use Eskimo again only if it were the last plane out at Armageddon.

The meeting itself went well: I schmoozed with some old industry friends and university colleagues; we enjoyed the Basque restaurant that I remembered from many past meetings despite the cold and slippery slushy sidewalks in downtown Reno; and my talk went well and was well attended, including two grad students who collared me after my talk to discuss their thesis work in space rescue. So, my ego was assuaged, although in retrospect not $800 worth, and especially not after the final Eskimo Airline affront:

We were to return to LA via a noon plane, and reached the airport at 10 to begin the check in process on the evil machine. But, this time, we were armed with our confirmation number, which the Agent at LAX had provided. We started the process and all went well until it asked for the "Destination?" We typed in 'LAX' and it asked "Destination?" We typed in 'Los Angeles' and it again asked "Destination?" I felt the tightness gathering around my chest. Fortunately the nearby Agent called out to find the problem. She told us, "Oh, didn't you know the flight had been cancelled?" No, we didn't, although we would have known had we been at home, since that's where they called to inform our answering machine of the change in schedule. They did put us on a 4 p.m. flight the same day, so we went back to the hotel and stewed and spent more money: altogether an ugly experience.

To cap it off, about an hour before my talk, I had run into a very old (from the '60s) friend and we caught up with each other's adventures in life. I casually remarked to him that, at almost 80, I would probably be the oldest living person to give a paper at this highly technical meeting. He replied, "I gave my talk yesterday, and I'm almost 83!" In true Linus fashion, "Rats", I said.

But, there's a happy ending! I wrote a 'Letter from an Outraged Citizen' to the president of Eskimo, including the text of the above story. In due time, I received a most welcome note from the airline's Customer Relations Supervisor, lauding my suggestions for improved operations AND REFUNDING THE AIR FARE FOR BOTH ME AND THE WIFE!

SPACE STATION ESCAPE VEHICLE –
40 YEARS LATER

R.F. Brodsky*,
Viterbi School of Engineering,
University of Southern California
Los Angeles, California 90089-1191, USA

Over forty years ago, the author and his associates at Space-General Corporation, a subsidiary of Aerojet-General, proposed and won what became a 1.3 million dollar contract to develop and test elements of a one person space lifeboat for crew rescue from orbit. The customer was the USAF Materials Lab. The vehicle proposed was a 1000 pound inflatable reentry paraglider utilizing a variant of the Rogallo wing design. During the life of this contract, similar one-time-usage designs, meant strictly for emergency use by up to six crew persons, were also proposed, but were not funded. This paper will disclose the work done in the 60's and will describe the author's unsuccessful, to date, campaign, starting in the early '90's, to have NASA consider its usage applied to the International Space Station (ISS).

ABSTACT OF RENO PAPER

Presented at the 43rd annual AIAA Aerosciences Conference; Reno, Nevada, January 10-12, 2005

THE END FOR NOW

www.ingramcontent.com/pod-product-compliance
Lightning Source LLC
Chambersburg PA
CBHW080726020726
47503CB00010B/2810